LEARNING

CAPITALIST

CULTURE

University of Pennsylvania Press
Contemporary Ethnography Series
Dan Rose and Paul Stoller, General Editors

A complete listing of the books in this series
appears at the back of this volume

LEARNING

DEEP IN THE

CAPITALIST

HEART OF TEJAS

CULTURE

DOUGLAS E. FOLEY

UNIVERSITY OF PENNSYLVANIA PRESS

Philadelphia

Library of Congress Cataloging-in-Publication Data

Foley, Douglas E.
  Learning capitalist culture: deep in the heart of Tejas/Douglas
E. Foley.
    p.   cm.—(Contemporary ethnography series)
  Includes bibliographical references.
  ISBN 0-8122-8246-9.—ISBN 0-8122-1314-9 (pbk.)
    1. Mexican Americans—Texas—Cultural assimilation—Case studies.
2. High school students—Texas—Social life and customs—Case
studies.   3. Capitalism—Texas—Case studies.   4. Texas—Ethnic
relations—Case studies.   I. Title.   II. Series.
F395.M5F65   1990
305.8'6872073—dc20   90-34686
                                                              CIP

CONTENTS

FOREWORD

It has been both a strange and a familiar pleasure to read Doug Foley's *Learning Capitalist Culture*. It is the most open and engrossing school ethnography I have seen—I thoroughly recommend it for readers across all the social sciences as an important addition to the growing body of empirical works in cultural critique. Of course I have criticisms to make, some of which I will mention. But I think this book is special in the way that it combines an historically located and contexted ethnographic picture (especially good in linking economic change, civil rights issues, and Latino-Anglo relations with detailed ethnographic evidence) with an associated theoretical project of *understanding* this picture through the development of theoretical categories of more general application. In my view it is the combination of theoretical and empirical work that makes for the only real possibility of advance in either. Doug Foley has indeed struggled and advanced on both fronts, and has produced a practical model of theoretically informed empirical work for us all to learn from.

It has been a familiar pleasure to read this book because, even though thousands of miles away and now many years ago, so many of the issues and scenes, ironies and tragedies are recognizable from my own experience and from the research for *Learning to Labor* (1981). It has been a strange pleasure because the setting for this study is so different from anything I know, and the actors—vatos, good-ole-boys, white trash kickers—like nobody I have met. The pleasure is both in realizing, mutatis mutandis, the very real commonalities of how capitalism is culturally reproduced in such widely different human, geographic, and economic circumstances, and in the sheer enjoyment of good writing, in being led through a fascinating cultural landscape and wanting to turn the page to find out more.

Of course the pages were not turned in total sympathy with the text. Even though the key focus, the proclaimed ethnographic and theoretical innovation, is on "expressive practices," and despite getting a good picture of Northtown—excellent in its political and economic and community backdrop—I wanted to *hear* more of the verbal exchanges within the "low status" groups. I wanted comparative evidence as to the degree of commodification or resistance to commodification in the expressive styles of the vatos and kickers, for instance. I liked the focus on football, status groups, and classroom exchanges, and understood the excellent placing of these in their "macro" contexts. But sometimes I missed a final delivery of the detailed life and range of "micro" events, locations, humor, and the trivial but creative passing of "dead time" within groups. Some of this gap was filled in by the researcher's reminiscences of his own earlier childhood, school, and college experiences. While I welcomed this (as well as the engaging honest and openness about the author's politics, motives, and relationships) as a productive response to and adaptation of "experimental writing" in anthropology, I also felt that I was asked to do too much unspecified work with the text. For me it infected the whole, frankly, with a certain sentimentalism—a too automatic solidarity of experience—and inflected it as well toward a particular, at times uncritical, male orientation. Still, what kind of pot am I to call this kettle black!! Part of the passion and integrity of the writing in this book come from a certain kind of masculine formation, a stance, a dignity, an honesty in the writer.

And I, myself, indeed felt truly like some kind of ghostly, closely traveling half brother, in the adventure of the theoretical journey reconstructed in the appendix. This was a stranger and deeper pleasure for me, and finally the source of the real and lasting value of the whole text. For, a continent away and well over a decade before I would meet him, here was another worker with very different materials to handle also rooting around with impatience and sometimes exasperation for a theoretical opening for ethnography, for a satisfactory way of finding *internal* links between personal and group experience, class structuration and the complex reproduction of capitalist formations. There was another anonymous traveler in another (new) world—skirting the marshes, traversing the long viewless valleys, avoiding the traps, peering over the precipices—pressing on perilously toward the same half imagined goal: an account of how at least a fragment of a capitalist social and cultural formation really worked without turning its "agents" into fools, dummies, and robots. Large tracts of the reconstructed journey with Doug Foley I have found quite exhilarating. They have changed me. I have learned from the lucid outline of Habermas, from the reaccommodation of his work into a classic "labor perspective," from the breathtaking reframing of Goffman as *critical* ethnographer, from the ambitious synthesis of anthropology, cultural studies, and socialist theory to produce the over-arching concept of expressive cultural practices. I have learned from this book new ways of understanding the class and capitalist specificity of many communications as well as the visceral importance of human communication in general—

to be fully dignified along with material production as humanly necessary, as embodying and arising from human labor.

And, of course, Doug Foley conducts the reader equally interestingly through my own work, and excitingly offers to get me out of what he says is my very own trap—seeing culture too simplistically as "ideological consciousness." A more expansive view of culture as expressive practices, he argues, would get me out of a "class reductionist" hole without losing the specificity of *class* cultures. This is also his project, and he produces a powerful general model in its pursuit. He argues that capitalist market relations produce general processes of the commodification of human expressiveness, of the attempted appropriation of all communicative labor. This is the essential dehumanizing cultural tendency of capitalist societies across the board: humans manage each other and their own performances in the same way they manage the production and circulation of commodities. We treat each other as objects, so our expressive cultural practices also become increasingly alienated and reified. Resistance to this process occurs not in cognitive ways, not through "penetrations" of dominant ideology (an impossible socialist ideology and consciousness) but through class-based speech and communication communities that keep alive *human* (not reified and alienated) expressive practices. To put the situation in a nutshell, working class and oppressed groups are more likely to treat each other as humans that are bourgeois groups, and to a greater or lesser extent this innoculates them against the commodification of their expressive practices. Unfortunately, the argument continues, the superior knowledge and experience of commodity forms of the bourgeois young gives them an ability to manage impressions and to maintain a social deceit in a variety of different social sites such as football, youth status groups, and classroom "making out games" in a way that low status groups cannot hope to match. The bourgeois group (or most of them) are thus guaranteed social prominence, school success, and ultimately economic power. The cultural logic of the capitalist system is thus enacted in every new generation.

The coherence of this argument and the illumination it throws on the ethnographic data quicken my sociological imagination. Whatever the criticisms and points to be made against it, there is a clear position here that is a touchstone for argument and a frame for evidence. It has been an influence directing my own current work toward "symbolic work," "symbolic creativity," and "grounded aesthetics" in the "ordinary cultures" of non-elite groups (see Willis 1990). Having said these things, however, I would like as well to enter some important caveats about Doug Foley's account of my *Learning to Labor*. I think the issue of "culture as socialist ideology" in my work is a hole he mostly digs for himself rather than just finding it there, though I certainly applaud the way he climbs out again. I would never argue that the lads' culture in *Learning to Labor* is socialist though I would argue that it contains materials that must be dealt with in any socialist reconstruction. The point of my ethnography was precisely to show the profane complexity of cultural experience, only a small part of which—partially, selectively, differently at different moments of the argument—is explicable in our theoretical forays. For me culture is a very commodious and profane conceptual bag. It is much, much broader than ideology. I would never equate the two. My notions of cultural practices and cultural production (in some ways rather close to what Doug Foley's theories refer to much more rigorously as expressive practices) produce *living* critiques and penetrations of dominant ideology only as a small (through crucial) part of their total effective presence. They often do so in eccentric, collectively unspoken rather than in individually verbal ways, and almost as the byproduct of the application of sensuous human capacities to immediate ends. I hesitate to use the word "cognition" at all to describe such processes. Furthermore, the in-built limiting structures here embedded as they are in sensuous, concrete forms are not in any conceivable sense a question of "false consciousness." It is not a mistaken or false perception, for instance, to experience class exploitation as concretely mediated and mitigated (for white men) and changed through gender and race power. These things are "real," too.

I mention these points not to try to keep the academic merry-go-round turning to my tune. I am trying to be faithful to a complex notion of living cultures as richly expressive—expressive of things highly likely (though never provably) to be connected, often critically, to the historically produced situations (including immanent logics of economic production) that locate them. The project of revealing what is expressed and its effects is contingent on all kinds of things and, of course, involves interpretation—what kind of social science is it that expects the meanings of things to be written on their faces? But this process is not the same thing as, and should not be discredited with the charge of being, "culture as ideology" or "socialism in waiting"!

Without leaving such critical spaces for "contents" (even if they are only interpretations), without allowing for some interpretive understanding of the embedded logics in rebellious impulses or social counter-forces, it is difficult, I would argue, to comprehend capitalism as a dynamic system whose contradictions are not only sites for cultural (and other) struggles but also sources for change and expansion. For me, the crucially interesting thing about cultural reproduction is how (really and potentially) critical resistant or rebellious forces become contradictorily tied up in the further development and maintenance of the "teeth-gritting" harmony of capitalist formations. The circuit of cultural reproduction, just like the circuit of capital (money-commodities-money), needs its own stages of *transformation*—where one thing becomes another thing unlike itself, which threatens the whole system as well as making it "go" by returning again finally in some expanded form to the original. We must take risks in trying to understand and present how the cultural system "goes."

I applaud Doug Foley's "expressive practices," and have learned from them and from how he gets to their formation, but I have a final worry about the extent to which they are describing only *reflections* of dominance and not transformed circuits of meaning with their own "go." The deceits and impression managements of the prominent students allow them to stay on top like their parents, but this is reproduction "top down." What do the vatos and kickers make of it all? Why do they go forward so vitally to their own confinement? They are lively enough, but is this to be understood only as communicative life for its own sake, important, even dominant as this emphasis must be? What are they resisting, fighting, "saying" (to risk falling into my "trap")? Don't they relate critically and illuminatingly to capitalist organization in more ways than simply resisting commodification of communication and being more human toward each other than toward other groups? How are such "contents" or critical impulses related, contradictorily, to the extension and tense stability of the system? If their expressive practices reflected or temporarily lifted only their subordination, the result would be too much stasis and pessimism (for me at least). In the Western context, at any rate, we would be left at best with the job of finding and classifying the remaining authentic communications in pockets of resistance to cultural modernity. I cannot help thinking that Doug Foley's final political position as expressed at the end of the book—that of the last man of the enlightenment bemoaning the irrationality of all apart from isolated special "men" of cultural distinction—itself reflects and is a product of something lacking in the theoretical position.

I believe there is another route, one which works from the irreducible strengths and innovations of the formulations around expressive practices, but which is more dialectical with respect to processes of commodification and which tries to speak more hopefully from the *inside* of dynamic change and its potentials. This route would explore the dialectical, contradictory (but nevertheless internal) links between expressive practices and their critical "content" and cultural reproduction around the central axis of the commodity form at the cultural level. Against the grain of reification in general, I would argue that cultural commodities have *widened* as well as set the field for ordinary people's symbolic work and creativity. The commercial leisure and entertainment industries keep returning to the streets precisely to find that creativity which cannot be found in the commodity process itself. And, the widened commodification of a widening leisure culture continually and creatively eats away at the Protestant ethic which still helps to drive the making of all commodities. This line of reasoning suggests questions to be *interpretively* directed at the vatos and the kickers. Is there something "rational" in their implicit and explicit views of school and work? In what contradictory ways do they use and become more developed by cultural commodities? Are there developmental potentials in how they exploit capitalism's yielding of leisure as the freest and most fulfilling zone of human activity? Why do their cultures exert a continuing hold on new generations even in kinder and more mobile times?

It is a tribute to the capacity and reflexivity of ethnography, and especially to Doug Foley's rangy version of it, that there are materials in this book to try to answer our questions. There are and will be, of course, many more questions than mine. The point is surely that we have a rich text here for development and interpretation. I have learned from Doug Foley's "expressive practices," and I very much admire the way in which the concept was forged through exposure to and struggle with *both* data and theory—as I say, a model. In my closing comments I have simply been trying to take up and continue the work of constructive critique. This is my version of the finest compliment it is possible to make: this book has lifted the possibilities of cultural critique.

Paul Willis
December, 1989

ACKNOWLEDGMENTS

Acknowledgments usually include long lists of people who have helped make the work possible. One's loving wife and long-suffering children, and colleagues, even if they ruthlessly penciled the manuscript, get tossed some gratitude. Sometimes authors' vanity gets the upper hand, and they list the tribulations of life that have left their work and careers mildewing in some musty study. Having suffered like Hamlet, I too am sorely tempted to gush on. God only knows how I would like to stick some pins of revenge into a couple of malicious colleagues, and to wax on about how friends revived me from bouts of despair. But the people who helped me with this text know how grateful I am, because friends argue over things. They really do not need publicity for their parts in my little drama, but I thank Jim Malarkey, Jan Nespor, Jeanne Caswell, James Brow, Harry Cleaver, Gail Kligman, Doug Kellner, Terri Greenwood, Karen Luzius, Walt Smith, Manuel Peña, José Límon, Vandra Maseman, Maria Reyes Abrams, Renato Rosaldo, Andrea Greimel, Bob Fernea, Ira Buchler, and Dale Koike. This manuscript benefited greatly from their comments.

I would also like to thank several new-found colleagues who were very helpful. Dan Rose, Paul Stoller, and Patricia Smith turned out to be editors who can take as well as dish out criticism. After editors who present outside reviews like death sentences, they were a breath of fresh air. In addition, Paul Willis turned out to be as likable as his lads. After I had spent years trying to improve on his seminal work, it was only proper, as the English would put it, that we would finally meet in his seminar at my university. Around the same time, we apparently both went searching in very different corners of the world for the "truth" about working-class cultures. My intellectual debt to him is made clear in the essay on theory.

The first part of the essay in Appendix A critiques Willis's theory of class cultures and shows how my perspective grows out of his work. I shared that essay and several rounds of tequila with Paul during his visit to Texas. At that time, he agreed to write a Foreword to this book which would lay out a more formal response to my critique of his work. That manuscript came to me before the final proofs were produced, so I have the opportunity to get in the last word—at least for the moment. The best way to "tune in" on our conversation is to read it chronologically. First, read Part I of my Appendix A, then the Foreword by Willis, and then my concluding remarks in the final section of Appendix A. I am enormously pleased that we had this exchange, which puts another kind of "dialogic frame" around this ethnography.

Finally, acknowledgments usually thank the "people" profusely for their friendship and free information. Obviously, North Towners' cooperation made this book possible. After fourteen years, some North Towners are probably sick of my coming around, and some may think this book stabs them in the back. This book criticizes what they take as good and natural. Living in other cultures, feminist friends, and left-wing books have shown me a darker side of American culture, and writing this book has forced me to let go of a few cherished memories. I can only hope that my friends in North Town will read this as a loving critique of the way we were all brought up, and that some will continue to accept me as a kind of honorary prodigal son.

I would like to dedicate the book to my two overachieving kids, Kristina and Greg. Their dreams for the future both inspired and embarrassed me into writing again. I also dedicate it to the working class kids in this story who had to endure the condescension of "the authorities." These heartbreakers have no right to act the way they do, but that never seems to stop them.

INTRODUCTION

This ethnography is about life in a small South Texas town that I call "North Town." North Town has been in the midst of a painful process of cultural and political change since the late 1960s. The Chicano civil rights movement since its inception has been challenging the vestiges of an earlier segregated racial order. The confrontation between Mexicanos and Anglos has created new tensions and problems for North Town youth. This is the story of how they are changing a segregated racial order and American society. This is also the story of how these youth learn a materialistic culture that is intensely competitive, individualistic, and unegalitarian. This "capitalist culture" of classist, racist, and sexist practices limits the impulse of the civil rights movement to create a more open, democratic culture.

This study shows how schools are sites for popular culture practices that stage or reproduce social inequality. The school is a cultural institution where youth perform their future class roles in sports, youth groups, and classroom rituals. The life style and values of middle class youth are held up to rebellious working class youth as the cultural ideal. The socially prominent youth learn a new communicative style and ethic and become adept at managing their images and manipulating adult authorities. These new communicative competences in the art of deceit prepare them to be future civic and political leaders. But as these youth gain materially, perhaps they lose a little of their humanity. This is the philosophical question that the study ultimately raises about our culture.

In some ways, this tale about growing up in America is a familiar one. Every medium from scientific studies to novels, TV sitcoms, and teen movies has explored the American youth scene. Margaret Mead claimed that Americans are so obsessed with youthfulness that our youth often become trend setters who socialize the adults. She and others have popularized the view that American youth have more autonomy and power than youth are accorded in traditional societies. Other social scientists claim that a "generation gap" and a distinct "youth counter-culture" exist in age-segmented America.

Other commentators emphasize how the media and popular culture constantly idealize and spotlight youth as a distinct market group. Rather than viewing youth as pawns of capitalism, some see them as a vanguard. Some social critics see youth counter-cultures as having an avant-garde political and social consciousness. Given such a range of views, "youth" has clearly become a cultural symbol that critics and admirers of American society continually interpret. The American intelligentsia periodically takes the pulse of its youth to assess the health of its civilization.

Another group of researchers and critics who study youth are more interested in how to create a state-financed public schooling system that educates the youth. Several studies of high schools ask why secondary schools are often so academically weak. These studies look at the motivations of youth and analyze how informal peer groups help or hinder the formal educational process. Most of these studies are more interested in practical policies for improving pedagogy, administrative practices, and the curriculum.

This study conceives of high schools as a site where American popular culture is enacted. It emphasizes the informal, cultural side of pedagogy and school organization. Life in North Town is presented through the eyes of youth, and this ethnography portrays how they experience football, teachers, classroom activities, status groups, dating, and race relations. The study is based on living in and visiting North Town periodically over a fourteen-year period. The original fieldwork was done over a sixteen-month period from 1973 through 1974. I also lived in North Town for six weeks during the summers of 1977, 1985, 1986, and 1987 and on numerous weekends. The youth I originally studied are now adults, and some run North Town and its schools. This ethnography captures the cultural and political ferment of the sixties and seventies and then asks these young adults to reflect on how North Town has changed in the eighties. Pseudonyms have been used for all of the people portrayed in this ethnography to afford them a measure of anonymity.

I am often asked by my university students to define what an ethnography is. After reading many "ethnographies," they develop a general idea, but, in truth, ethnographies are as varied as the preoccupations of ethnographers. Renato Rosaldo (1989) and George E. Marcus and Richard Cushman (1984) have usefully outlined and critiqued the narrative conventions of an earlier "realist" style of ethnography. Such texts, which became the accepted convention, were written from the detached perspective of the invisible, omniscient, objective observer. This trained scientist lived in exotic cultures to discover the order and coherence of a particular group. Frequently, these holistic, orderly portraits were presented as if living in and understanding a strange culture was an unproblematic task.

Scientists supposedly carried out such field studies with rigorous, dispassionate, systematic methods. The posture and tone of the text was always a high-minded, scientific search for the universal laws of human cultures. More recently, in the wake of revolts in the philosophy of science, anthropologists have begun writing "experimental" ethnographic narratives. What presently constitutes an authoritative text has become problematic. The old "realist" texts are now seen as a set of rhetorical conventions to convince the reader that the hand of a dispassionate, objective scientist rendered a reliable, valid text. Ethnographers now discuss the poetics and politics of ethnographic writing, and the avant-garde takes its cues from critical theories of writing, texts, and symbolism. The feelings of ethnographers have begun appearing in these texts, and some texts have taken a decidedly literary turn. Extreme truth claims that one's ethnography is an objective, scientific rendering of the culture are now downplayed.

Some contemporary ethnographers argue that a strong we/they dichotomy may pervade interpretation and reify those studied into an imaginary "other," or ficticious object to study. That criticism entreats ethnographers to search for ways of being "dialogic" and putting themselves into the account. Being dialogic with the subjects of the study has many meanings, but it generally suggests a greater intellectual openness and political and emotional vulnerability on the part of the investigator. Ethnographers drop their scientific pretensions, toss their pith helmets and imperial advantages, and close the distance between themselves and the imaginary other being studied.

I have been intrigued and puzzled by these developments in my field. Intrigued, because I have long felt constrained by the conventions of thinking of myself as a scientist who is writing a scientific, realist text. Puzzled, because some of these new "experimental ethnographies" seem even less accessible than the old realist texts. Such texts are sometimes filled with ethnographers ruminating over the epistemological perils of studying "the other." Experimental ethnographic texts derive their authority from the author's tone and posture as a reflective, skeptical, philosopher-poet. Unfortunately, surrealist and post-modernist ethnographies, like surrealist and post-modernist art, can be as opaque as they are imaginative.

Although this revival of philosophical relativism will no more save the field than earlier "new ethnography" movements did, it does help shatter lingering positivist fantasies. Moreover, this new ferment and experimentation opens up intellectual space. The genre of ethnographic writing will undoubtedly change in the coming years. Although often more engaging than much social science writing, ethnographies are rarely as touching and intimate as good literature and cinema. According to my students, ethnographies are "pretty dry stuff." Too many ethnographies are written largely for other ethnographers. Consequently, they are filled with arcane academic discourses that make little sense to non-professionals. In the end, the peoples and cultures portrayed tend to be subjugated to a theory-driven text that showcases the author's thesis.

Ethnographies do exist that are quite bold, dramatic, and entertaining to read, but they risk being condemned to the category of "popularized accounts" or "passionate ethnographies." Getting your work labeled that way is the academic kiss of death. The long nose of the academy looks down on ethnographers who make too strong a play for public acclaim and acceptance. If you become a popular "popularizer" like Carlos Castaneda, you can, of course, laugh all the way to the bank. Most of us, however, are humble drones who toil on topics of more limited appeal, and we either succumb to established narrative conventions or cannot write well enough to shatter them.

I have been influenced by these debates and have tried to write an intimate, engaging, and "popular" text that is also reflexive and critical. This "realist text" tries to bridge the we/they split with a narrative language filled with real people and events and less technical jargon. Reduced to its most basic level, an ethnography is simply a record of the ethnographer's experience with a group of people. How skillfully this personal record is recounted can vary a great deal. Two recent experimental ethnographic narratives that I like are Barbara Myerhoff's *Number Our Days* (1978) and Dan Rose's *Black American Street Life: South Philadelphia 1969–1971* (1987). They have a personal, autobiographical quality that deftly captures the scene and people and what the ethnographer did and felt. In very different ways, they have served as models for narratively representing the youth scene of North Town.

Unlike these monographs, however, this ethnography concludes with extended reflections on theory and on field methods. I have consciously separated my description of a people and their place from a technical, theoretical discussion of the interpretive framework guiding the study. These technical discussions of ideas are radically different from the ethnographic narrative about North Town. They are written in this peculiar language that I have learned to speak with other academics. I have tried to make these essays accessible to non-specialists, but they do assume some familiarity with social theory and methodology. Non-specialists will find parts of these essays more difficult to understand than the ethnographic text.

The essay on social theory, which lays out my assumptions about culture and class, helps explain why this particular ethnography took the shape it did. Those concepts are the intellectual foundation of the descriptive ethnography, which would look nothing like it does without those ideas. Readers who are not social scientists must be aware that ethnographies always have some guiding ideas. Ethnographers are not recording machines that simply present "facts" that speak. Ethnographers filter their experiences through ideas and values that they use for making these "data" have meaning. In the end, ethnographic portraits may say as much about the author as they do about the people being studied.

Writing this ethnography in two distinct dialects or narrative styles has an important methodological function. It is my way of demystifying and laying open the whole process of producing or constructing a "scientific ethnography." The theory and methods essays make my perspective obvious and tie it to my personal experiences. This arrangement makes the text easier to evaluate and criticize. I have tried to portray enough of how I worked in the field and the library to reveal the constructed character of this account. Ethnography is the craft of writing critical, reflective empirical accounts of your personal fieldwork experiences. C. Wright Mills (1959) calls it "intellectual craftsmanship," and it requires a great deal of "sociological imagination." This ethnography is myself trying to think critically and imaginatively about my country and how these youth and I have been shaped.

As subjective as that definition of ethnography may seem to some, I still believe in the ideal of objective ethnographic accounts. There is a historical and cultural reality that we inherit and must critically reflect upon, if we are to evolve as a species. On the other hand, I can only believe in a kind of consensual, perspectivist view of truth and objective accounts of this historical reality. We can at least grope around in disciplined ways to figure out the meaning of the shadowy, ever-changing social world that we inherit. We can give our approximations of what is true about North Town and ourselves. Ideally, the point is to produce a text that is open enough that even non-specialists can engage it critically. Successive generations will undoubtedly find new ways of reading this text.

ONE

The Civil Rights Movement Comes to Town

The Setting

We arrived in North Town a year after the Chicano civil rights movement had burst onto the local scene. Our research team of three found lodging in a large, old, two-story Victorian house in the center of town. The house was located near the county courthouse and the main Protestant churches in the old Anglo section. The neighborhood had become predominantly Mexican American and was showing signs of gentrification. Perhaps prophetically, young Mexican American professionals were renovating houses that symbolized declining white power. From our upstairs apartments, the old county jail was visible. This relic no longer held prisoners but seemed filled with the ghosts of a segregated past. People told colorful stories about Sheriff Cameron, a tough-talking Anglo who yanked Mexicano troublemakers out of rowdy cantinas. At night, we sat on the porch and drank a beer to those poor souls who languished in Sheriff Cameron's jail. The sheriff's legend was as vivid and steamy as a South Texas summer. His memory and deeds still haunt this small agricultural town of 8,000 people.

North Town sits in a vast dry and gently undulating plain of former rangeland. Modern farmers with tractors and irrigation systems have battled to convert this rain-starved land into farmland. They grow watermelons, peanuts, and cotton among pastures and feed lots full of cattle. The country is a checkerboard of open farm land and pastures dotted with scrubby mesquite trees and brush. The town is close enough to San Antonio for working in the military bases or weekend shopping, and far enough away to be more than a bedroom community. North Town is a typical South Texas "county seat town." It is the seat of government and the distribution center for a productive agricultural county. A few people also harvested a little oil when prices shot to thirty-two dollars a barrel in the 1970s.

The town still has the feel of two separate towns, one the old Mexican town with its tiny, shabby corner grocery stores and taco stands, and the other a well-kept downtown of car dealerships and small family-owned pharmacies, cleaners, and appliance and five-and-dime stores. Various public buildings, larger grocery marts, furniture stores, and funeral parlors also display old North Town family names. A long, well-paved four-lane main strip runs from the center of town to its outskirts. Like most commercial strips, the town's outer perimeters are dotted with welding shops, nurseries, gas stations, and electrical and plumbing shops. What is uniquely South Texas are the agricultural sheds. They ship the town's lifeblood to supermarket chains throughout America. And as in most small-town strips, national chain stores are muscling into the local economy. Walmart, HEB supermarkets, and a host of fast-food places— Pizza Hut, Sonic, and Golden Chicken—chase the small wages of most North Towners.

During weekends, the strip is alive with teen-agers and young adults cruising, talking, eating, and drinking. Other places that catch the eye are the churches and the high school and its football and baseball fields. When North Towners are not home watching television or video movies, or barbecuing and drinking beer, they are going to church services or watching their kids play sports. The pace of life is relatively slow, friendly, and unruffled. North Town is a quiet place, despite occasional fights in the town's cantinas and one night club. There are no urban gangs and few brutal crimes. People generally feel safe walking around, and residents will tell you that "this is a good place to bring up kids."

The worst problems in North Town are those caused by chronic poverty. Since the turn of the century, Mexican nationals have come to North Town to pick cotton and vegetables. As the years passed, many became citizens and now work in non-agricultural jobs or languish in the economists' category of "underemployed." The town has an unemployment rate of at least 15 percent, and perhaps as high as 40 percent of the households have only one parent. Many families live in substandard houses and are forced to rely on food stamps and Aid-to-Dependent-Children payments to survive. Like most small towns, the youth increasingly migrate to the city to find good jobs. North Town leaders find it difficult to compete with the cities to attract industry. Without signs of growth, recruiting new teachers, professionals, and budding small entrepreneurs has become difficult.

North Town rises and falls economically with the whims of Mother

Nature and the national agricultural market. As machines have taken over production, the number of farms and ranches has decreased. Fewer and fewer Anglo patrons remain to run the economy. Moreover, the national chains are displacing the local Anglo merchants, and a new crop of Mexicano teachers, social workers, health care experts, and professionals are replacing the Anglo service workers. North Town is now 85 percent Mexicano and rising. As the years go by, the desert regions of northern Mexico seem to be reclaiming this early Mexican frontier town.

The Modern Civil Rights Movement Comes to North Town

I settled into North Town with a strong sense of coming home to rural America. Except for the stiffling summer heat and the strong Mexican flavor in the town's food, music, and speech in the streets, it could have been my hometown of Tama, Iowa. I began "hanging out" at the local schools and engaging the kids and the community political leaders in conversations. The local Mexicano political movement, then called the Ciudadanos Unidos (United Citizens), had just won the school board and city council elections.

Upon winning the city council and school board elections of 1973, the Ciudadanos Unidos publicly announced its existence. The sudden, triumphant emergence of an organized Mexicano political group convinced most Anglos that a Chicano conspiracy had "taken over." Many Anglos felt that the Mexicanos had "tricked" them and had "stolen the election." Within six months after the elections, the new Mexicano politicians were labeled "communist." Prominent local businessmen and ranchers organized the Better Government League (BGL) to fight this communist conspiracy. They drafted the following statement of purpose in English and Spanish and vigorously tried to recruit local Mexican Americans into their group:

North County Better Government League is an organization of and for the people of North County. Its primary purpose is to actively promote good, representative government which is responsive to all the people and their needs.

The organization is for supporting those candidates which are of the highest caliber, personal integrity, background, and experience which qualifies them to serve.

The organization is for keeping more than one political entity available in North County to insure that all people have a true possibility to express themselves through elected representatives.

3

The organization is for a viable community which can prosper and grow economically for the benefit of all our citizens. We want community harmony and everyone working together to accomplish common goals.

We are for full utilization of the abilities and talents of all our local people and equal opportunity for all without regard to political beliefs.

We support the concept of local people in positions of authority which represent the interest of local people.

We are for school systems that have as their main purpose the education of children without using them as tools for political purpose. We are for respect and obedience in the home and on and off the school campus.

The organization is for sound, honest, and qualified law enforcement. We support law and order with fairness to all concerned.

We are for freedom of our religious institutions from political turmoil and upheaval.

The organization is for freedom for all people to participate and express their political beliefs without fear of intimidation.

We are for sustaining our country and its communities as a good place to live and raise our families without prejudice and fear. We are for the projection of a non-controversial attitude which will cultivate respect and interest among other people in becoming a part of our area.

The BGL had limited success in recruiting Mexicanos into their organization. A few local Mexicano businesspeople, denounced by others as "vendidos" (sellouts), did openly join the group. Most of the original Mexicano BGL members were employees of Anglo farmers and ranchers. Juan Luna, a postal clerk, was selected as their candidate for mayor. He subsequently won, and remained a staunch advocate of a more accommodating, "diplomatic" view of race relations.

The BGL, which had approximately a hundred active members, was continually beset, however, by potential splits among its much larger voting membership. The more extreme ideologues on race relations wanted to punish Mexican Americans through large-scale firings of known Ciudadanos sympathizers. They also wanted to end all "federal give-away programs" such as Head Start, food stamps, Bilingual Education, and Aid-to-Dependent-Children. Moreover, they were not prepared to sponsor Mexican American political candidates or accept the Mexicanization of the local social service agencies. In contrast, moderate BGL members sought a more conciliatory program of expanded social services. They were more pragmatic and less ideologically conservative about accepting the liberals' federal poverty programs. They also wanted to sponsor and form political alliances with "sensible" Mexican Americans. They understood that they were demographically outnumbered (70% vs. 30%) and that the times were changing.

These two Anglo factions tended to divide along class lines. The more well-educated, prominent businesspeople and landed gentry were moderates who sought to reform the racial extremists. The less well-educated Anglos and some farmers and ranchers were the "red necks" who sought to punish disloyal, ungrateful Mexicanos. Members of the two BGL factions referred to each other as "dumb red neck types" and "stuck-up, know-it-all types." Disagreements ensued over the parties' proper public image, their philosophy of race relations, and various school board and city council policies.

The BGL's primary goal was to regain political control of the city and school board and to crush the Ciudadanos threat. The BGL quickly raised $10,000 for an election challenge and grand jury hearing into possible voting irregularities. They also accused two Mexicano city clerks, considered Ciudadanos loyalists, of tampering with the write-in ballots. The BGLers contended that the city manager, a young lawyer, had masterminded this plot to destroy fair city elections. They believed that this "city hall crew" was criminally conspiring to end free democratic elections. A grand jury of predominantly BGL sympathizers summoned hundreds of allegedly illegal Mexicano voters to appear before the court. Mexicano activists called the grand jury investigation a racially motivated vendetta to intimidate voters and destroy their party. The grand jury investigation became the single most important symbol of Anglo power or "realpolitik."

The other intimidation tactic Anglos used against Mexicano voters was "economic blackmail." A number of Mexicanos reported that they were threatened with firings and salary reductions if they did not vote against La Raza, the "radical" segment of the Ciudadanos. One frequently mentioned example of economic intimidation occurred on the school board. The school board president was accused of "blackmailing" another Mexicano board member, a vegetable farmer. The story went that if the Mexicano board member did not vote with the Anglos, the school board president would rescind his land lease. After a few months, the Mexicano board member became conspicuously absent from all school board meetings. This left the board racially divided, three to three. The school board "blackmail affair" became the other key symbol of Anglo power.

As the racial conflict deepened, the newly formed Ciudadanos Unidos organization, which also had approximately a hundred active members, developed its own ideological factions. The majority group, the moderates, controlled most of the school board and city council seats. The BGL's grand jury investigation provoked the "young turks" in Ciudadanos. As the conflict intensified, they urged Ciudadanos members to form a chapter of the Partido Raza Unida. A handful of local businesspeople, farmers, and college students were inspired by the success of José Angel Guttiérez in nearby Crystal City. Ciudadanos "radicals" wanted the "moderates" to emulate more closely the Crystal City model of reform. First, they hoped to pursue federal monies and programs more aggressively. Second, they advocated a more aggressive confrontational style of race relations. Third, they wanted to define more narrowly who was a "real Chicano." As in Crystal City, North Town's radical Chicanos wanted to label any Mexicano a vendido who was unwilling to openly confront the gringos.

Despite their different styles of race relations, the two Mexicano groups were similar in many ways. Ideologically, both factions subscribed to the philosophy of mainstream liberal democrats. They wanted to expand the welfare state's social service programs for the poor. They were more concerned about social issues and programs than about fiscal frugality and a strong national defense. In class terms, these two Ciudadanos factions were also essentially the same. They represented the emerging Mexicano middle class and had similar levels of education and income. Culturally, neither faction was more assimilated than the other. Generationally, the "radicals" tended to be a younger group of aspiring political leaders.

Ultimately, a small group of radicals took control of the Ciudadanos organization, and in 1974 the group officially became Partido Raza Unida. A local farmer, Manuel Ramírez, an outspokenly angry man, became the new leader of the reconstituted group. This transformation of the Ciudadanos to a chapter of the Raza Unida Party occurred because the moderates did not contest it. The moderates became convinced that an enraged Anglo community and its vendido allies could defeat a disorganized, inexperienced, and extremist Raza Unida group. They felt that North Town was not ready for such a confrontational approach to race relations. Rather than argue, they quietly acquiesced and participated much less in the next election. Raza Unida proceeded to run an angry racial campaign against the gringos and lost by a two-to-one margin. The moderates' plan was to regroup and reconstitute themselves after the election loss, which they subsequently did.

A Diversity of Views in the Movimiento:
The Diplomat and the Militant

Within the Mexicano community, a wide variety of views existed on ethnic politics and race relations. Two men became key symbols in the public discourse over the best way to conduct race relations. Their views on racial politics and the past articulated what many North Town Mexicanos felt:

Mayor Juan Luna, the Diplomat and "Vendido":

> Myself, I wasn't fighting for one side or the other. I told them, I can get a lot of things done, and I am going to do it. But I am going to try and negotiate. As long as I keep doing what I have been able to do, I think I can stay in as mayor as long as I want to, because I am not trying to put the shaft on anybody. I am trying to better the town as a whole. I don't want one side to be on top . . . I just think it's a big problem that has to be worked out by both sides working together, and I would much rather sit down and talk to my enemy than to fight him, right? Let's sit down and try to work something out, no use taking punches at each other and not accomplishing anything . . . Well, I can't go all the way to the other side of town and punch out a guy, just because his daddy beat up my daddy. You can't live in the past. If you ever intend on progressing or bettering yourself, you have to look ahead. These people are fighting a fight that is long gone . . . By the middle sixties things were changing quite a bit. Mexicanos were getting better educated and doing a lot of their own thinking. They had the opportunity to progress, whether they wanted to or not, depending on them . . . Lately, there are so many ways. You can go get all kinds of help to educate yourself, get a college degree or whatever you want . . . I guess you have to go with the majority of the business people and the large land owners, ranchers, or farmers, whether they are Anglo or Mexicano. They can do their job, and there are not many Mexicanos that can provide that for the people . . . Well, there *are* people that are discriminated against, but not because of their coloring, but because of their character. I mean, if you get into a place and act like you own the damn thing and do what you want to, and that place belongs to somebody and it cost them money to build, that's not right. You can't just go in and destroy things and do as you damn well please. If the people that own it throw you out, that doesn't mean that they are discriminating against you.

Manuel Ramírez, the Militant Chicano:

> Since I have become active in politics, I have been called "puto" [sexually promiscuous], "joto" [homosexual], and "ratero" [a thief]. They have hurt me deeply. The people advised me to stop, but I understand from the scriptures that somebody has to be a martyr. I'm single. I have nobody to cry for me, nothing to leave behind. They will just bury me. I'd rather fight for equality. I

believe, like Emiliano Zapata, that the land belongs to those who work it. But here in Texas the Chicanos work the lands, but they are administered by the Anglos. I'd rather fight injustices in this world than to say I didn't . . . In the Bible it says Christ freed men. He broke the chains of slavery. Christ said, "I am the light, follow it." I'm trying to do that, but the rich and the educated still take advantage and abuse us. I have to be an example. I knew that when they beat the shit out of me, and I almost died. I knew that I lived to do something more . . . Once economic reprisals start, too many people want to play it on the safe side. They wanna be with the Democrats. Mexicanos aren't politicized for a party. They don't know what it stands for, what is chairman, conventions, precincts, the role of leader. They think they are ready, but they don't know the laws and the power of the opposition, how hard the struggle will be . . . I have tasted the bitterness of Anglo society. To whites, the color is the difference. Race is the key to getting elected. I told these people! Now *they* are being called communists! Now *they* are being dragged into court! People are being threatened, if they vote. They will lose their jobs. Mexicanos can stand up for their rights, but losing your job is different. It will take time, my friend, but that is one thing that Chicanos have got, time. We got no money, but we got plenty of time.

The discourses of these two men eloquently portray fundamentally different world views. Mayor Luna expressed little anger and racial hostility toward Anglos. Yet, he clearly expressed a racial consciousness when he talked about "them" and "us," and his preference for "working with the enemy." He was optimistic that racial discrimination had declined and that the society had opened up to Mexicanos. He emphasized that, if one wanted to get ahead, one had only to be respectful and show respect for private property. He tended to caricature radicals as living in the past, being disorderly, and trying to get revenge. In contrast, he portrayed himself as a sane, reasonable man who had worked hard and behaved properly to accomplish what he had. He saw himself as a humble, optimistic, cooperative man who was a model of how to get ahead. For Mayor Luna, race was not a very important factor in politics and everyday relations. He wanted to forget the past so the races could get along and move forward.

In stark contrast, Manuel Ramírez expressed deep anger at the racial discrimination he had experienced. For him, Anglo society had changed little and had made few concessions. Far from being reasonable and accommodating, Anglos had reacted violently to his demands, and he had been personally beaten by an Anglo peace officer. This incident left him martyred and deeply committed to battle racial injustice. He compared himself and his cause to those of Jesus Christ and Emiliano Zapata. Like these two great historical figures, he saw himself fighting for the poor, downtrodden Chicanos against the rich Anglos. He was deeply pessimistic

8

about his people's will to fight and to follow him, but was dedicated to battling Anglo racism and privilege. For Ramírez, race was an ever present factor in North Town politics and human relationships. Rather than forget the past, he wanted to remember and use it to build a sense of racial injustice in his people.

Between these two extremes lay the rest of the North Town Mexicanos. The majority of Mexicanos refused to get involved in either political group. Many ordinary working class Mexicanos expressed a deep distrust of all "politicos," regardless of race. They avoided being identified with any particular candidates or political groups. Their attitude on race relations was neither extremely accommodationist, nor extremely militant. They wanted race relations to improve, but unlike Mayor Luna they had not tasted the good life and did not expect to. They were neither as optimistic as the Mayor nor as bitter and pessimistic as Mr. Ramirez. They were resigned to their poverty, and their hopes lay in educating their children.

After the initial Mexicano revolt, the Anglo-controlled BGL won the subsequent city, school, and county elections and the Raza Unida party lost nearly all its supporters. From 1974 to 1979, North Town enjoyed a brief respite from ethnic confrontations and politics. Manuel Ramírez, the dedicated militant, ended up establishing a rural health clinic called El Sacrificio. The moderates revived the old League for United Latin American Citizens (LULAC) civic organization, raised college scholarships for the youth, socialized together, and quietly plotted their return to politics. In short, the political cauldron bubbled away until new public confrontations surfaced.

More Ethnic Confrontation: The Second School Board "Takeover"

In 1979, North Town politics took an unexpected turn. The "vendido" mayor, Mr. Luna, found himself in trouble with the Anglo community, which disliked some of his policies. First, he resisted firing his city manager, a friend and a talented federal grant writer, who had been widely criticized for a drinking problem and lax administrative practices. Second, he sponsored the opening of a large Walmart department store. This national chain store quickly undersold and ruined several small Anglo merchants. Third, he "meddled" in the Anglo-run school board and became involved in a bitter dispute with the board president, his sister. A number of disillusioned Anglos convinced a newly arrived Anglo businessman to run against Mayor Luna.

These developments forced Mayor Luna to seek a reconciliation with the radicals of Ciudadanos Unidos. In 1979 the embattled mayor and the LULAC moderates forged a temporary reunification of the Mexican American community. Several new leaders in LULAC convinced the old radicals that the mayor could be trusted. Meanwhile, rumors abounded in the Anglo community that their moderate mayor "had gotten into bed with La Raza." A new Mexicano conspiracy appeared to be underway when the alliance's candidates beat a slate of Anglo-sponsored candidates for city council by several hundred votes.

Soon after the city elections, the new alliance helped elect three more Mexicanos to the school board. By the spring of 1980, North Town was watching a rerun of the 1973 confrontation. During the "quiet years" from 1974 to 1979, the old Ciudadanos group had regrouped and added several new, energetic professionals. The more activist Mexicanos had regained a majority on the school board and city council. They felt that the North Town schools needed changes in administrative leadership, teacher evaluation, and curriculum. They boldly hired North Town's first Mexican American school superintendent and a Mexican American athletic director from the Rio Grande Valley.

The board's school reforms quickly bogged down in a conflict with their new Mexican American superintendent. Within months, relations between the board and the superintendent deteriorated. He was considered insubordinate for failing to provide information needed for the proposed curriculum and evaluation reforms. The opposition claimed that the superintendent's only shortcoming was his unwillingness to go along with a "Chicano takeover" of the schools. Conversely, Mexicano activists accused Anglos of supporting an incompetent superintendent to discredit the new independent Mexicano school board.

Within a year, the board was "calling for the superintendent's head." They conducted a series of heated meetings that culminated in a controversial hearing, which the community watched on closed-circuit television. The superintendent was ultimately charged with twelve major deficiencies, including managerial and fiscal incompetence. The following day, approximately fifty students, many of them graduating seniors, staged a one-day boycott and protest in support of the superintendent. They were led by several children of prominent Anglo families and by the daughter of a Mexicano school board member. This brought in the San Antonio media, which played up the irony of Anglos supporting the first Mexicano superintendent against an all-Mexicano school board.

The local newspaper carried strongly worded editorials calling the board "Crystal City Clones." The board was portrayed as seeking to drive out Anglos and ruin the schools in the same manner as Crystal City "radicals" had. The four Ciudadanos-type board members were ridiculed as the "fabulous four," and were portrayed as setting themselves up as dictators to rule over Anglos. Rumors swirled among students that the Texas Education Agency would censor the district and make their diplomas worthless. Many Anglos privately threatened to leave town if the school board was not thrown out of office.

The new ethnic superintendent had stirred up old, bitter racial feelings. When unable to work with the all-Mexicano board, he apparently leaked information from executive meetings to Anglos. He accused board members of making inflammatory, anti-Anglo remarks and portrayed them as plotting to fire Anglo teachers and favor Mexicanos. Although the board members denied these charges, the new Mexicano athletic director/ football coach did apparently make many disparaging racial remarks. According to fellow coaches, he occasionally showed up late for practice, and he was also arrested in a drunken brawl. One radical board member was also accused of frequently visiting the schools to "spy on teachers." The Mexicano director of federal programs was also accused of inflating the migrant education rolls with non-immigrant children. Conservative ranchers and businessmen screamed "giveaway program," and revived the old images of ethnic favoritism and fiscal corruption.

In 1981 ex-BGL leaders rallied together and ran a new slate of moderate Anglo candidates to defeat the revival of La Raza militancy. As local politics heated up again, the newly elected Mayor Luna returned to the Anglo fold to crush this new radical threat. As in 1974, the Mexicano moderates retreated to the sidelines to let local politics "cool off." This left a handful of militants to run a strident, ill-fated campaign. Confused Mexicano voters stayed home in droves, and a poorly organized slate of militant candidates lost by a two-to-one margin. The ethnic confrontation of 1981 replayed the past, as if orchestrated by the ghosts of the 1974 campaign.

The Political Leaders of the 1980s: A Personal Ethnic Feud

Only two North Town "ethnic" politicians of the seventies survived as strong local leaders in the eighties. Alberto Alonzo, a former labor contractor and businessman, developed a dedicated following among low income Mexicanos. Abandoning the idea of a separatist political party, he and other Ciudadanos moderates became liberal Democrats. They wrested control of the county Democratic Party from local Anglos and helped get Mark White elected governor. Commissioner Alonzo was then rewarded with the chairmanship of the regional government council. For a time, he approved all grant applications from the region's counties. In addition, he was also elected to the executive committee of the state Democratic Party. Alonzo became North Town's first Mexicano to have real influence in the state Democratic Party.

In contrast, County Judge Sam Warren, a former school teacher and successful rancher, became the strongest North Town Anglo politician. The support of Mayor Luna's faction helped him build the town's only enduring interracial alliance. Because he spoke fluent Spanish and "worked the barrio," Judge Warren also developed his own following among low income Mexicanos. Like all Texas county judges, he helped people get county medical care, drug counseling, lenient treatment in police matters, and various jobs and favors. His eight years as county judge were free of scandal, and some Mexicano activists privately admitted that the judge supported various community health, recreational, and social programs that benefited Mexicanos.

Judge Warren proved to be a fierce opponent of anyone he considered a racial extremist. He attempted to prove that Commissioner Alonzo misused road equipment. In addition, the judge instituted a unitary system of road maintenance equipment under a county engineer. He claimed to be "modernizing" the county, but Commissioner Alonzo saw the program as a political attack on his road-paving activities. The commissioner accused the judge and others of harassing him about his son's liquor license, his use of county road funds, and a variety of other incidents involving two of his sons.

The local media continued to give extensive coverage to the conflict between the judge and the commissioner. When racial tempers flared, each side had a media organ that would put the best face on its particular cause or champion. The local paper ran anti-Alonzo commentary, and the radio ran news coverage that cast Alonzo in a more favorable light. Amidst this swirl of opinion, the judge and the commissioner became enduring political enemies. Each minimized the importance and ability of the other, but they were worthy adversaries. Each had his own following; each had his detractors as well. Opponents labeled the judge "lazy," "arrogant," and "cynical," and the commissioner "the godfather," "corrupt," and "anti-Anglo." Militants on both sides saw the conflict as symbolizing the Anglo–La Raza confrontation, but others saw it as a personal feud that hurt the community. These two proud South Texas machos survived to blow the trumpet of electoral battle another day. They remained committed to defeating each other, and convinced that they were doing what was best for the community.

As of 1987, electoral politics in North Town had entered a transitional, unstable period. No one knew whom to trust or what alliance to make. North Town's original Ciudandanos Unidos leaders were anything but united against the gringos. Serious splits had developed among North Town Mexicano political leaders. Mexicano businesspeople and professionals were slowly losing their image as "radicals," however. These activists had been quietly raising families and doing public service since the original confrontations in the early seventies. Their old ethnic political organizations had died, and so had much of the militant rhetoric about "killing the gringos." There were new signs of greater acceptance of this emerging Mexicano middle class by Anglos and moderate Mexicanos. But there were also signs that this new generation of Mexicano leaders easily lost their Anglo supporters when racial tensions heated up. Many North Towners still puzzled over why their town had experienced recurring racial conflict over the past twenty years.

Why Did North Town Race Relations Finally Explode in the 1970s?

Initially, we had no plans do a historical study of North Town, but the more "ethnic politics" confused us, the more we retreated into the recollections of old-timers and the historical records. Ultimately, we came to see the seemingly unexpected arrival of an "aggressive" ethnic movement as an eighty-year process of changing social class relations. Our original community study (Foley et al. 1988) described in great detail the region's economic transformation from a semifeudal cotton sharecropping economy (the Rancho era, 1900 to 1930) to a wage labor economy based on migrant labor (the Colonia era, 1930 to 1960).

As agriculture in North Town became fully capitalist in character, a major recomposition of the community's class structure occurred. The old semifeudal relationships of patrons to their peons was transformed into a modern, more impersonal, antagonistic wage-labor relationship during the Colonia era. As North Town's tenant farmers became a rural working class of vegetable and fruit pickers, they forced the local landed gentry to mechanize production and to accommodate to their northern migrations. From the 1930s on, the growers mechanized their production of vegetables as much as feasible to control their labor force. In addition, they came up with better ways to manage workers. Local growers created a kind of labor aristocracy of selected North Town Mexicanos who became the permanent field hands, managers, machinery operators, and contractors. These local Mexicanos helped manage a broader base of illegal, bracero (guest worker), and less fortunate local Mexicanos.

The emergence of these new Mexicano community leaders who managed the labor system was rooted in the northern labor migrations of the 1940s and 1950s. The work histories of numerous small businesspeople and labor contractors showed how skillfully some Mexicanos used the labor migrations to the north to accumulate capital. The most enterprising migrants became "free wheelers" who had their own cars or who became troqueros (truckers) and labor contractors. Such migrants negotiated concessions from their southern patrons about going north earlier in the spring and returning home later in the fall. Meanwhile, they arranged higher paying, more extended work periods with their northern patrons. In effect, they skillfully played off the northern growers against the southern ones. They also made additional money transporting friends and relatives and organized their extended family into a household of laborers. The women and children of the family worked alongside the men in the fields.

Upon returning to North Town, these more entrepreneurial migrants reinvested their savings in the small stores and rental houses of North Town's "Mexican town." They took advantage of the urbanization of North County, which followed the passing of the sharecropper system of production. Most North Town Mexicanos moved from the isolated ranchos into Mexican Town during the Colonia era (1930 to 1960). This provided new Mexicano entrepreneurs with many investment opportunities. The great labor migrations to the North, as exploitative as they were, had important implications for the class and racial orders of South Texas towns. The contemporary Mexicano leaders that we observed running businesses and practicing ethnic politics in the 1970s and 1980s can trace their families' rise to the northern migrations.

Perhaps even more importantly, the northern migrations also had a liberating effect on the Mexicano working class. Increasingly, the average Mexicano fieldworker no longer depended on his southern patron for everything. He no longer lived on an isolated ranch. His children now went to a segregated Mexican school in town, and families had their own Mexican Catholic, Baptist, and Methodist churches. He and his family migrated north and worked for higher wages for at least six months of the year. He was, in short, far more autonomous than under the earlier paternalistic, semifeudal ranching and sharecropping system. This new autonomy was expressed in greater demands for schools, social services, and independent political leaders.

Gradually, this restless working class and its new middle class leaders began to challenge the old racist Anglo political order. During the Colonia era, various small-time Anglo politicians, county judges, and sheriffs developed "political machines" of loyal Mexicano brokers and voters in the new "Mexican town." As the agricultural production system became fully capitalist, the form of Anglo political control and the extent of Mexicano political disenfranchisement changed. In the earlier Rancho era, the landed gentry had controlled voters through isolation, ignorance, heavy indebtedness, and extensive disenfranchisement. In the Colonia era, the growing economic autonomy of the town-based migrant wage laborers forced Anglos to develop a more indirect, brokered system of political enfranchisement. Small-time Anglo politicians and their loyal Mexicano brokers, often labor contractors, ran carefully orchestrated campaigns with low voter turnouts. These trends became pronounced after World War II, and several Anglo political leaders forged tenuous political alliances with Mexicano politicians. More progressive Anglo leaders began incorporating Mexicanos into a slowly crumbling segregated racial order. Mexicanos were appointed to city positions, and they were "invited" to run for the school board. The children of selected Mexicano families began going to the Anglo schools before the schools were officially desegregated. Various church groups also began promoting interracial youth groups. These changes were opposed by more conservative elements in the Anglo community, but the national civil rights movement's effects were clear by the 1950s and 1960s.

Even more visible was the growing militancy and rising expectations among the Mexicano people. Historically, ethnic working class struggles have been occurring in South Texas since the early 1900s (Zamora 1975; Nelson-Cisneros 1975). Our community study emphasized that the Mexicano working class, not the various formal civil rights organizations, was the real basis of change. The working class struggle had grown stronger by the early 1950s. Mexicano workers resisted racism through work stoppages, confrontations in bars, complaints at schools, and fights between youth. As their collective anger built into a series of small, periodic defiances, a new desire for change emerged. New home-grown community leaders appeared to articulate these new expectations. Out of this seventy-year period of class recomposition emerged the Comissioner Alonzos, Judge Warrens, and Mayor Lunas that eventually struggled to control North Town politics.

15

Cultural Politics: Mexicanos Construct a New Popular Memory

Another important way we came to understand "ethnic politics" was as a cultural process in which the old segregated racial order was redefined. Various historians (Hobsbawm and Ranger 1983; Samuel 1981; Johnson et al. 1982) have noted that any process of cultural change involves ordinary people constructing and reconstructing the meaning of their own history. In this view of "ethnic politics," North Towners were using remembrances of past race relations to redefine the present. This shared popular memory—what was remembered and forgotten, what stories were told to justify present actions—was a crucial part of conducting contemporary race relations in North Town.

During the post-World War II era, the Mexicano people began advocating the dismantling of the segregated racial order. As North Town desegregated its public institutions in the 1950s and 1960s, the cultural rules governing everyday race relations changed. Gradually, Anglo public demeanor in social relationships became more respectful. Mexicanos reported more cordial, friendly treatment in stores and at the post office and city hall. Physical territories and spaces in the town once considered "Anglo" and "Mexican" began breaking down. Mexicanos were no longer afraid to go downtown or to the public schools. The County Court House was no longer exclusively Anglo. Mexicanos perceived a growing Anglo respect for "their" churches, children, cantinas, and restaurants. Along with this greater public respect and accommodation came a new-found sense of freedom to move and act more as equals.

This greater sense of freedom also kindled a continuing desire in Mexicanos to tell their children about a cruel, uncaring past. The North Town Mexicano community was filled stories of racial atrocities to justify the present political revolt or break with the past. The political movement unleashed stories about cruel Anglo patrons, sheriffs, and money-lenders, and about loyal workers being replaced by tractors and combines. There were stories of brawling, disrespectful Anglos in their cantinas, and of patrons who sought to make Mexicanas into mistresses. For the Anglo leaders who had pretensions of being liberal, there were stories about how they treated their maids and household help. Mexicanos also told stories about positive, heroic, and honorable resistance. Homilies about standing up to "gringos" and jokes about "gringos" were part of everyday conversations. Telling the tale of this bitter past was a vital part of creating a new popular cultural and political consciousness (Foley et al. 1988).

Chicano activists located their strength in this past. Only those who sought to be diplomatic and accommodating avoided using the past to construct a new present. Mayor Luna's appeals to "forget the past" illustrate perhaps the most fundamental difference between him and the militant Manuel Ramirez. The deepest connotation of being a "vendido" was practicing a kind of social amnesia about one's past. Vendidos sold out their historical roots. Conversely, cultural nationalists entreated their followers to remember the bad and good of it. To some extent, most contemporary North Town Mexicanos have followed the cultural nationalists' efforts to create a new cultural pride among the people. The most obvious signs of the nationalists' impact were in the everyday cultural practices and attitudes of ordinary Mexicanos.

In short, a major cultural transformation had taken place in North Town racial/ethnic relations. The old, restrictive rules of being "seen but not heard" and of "staying in one's place" were no longer practiced. The Mexicano people had shattered the social territories that Anglos assigned them, and they had created their own social, expressive space. Of course, there were still Mexicanos who avoided associating with Anglos and who were inactive in public affairs. Older Mexicanos often marveled at the brashness and openness with which young Mexicanos walked about and expressed themselves to Anglos. These new patterns of more open, assertive behavior evoked many we-had-it-worse-in-the-old-days stories from old-timers. Such an ongoing dialogue between the generations confirmed the importance of never returning to their bittersweet past—except for the telling of tales.

More Cultural Politics: The BGL Construct a New Political Rhetoric

In the face of these new assertions of cultural pride and self-determination, North Town Anglo leaders were forced to legitimate their current political and economic prominence on new grounds. The old norms of Anglo racial and cultural superiority were losing their credibility. Increasingly, Mexicanos believed that the past was unjust, and that they were the social equals of Anglos. Moderate BGL Anglos realized that extreme racial ideology and prejudice had become anachronistic in a desegregating racial order. These "modernizers" of traditional racist ideology actively battled hard line "red necks" who evoked Anglo racial privilege with comments such as, "Mexicans are too dumb and crooked to run things," "Mexicans can't manage money," "No Mexicano is ever going to be good enough to give me orders."

Some Anglos sought to distance themselves from this racist ideology that Mexicanos were culturally and intellectually inferior. These policy-makers used a more liberal rhetoric about serving the Mexicano and Anglo populations of North Town equally. This new political discourse created internal dissension within the BGL, however, and school board politics became the center of controversy. In several policy decisions, the moderate BGL leaders sought to persuade "reactionary red necks" and "radical Chicanos" to accept the legitimacy of their authority. The moderate Anglos generally sought to justify their policy decisions on non-racial grounds: rule by law and legal procedure and greater tolerance for cultural difference.

The first new basis of legitimacy, rule by law and legal procedure, was an explicit statement against La Raza's alleged criminality and totalitarian character, and for Anglos' alleged capacity to be rational and objective. The BGL represented themselves as saving the American democratic tradition of rule by law. They hoped to give these "ignorant," inexperienced new Mexicano politicians a lesson in civics. Their decisions, which they considered "fairminded and democratic," were supposed to be in stark contrast to the "illegal, criminal, and communistic" behavior of the new Mexicano city council.

The second new basis of legitimacy, greater tolerance for cultural difference, was a public posture that distanced moderates from the old Anglo ideology of cultural superiority. Adopting this posture tacitly acknowledged the Mexicanos' emphasis on cultural pluralism and equality. These new Anglo politicians sought to transform the cultural basis for traditional race relations. They wanted to signal that a new kind of Anglo political leader had emerged who was responding to Mexicano demands. These new Anglo leaders rhetorically portrayed themselves as fairer and less racially bigoted than past Anglo leaders.

The BGL Legitimates Its Authority in the Schools

The ongoing cultural process of redefining the old segregated order often centered on who controlled the schools and the minds of future generations. School politics became the issue that evoked the most fears and passions in North Towners. A series of incidents illustrate how North Towners struggled to redefine a racist past and live with a new, uncertain present and future.

The first school board controversy that symbolized this new political discourse occurred over wearing Raza Unida political buttons in school. A junior high principal decided, without board approval, to "crack down" on "trouble-makers" wearing provocative political buttons. Several teachers took buttons off the students, and the principal gave a long impassioned lecture to the student council. He compared the Raza Unida to Nazi and Communist movements that threatened freedom and the American way of life. Quite predictably, the student council included several students from the families of Ciudadanos activists. The president of the student council was the son of one of the Ciudadanos school board members.

The next morning, an angry delegation of twenty parents demanded that the superintendent either muzzle or fire the principal. The key leaders of the delegation were Ciudadanos activists. The school board quickly rescinded the principal's unilateral decision and announced their agreement with recent rulings protecting freedom of speech in schools. During the school board hearing, the principal was publicly reprimanded and forced to apologize to the Raza Unida party leaders. Most teachers and a number of BGL members regarded this as a capitulation to La Raza radicals.

On another occasion, the board found it necessary to rule on a case of two Anglo football players caught drinking beer at a livestock judging contest. Both boys were seniors in good academic standing, and many Anglos considered them "leaders, fine young men." The board, following its rule on such matters, suspended both boys from school for the remainder of the year. During a well attended, emotional hearing, the board reaffirmed its position of following the letter of the law. A number of speeches portrayed the board as fair and impartial people who punished "all students." They followed the stated rules, as they said, "to the letter of the law."

The aftermath of both these incidents illustrates the ideological rupture in the BGL ranks. In the first case, Anglo hard-liners agreed with the principal's assessment that wearing a La Raza button was provocative and against American democracy. They felt the board was "a bunch of appeasers." One rancher commented to me:

> This is another damn give-away program, if you ask me. We can't let these thugs push us around. What in the hell is this goddamn school board trying to prove? They don't need to give in to that bunch! It will just make them try to get away with more on us. We can't be making concessions with these people or it will be "gimme this and gimme that" from now on.

In the second incident, a group of angry Anglo parents castigated the board for "bending over backwards to show the Mexicans that Anglos could be strict with their own kind." In the eyes of many local Anglos, the board was being too legalistic. During a heated argument, board critics

19

pointed out that several Mexican boys caught drinking during the previous year were not suspended. Dissident Anglos read the board's statements and actions as unnecessary political pandering. They resented the loss of informal Anglo privileges.

The political buttons and drinking incidents illustrate the moderate BGL leaders' attempts to legitimate their authority on the grounds of rule by law and legal process. Indeed, the essence of a modern rational-legal society is a set of public bureaucracies that serve all citizens fairly. Theoretically, modern impartial, rational, efficient rules replace traditional, inherited cultural practices and priviledges (Weber 1947). In this case, the rules and legal procedures of the school bureaucracy had to be spelled out more carefully. These new Anglo moderates were trying to create decision-making processes that were, or at least appeared, more legal and rational and less cultural or racial.

This process of legitimation was also evident in a variety of everyday school policies and practices. School administrators and teachers were generally put on alert to be much more careful about provoking racial incidents. First, the board initiated a more liberal hair and dress code policy. They clearly established what constituted neat and properly groomed hair and dress. In creating this new policy, various board members made several speeches emphasizing that they now had a clear, objective basis for sending offensive students home. The main students this affected were the working class Mexicano males, the "vatos" (cool dudes) who dressed unconventionally and wore long hair. The new policy made it more difficult for Mexicano political activists to make a racial issue out of the vatos' expulsion and punishment.

Second, the system of discipline was also reorganized. The previous liberal principal was replaced with a former football coach who had a reputation for firmness and fairness. The board also replaced the school counselor and created a new vice principal position. According to teachers, the whole tone and style of the high school administration changed. The counselor was requested to help any and all students get into some college, if they had any aspirations. The new counselor, whose wife was Mexican American, never tired of saying that "there was a place for anybody and everybody in some college, regardless of race, creed, and school performance."

Perhaps most importantly, the vice principal established a "rationalized" system of punishment. The key to his system was a card file on all student offenders. Each student who had ever been sent to the central office had a "record." All previous unexcused tardinesses, detention-hall sentences, and referrals from teachers were listed. The previous offense then became the basis for interrogating offenders. Any tongue-lashings, "licks" (paddlings with a board), and suspensions given out were based on one's record. The vice principal always pointed out that he was acting strictly on evidence, not his personal views of the offenders.

Third, policies toward class placement and evaluation were also shrouded in rhetoric about the objective technology of tests. The principal strongly defended the placement of more than 50 percent of the Mexican American students in "practical classes" that were all-Mexican. He contended that they were not being discriminated against; regrettably, their test scores were simply "too low to qualify for placement in advanced classes." Within these courses labeled "practical," North Town educators claimed to be "creating an opportunity for the low-achieving student." They used books with only fourth and fifth grade reading levels and simplified the objective exams in practical high school classes. These practices artificially raised the achievement scores of practical students.

In addition, teachers then coached students, practiced tests, and frequently gave re-tests. Once the test scores had been raised through these means, low-achieving students could be "socially promoted." Lower academic standards and expectations were instituted through the rhetoric of "equal opportunity for the low achiever." Everyone deserved a chance to feel successful. This image of "academic success" was strongly contested by the new Mexicano middle class, however. They interpreted these kinds of concessions to "quality education" as an Anglo attempt to deny Mexicanos an equal education. Particularly the Ciudadanos school board members felt that principals and teachers were not "tough enough on our Chicanitos." Taken together, all the previous policy practices initiated by the school board represented a systematic response to the politicization of local race relations.

In addition to these school policies, the BGL leaders also sought to make a number of concessions on the expression of Mexican American culture. Most teachers and students reported that the rules against speaking Spanish had already been relaxed before a strong civil rights movement emerged. Indeed, the general attitude towards Spanish was extremely permissive. It was the informal language of the hallways and classrooms. Students frequently shifted into Spanish to hide comments from teachers. This "code switching" between languages was done often and with impunity.

A more dramatic illustration of concessions toward Mexicano culture and language was the board's sponsorship of a bilingual education program for children who spoke little English. A number of school board meetings were filled with conciliatory speeches about the need for bilingual education. Following the 1974 Texas Bilingual Education Law, if the parents of twenty limited English proficient (LEP) children requested a bilingual classroom, a school district was required to provide such an instructional setting. The activist women leaders in Ciudadanos Unidos requested such programs, and the school board responded.

In addition, other federal programs (Title I and Title VII) for the culturally different and economically underprivileged such as Head Start, Free Lunch, and Migrant Education were also instituted or maintained. These changes followed the creation of a single, integrated school district in 1971. Generally, the BGL school board members were "liberals" on a number of federal programs that many local Anglo ranchers and farmers considered "give-away programs" and "federal government meddling." The Anglo board members expressed non-ideological, pragmatic views toward making concessions to Mexicano demands for more federally sponsored school equity programs. This posture represented a distinct break with the school policies of the 1950s and 1960s.

The school board took numerous opportunities to portray their new policy orientations in public meetings. The problem with such verbal portrayals was, however, repeated inconsistencies in their behavior. Local Ciudadanos leaders never tired of pointing out this difference between the political rhetoric of Anglo leaders and their actual deeds. For example, the school board advocated bilingual education, but they understood bilingual programs as compensatory, transitional programs designed to teach English. They were not interested in maintaining the language and culture of Mexicanos. In fact, the board vetoed any attempts to introduce Chicano history and culture. During various school board discussions, the idea of "Chicano history" was called "un-American" and "political propaganda." The board had little interest in any formal curriculum that would promote the ethnic consciousness-raising process that Chicano cultural nationalists extolled.

One of the most telling incidents occurred over the painting of toilet walls. The school board accused the director of the Head Start Program, a suspected Ciudadanos sympathizer, of turning the bathrooms into a political billboard. The director had organized parents and various volunteers to fix up and paint their building. They painted the bathroom walls in bright yellows, blues, and greens. The decor included a golden rising sun and a brilliant rainbow. Everyone from the parents to the children admired their colorful new building. When the school board heard about the new color schemes it quickly investigated. Several BGL members claimed that the Head Start staff had painted an "Aztec sun," which was being used as political propaganda. The board ordered the bathrooms repainted

22

a standard beige color. The director was informed that noncompliance would be considered an act of insubordination and defacing school property. After much teeth-gnashing, the walls were repainted beige.

Finally, BGL leaders also tried to create community events that symbolized their positive view of Mexicano culture and harmonious race relations. One conspicuous example was the Chamber of Commerce's Fourth of July celebration. The affair included a number of games such as a cow chip throwing contest, food booths, and a variety of local performers who entertained people. The afternoon program was conspicuously interracial in design. The Catholic Church's all-Mexicano choir sang "America the Beautiful" and the "Battle Hymn of the Republic." One prominent BGL leader made sure I noted that these young Mexicanos were patriotic and were getting along well with Anglos. The program included several high school students dancing an "Aztec Dance." The Aztec dance was followed by an Anglo country western singer wailing out a song about his lost love. The interracial theme was extended to the evening dance, which had both a country western band and a Mexicano con junto band. These events purported to symbolize the Chamber of Commerce's commitment to cultural pluralism.

Ten years later, I witnessed a very similar event (minus the Mexicano choir singing "America the Beautiful") called the "Annual Peanut Festival." This time the general Chamber of Commerce, which now included several Mexicano businesspeople, and the Mexican American Chamber of Commerce jointly planned the festival. As before, the political leaders took pains to point out the celebration's significance for racial harmony. Unlike the earlier event, former Ciudadanos and BGL leaders both promoted the event. Such public celebrations to encourage racial harmony were also apparent in occasional church-sponsored events and church youth groups.

In summary, the local school board politics staged the complex process of constructing a new popular conception of race relations. North Towners battled as much over their differing definitions of reality as they did over the actual control of their public institutions. A new political discourse on race relations emerged from these ethnic political confrontations over schools. In the end, actions like painting the Head Start bathrooms beige were far more persuasive than rhetorical speeches about bilingual education programs or patriotic Fourth of July celebrations.

When both groups confronted the meaning of their past, a profound difference in perspectives emerged. Mexicanos saw how closed and defensive Anglos were in the discussions over a Chicano history course. The idea of teaching the stories about racism, the migration, the old sheriffs, the Ku Klux Klan, and various Chicano heroes met with stiff Anglo resistance. Indeed, the local schools were generally not a place that openly and officially dealt with the town's "racial problem."

North Town Schools: A Case of Social Amnesia on Racial Issues

After a few months of fieldwork, it became clear that the schools made racial issues their best kept secret. Teachers avoided any discussion of the "La Raza threat," and the idea of discussing this ethnic conflict frightened most of them. I was initially struck by how little open discussion over these issues occurred in classrooms. In countless hours of observation on the school grounds and in classrooms, I saw only three teachers discuss the race question openly. After a few months, I began asking teachers why they avoided this topic. Over and over again, they gave the reasons this teacher did:

> I try to stay away from any discussion of racial stuff and La Raza, because you never know what these kids will say to their parents. One time, I presented some stuff about the birth control controversy, and the principal asked me if I was advocating birth control to Catholics! If I let them talk about La Raza, I guarantee you that some parents are going to get on my case for advocating racial violence or communism or something bad. Sometimes these kids don't like you, so they just wait for something to use against you that they know their parents hate. Or sometimes, they just misunderstand the difference between discussing an idea and being for an idea. I don't think most of them ever discuss anything objectively. If we started talking about this stuff, somebody would also get mad and start cussing out the other side. It might even lead to fights right then and there, or afterwards. We aren't ready to talk about this kind of stuff around here yet.

Other teachers said that they were afraid they would lose their jobs. Many perceived the school board as ready to make sacrificial lambs of them. Most agreed in principle that the school should be open and innovative about race relations. In practice, however, teachers felt that there was too much political pressure to promote a "racial dialogue." Teachers talked openly about their own views of local politics and race relations, but they avoided such discussions in their formal lessons.

Topics often came up that lent themselves to such discussions. For example, the government teacher taught a unit on third party politics. He spent several days describing the pluralist theory of American politics. He explained how more "radical" third parties periodically challenge the two major parties, the Democrats and Republicans. This proved to be exactly what happened to the Partido Raza Unida in North Town. The town was a living laboratory of how American politics work, so I asked him at the time why he didn't use Partido Raza Unida as an example of his theory. He told me that it was too controversial for either students or parents to discuss calmly.

Shortly after the government unit on third parties, I observed a discussion on Thoreau's "On Civil Disobedience" in English class and a discussion on the black civil rights movement in American history. Both teachers studiously avoided drawing any parallels to local events, because they feared controversy and political pressures. One of the more advanced students defended teachers in the following way:

> The administration doesn't like Mr. Ray, because he lets kids express their opinion about all sorts of things. Then some dumb kid goes home and tells his parents, who complain to the school board, and they give Mr. Ray hell. For example, one day we were talking about the good and bad aspects of tobacco, and this kid tells his parents that Mr. Ray told us everybody should smoke. So he catches it, and everybody got real mad. It's stupid, we can't even have a good discussion . . . Yeah, we have discussed the political problem this town has a couple of times. It came up on a couple of essays people wrote, so we discussed it. This one Mexican kid said North Town should be free enough to let Mexicans have their own party. Several of the Anglo kids really didn't like that, but they didn't say too much. Mr. Ray let the kid have his say, and a couple of us said we thought they were too extreme. Nothing really happened. Nobody freaked out about it. Mr. Ray didn't say too much one way or the other. He mainly let us talk.

I witnessed a similar discussion in Earl Ray's class. There was considerably more tension than the student implied, but neither side was willing to take the conversation too far, and Ray steered it rather quickly to another topic. He expressed a good deal of frustration about not being able to discuss many sensitive topics openly or in depth.

His views were shared by a young assistant band director straight out of the University of Texas. He characterized himself as "a frustrated white liberal" who was going back to the safe confines of the city:

> I can't deal with all this hatred. They need to start group dynamics in about third or fourth grade and get all this out in the open. I've done my bit at Brown school [a private school for emotionally disturbed youth] for two years. I'm not a social worker. I just want to run a nice quiet band somewhere. The biggest thing I see here is everybody tries to avoid the problem. Teachers feel that if it really does come out, the kids and they won't be able to deal with all the hate

25

and misunderstanding under the surface. There is a lot of fear about it. I know I can't, and I've had some experience with this kind of stuff between the races at the Brown school.

We also experienced this social amnesia very directly when we asked people to review a draft of our book. The issue of publicly acknowledging the town's bittersweet historical past resurfaced. Some North Towners called our book "propaganda for La Raza" and accused us of being racially biased. For Anglos, we had allied with Mexicano cultural nationalists in using the past "against the Anglos." In some sense, I was a traitor to my own race because I had no amnesia about the town's racial past.

While BGL Anglos and Mexicanos generally wondered, "What good would this book do?" many Mexicano reviewers wanted the real names used in the book. They also wanted a Spanish version for their old-timers to read. They made glowing comments about how "no one has ever told their story before." Of course, what they meant was that nobody had ever written an "official history" of their story. When a number of Mexicanos read an early draft of the book, they recognized the stories reported as "the same stories that I heard growing up." For many Mexicanos, our account was true because we had taken our place alongside the elders as their storyteller. Unlike the elders, however, we were outsiders and would be telling their story to a much larger audience. As one reviewer said, "Maybe you will tell the feds, and somebody will come in here and clean up this town."

Even today, the schools still seem to have a policy of social amnesia about our book. Nevertheless, the local radio station, run by a Mexicano activist, publicized and sold it. The station also taped an interview with me discussing the book. In addition, one city manager ordered copies for the city employees, and the bilingual education program director purchased several copies for incoming teachers to read. According to the city librarian, approximately six or eight high school students a year check out the copy in the public library. One social studies teacher said students used it for reports, but the school library has no copy because it "might stir up bad feelings." We could not be trusted to tell the story of North Town's racial past.

North Town political leaders also had little trust in their own teachers to explain the town's "racial problem." They doubted that teachers and their children could rationally discuss racial feelings. But as the subsequent discussions on school sports, dating, and classroom interactions will illustrate, some teachers and coaches did informally mediate racial feelings and conflicts. Some courageous examples of relatively open, conflict-free dialogues occurred, in spite of many community leaders' unspoken policy of social amnesia.

The Racial and Political Legacy of North Town Youth: A Summing Up

This, then, is a little of the political and racial legacy that North Town youth inherited. This is the historical context in which North Town youth grew up. Understanding the behavior and events in the schools is impossible without a sense of the historical baggage these youth must carry. At times, they were merely reenacting the town's traditional patterns of privilege. They enacted much of this legacy as they played football, dated, and did their classroom schoolwork. At other times, these youth were charting a new course and breaking with their inherited past. It is to these matters, then, that we must turn. Hopefully, this tale will capture the complexity of these tumultous times as it illustrates why schools are a site of popular culture practices that stage social inequality.

TWO

The Great American Football Ritual

In the fall, North Towners enliven community life with a peculiarly American ritual. Every Friday night, North Towners avidly support their high school football team. Growing up American, especially for many males, involves participating in competitive school athletics. This chapter is a cultural analysis of football that emphasizes how fundamental American values are learned and transmitted. This community ritual socializes North Town youth to carry on a number of traditional cultural practices governing class, race, and gender relations. What follows is an account of the football season I experienced in North Town.

The Pep Rally: Building Solidarity and Reproducing Gender Roles

Students, whether they liked football or not, looked forward to Friday afternoons. Regular seventh period classes were let out early to hold a mass pep rally to support the team. Most students attended these events, but a few used them to slip away from school early. During the day of the pep rally I attended, I heard a number of students planning their trip to the game. Those in the school marching band (80) and in the pep club (50) were the most enthusiastic. This trip meant getting out of the house, relatively unsupervised, for eight or ten hours. Students were plotting secret rendezvous with boy and girl friends or were fantasizing about fateful meetings with their unknown true loves. Fewer students and townspeople than usual would follow the team on this first long road trip.

Nevertheless, as on most Fridays, teachers and students were talking about "the game." Some teachers engaged the players in lively banter during classes about "whipping" Larson City. In senior English class non-players entreated the players to get "revenge" for last year's defeat. A long analysis of last year's bad calls, missed kicks, and fumbles ensued.

The history of this event had already been reconstructed, and those students interested in it shared that moment with the players. Players and non-players collectively plotted and reveled in mythical feats of revenge. There was much brave talk about "kicking their asses this year."

Some North Town high school students considered the idea of young males in padded armor crashing into each other "dumb" and "boring." Some North Town adults also thought that sports was "silly" or "too rough" or a "waste of time." Generally, however, most North Town students, like the adults, looked forward to football season and these Friday night games. The games enlivened the community's social life. Enthusiastically supporting "the team" meant supporting your town and your way of life. Adults, especially the local Chamber of Commerce types, articulated this view even more than the students. Community sports was the patriotic, neighborly thing to do. Many kids in school felt deep loyalties to support their team. Others, as we shall see, used these community events to express their disgust for the game and the players, hence for "respectable," mainstream society. Whether they loved or hated football, most students were glad to get out of classes and attend pep rallies.

This Friday afternoon, the pep rally started like most school pep rallies. As the last bell rang, the halls were crammed with students rushing to put books away and to find their friends. Having reunited, pairs and groups of students pushed and shoved their way into the school gym. Different students claimed their rightful territories on the bleachers facing the microphones. Months later, after knowing the kids better, I could see the pattern to this mad scramble for seats. It was all age-graded, with the older, most prominent students taking the center seats, thus signaling their status and loyalty. Younger first-year and second-year students sat next to the leaders of the school activities, if they were protégés of the leaders.

In sharp contrast, knots and clusters of the more socially marginal students, the "druggers" and the "punks and greasers," usually claimed the seats nearest to the exits, thus signaling their indifference to all the rah-rah speeches they had to endure. The "nobodies" or "nerds," those dutiful, conforming students who were "followers," tended to sit in the back of the center regions. Irrespective of the general territory, students usually sat with buddies from their age group. Teachers strategically spread themselves out at the margins and down in front to assist in crowd control.

The pep rally itself was dominated by the males, the coaches and players. They were introduced to the audience to reflect upon the upcoming contest. In this particular pep rally, the team captains led the team unto the stage. All the Anglo players entered first, followed by all the

29

Mexicano players. Since one of the team captains was Mexicano, this entrance by racial/ethnic group was particularly noticeable to an outsider. The coaches followed the players in, and the principal, Bill Wicks, himself an ex-player, gave the floor to the head coach, Roberto Trujillo. Coach Trujillo started out with the classic pep talk that introduced the team captains. They came forward and spoke in an awkward and self-effacing manner, thus enacting the ideal of a sportsman—a man of deeds, not words.

The first stuttered through several "uhs" and "ers" then quickly said, "I hope y'all come support us. Thanks." The crowd screamed and yelled. I said sarcastically to the kid next to me that the captains were "some speakers," and he shot back a puzzled "yeah?" I recalled the dread we always had about making these obligatory speeches. Then as now, kids expected their jocks to be inarticulate—as the cliché goes, "strong and silent types." Another, more confident player, the quarterback and team captain, said, "Coach Trujillo has made us work real hard to get ready for Larson City. We are ready to give them a good game." His speech evoked the players' loyalty to their coach and their dedication to hard work, and the hope that these qualities would bring victory.

Coach Trujillo then followed up and elaborated upon these themes. He also brought up the theme of revenge in a low-keyed way. Last year's defeat at the hands of Larson City was evoked to jibe the present seniors that "this would be their last chance to beat the Raiders." Since Larson City was not a longstanding, traditional conference rival, getting revenge had less meaning than beating arch-rival Hodson.

Between the brief comments made by players and coaches, the cheerleaders and pep squad tried to involve the student body through cheers. A small contingent of the eighty-piece marching band tooted and banged out the proper drum rolls for the speakers and cheerleaders. Other band members dispersed among the crowd and helped the pep squad lead cheers. Being a part of the band was an important way of establishing one's loyalty to school and community. Later, during the game, the marching band would entertain the crowd at half-time while the players rested. This half-time performance also showcased the youth of North Town.

The Marching Band and Band Fags: The Male Gender Boundary

The quality of the marching band was as carefully scrutinized by some community members as the football team was. The band director, Dante

Aguila, was keenly aware of maintaining an "excellent" winning band. Like sports teams, marching bands competed in local, district, and statewide contests and won rankings. The ultimate goal was winning a top rating at the state level. In addition, each band sent its best players of various instruments to district contests to compete for individual rankings. Individual band members could also achieve top rankings at the state level. Some community members, themselves former band members, supported the marching band as much as the team itself. The marching band was also a major symbolic expression of the community's unity and its future generation of good citizens and leaders.

A certain segment of the student body began training for the high school marching band during their grade school years. Band members had a very different view from football players about participating in band. For them, being a band member was a highly valued extracurricular activity. The band was filled with students who tended to come from the more affluent families and have better academic records. The more marginal, deviant students perceived band members as "goodie goodies," "richies," and "brains." This characterization was not entirely true, because the Band Booster Club made an effort to raise money to help low income students join the band. Not all band students were top students, but many were in the "advanced" or "academic" tracks. Band members were generally the students with "school spirit" who were proud to promote loyalty to the school and community. As one local city councilperson was fond of saying, "Band kids are the best kids in this town."

The view that they were the "cream of the crop" was not, however, widely shared by the football players. Female band members included a wide range of young women; some were studious "homegirls," but, like the pep squad, a large number were socially prominent and "cool." On the other hand, "real men" supposedly did not sign up for the North Town band. According to the football players, the physically weaker, more effeminate young men tended to be in the band. The young men who belonged to the band were considered "band fags." The only exceptions were "cool guys" who did drugs and had their own rock and roll band, or guys from musical families who planned to become professional musicians. Indeed, the players seemed to perceive male band players as eunuchs in their royal court. These males were sometimes derided and picked on as "sissies." Occasional gender jokes were made about their "not having the balls" to date the "cute" female band members. Jocks perceived them as no competition for dating the attractive young women in the band and pep club.

Jocks swore that band members walked and talked in more effeminate ways than other males, but I was never able to perceive the difference. These conversations on the differences between males evoked numerous memories about the same prejudices in an earlier era. The main masculinity tests "real males" in the late 1950s orchestrated for band "homos" was to punch their bicep as hard as possible. If the victim returned this aggression with a defiant smile or smirk, he was a real man, if he winced and whined he was a "wimp" or worse, a "homo." In my observation, to "punch out" someone's bicep was still a common masculinity test, the other variations being pinching the forearm and rapping the knuckles. All these tests of pain thresholds were still being practiced, and were preludes or provocations to actual fighting. What had changed was the terminology for "effeminate males," the term "fag," which meant a cigarette in the 1950s, having replaced "homo" as the preferred invective.

Punching and pinching each other were types of male taunts that marked joking, buddy relationships. Such "tests" or ritualized forms of insult could, however, escalate into fights between two aggressive, dominance-oriented males. This kind of male play served a somewhat different purpose when directed at "effeminate males." The more physical males enjoyed terrorizing the effeminate ones in this manner. These were small, daily ritual degradations, moments when some males physically "picked on" other males. There was nothing dishonorable about physically superior males reaffirming in small ways their place in the pecking order. But to fight the weaker males would have been considered a mismatch and dishonorable, bullying behavior.

For the most part, players themselves rarely engaged in this type of behavior toward male band members. Jocks generally looked on with amusement and egged others on to enact this culturally defined boundary between effeminate and masculine behavior. Male "hangers-on," those hoping to "hang with" the jocks, were usually the "hit men." Being "real" and "secure" men, the jocks had to show restraint toward dominating obviously weaker males. It was this show of restraint that signaled their power and prestige.

Cheerleaders and Pep Squads: Reproducing the Female Gender Role

As in most pep rallies on the Friday I am describing, the cheerleaders were in front of the crowd on the gym floor, doing dance and jumping routines in unison and shouting out patriotic cheers to whip up enthusiasm for the team. The cheerleaders were acknowledged as some of the prettiest young women in school, and they aroused the envy of "nobodies" and "nerds."

Male students incessantly gossiped and fantasized about their "reputations."

One frequently told story was about a pep rally when students started throwing pennies at Trini, a cheerleader. Initially, this curious story made no sense to me. Trini struck me as the perfect all-American girl next door. She was "cute and perky," got above-average grades, and was on her way to college, a good career, and marriage. She also dated an Anglo from another town. Trini complained, however, that she could not wait to "blow this town" because "people here acted like animals" toward her. She was very outspoken, which may have been the reason for the mass penny pitching. That incident, and the relentless gossip about her being a "slut" and "gringo-loving whore," had cut her down to size, but being strong-willed she would not quietly accept these put-downs. She lashed back, criticizing people for being small-town and small-minded.

The rest of the girls, four Mexicanas and two Anglos, were of more or less the same physical and social type. One of the Anglo girls was particularly athletic, which often prompted Anglos to make negative comparisons with a Mexicana, who was popular but considered a bit plump. Students invariably had their favorites to adore and/or to ridicule. They told contradictory stories about the cheerleaders. When privately reflecting on their physical virtues and social status, they saw "going with a cheerleader" as guaranteeing their coolness and masculinity. Particularly the less attractive males plotted the seduction of these young women and reveled in the idea of having them as girl friends. When expressing their views publicly to other males, however, they often accused the cheerleaders of being "stuck up" or "sluts."

This sharp contradiction in males' discourse about cheerleaders makes perfect sense, if one remembers that males talked about these young women as objects to possess, dominate, and gain status through. Conversations among males about these females were rhetorical performances that bonded males together and established their rank in the patriarchal pecking order. In public conversations, males often expressed bravado about conquest of these "easy lays." In private conversations with intimate friends, they expressed their unabashed longing for, hence vulnerable, emotional need for these fantasized sexual objects. These highly prized females become, therefore, dangerous, status-confirming creatures that were easier to "relate to" in rhetorical performances than in real life. Only those males with very high social status could actually risk relating to and being rejected by the cheerleaders. The rest of the stories these young men told were simply male talk and fantasy.

The one exception to this fantasized, contradictory, adoring yet envious view of cheerleaders was Martha, a somewhat shy, plump, likeable cheerleader. She was homey and simple, a kind of earth mother symbol of fecundity and domesticity. Unlike many of the cheerleaders, she was neither cool nor upwardly mobile. She lacked a reputation as a "wild, swinging boozer." She was simply Martha, the kind of woman who would become an "ideal wife and mother," and who would maintain a good religious household. In Martha, most "nobodies" could see a respectable, successful representation of themselves. She was the life that they would eventually live. She was the one cheerleader who seemed above the leveling influence of gossip.

Many young women who were not athletic or attractive enough to be cheerleaders nevertheless wanted to be. Such young women often joined the pep squad as an alternative, and a strong esprit de corps developed among the pep squad members. They were a group of fifty young women in costume who came to the games and helped the cheerleaders arouse crowd enthusiasm. This group also helped publicize and decorate the school and town with catchy "team spirit" slogans such as "Smash the Seahawks," "Spear the Javelinos." In addition, they helped organize after-the-game school dances. Their uniforms expressed patriotism toward the team, and pep squad members were given a number of small status privileges in the school. They were sometimes released early for pep rallies and away-from-home games.

Teachers were often solicitous to pep squad members and labeled them "good students." Pep squad members were usually students who conformed to the school rules and goals, thus were "good citizens," but being in the pep squad also afforded them an opportunity to break home rules. On road trips, these young women momentarily escaped parental supervision and had public opportunities to attract and flirt with young men from other towns. This helped establish their gender status among other students as more "hip," even though being in pep squad was a "straight" activity. Students and some teachers joked with pep squad members about "getting out of the house" to go to the games for romantic reasons. These young women had, therefore, a strong supporting role in the pep rallies and the whole sports scene.

This Friday's pep rally ended with the usual speeches exhorting the young boys on to victory. As the last drum roll echoed, students rushed to the exits. The end of pep rallies usually struck fear into the hearts of most teachers, who had to control a student body escaping to their weekend fun. As the team filed out, Coach Trujillo asked, "Is that how they do it in Iowa?"

I wanted to say: "It sure is, but we never had any Mexicans to march in last." Since discretion is the better part of valor in anthropological fieldwork, I actually replied, " Yep, it sure is. So are we really going to beat Larson City?"

A long, somewhat nervous conversation followed in which the Coach conveyed to me that I would soon find out he was controversial and needed to have a winning season to avoid being fired.

A Mexicano Coach on the Firing Line

Coach Trujillo, being North Town's first Mexicano coach, had inherited what most townspeople considered the "best crop of players since North Town made it to regionals in the fifties." Considerable controversy had already set in among the Booster Club supporters. They had opposed the board's hiring of Coach Trujillo over a popular local Anglo coach, both native sons.

Coach Trujillo's father ran a dance hall that alternately hosted Anglo country western and Mexicano con junto music. More importantly, his father was one of the charter members in the new BGL political organization. This alliance with the Anglo BGL made him and his son "vendidos" in the eyes of many Ciudadanos members. His son, actually not a politically involved person, had a reputation as "a nice man, but a little weak." He was, however, the perfect compromise candidate for the BGL liberals who controlled the school board. Coach Trujillo was a native son, college educated, polite, respectful, and generally mild-mannered. His previous coaching record, though not exceptional, was considered acceptable. Most importantly, he was from a successful middle class Mexicano family who renounced the extreme views of La Raza. Some people noted the similarity in his style to that of Mayor Luna. He was the BGL liberals' model of an accommodating, reasonable Mexican.

A number of BGL Anglos were outraged, however, with this appointment over the Anglo coach, Jim Ryan, who had the distinction of having led North Town to their only regional finals. He was also a likeable "good old boy" type who was very approachable and had deep South Texas roots. Liberal BGLers viewed him as a poorly educated "red neck" who could never portray the new ethnic tolerance they imagined themselves representing. Coach Ryan was a staunch conservative who constantly railed against communists, welfare loafers, and La Raza radicals. Many Mexicano players actually considered him a good disciplinarian and coach, but a number also felt that he was indeed partial toward Anglo players.

35

Coach Trujillo, on the other hand, was considered too friendly and "soft on the players." Stories circulated about his "easy practices" and "indecisive play calling." What many of the critics wanted was a "military style coach," a stern disciplinarian. They constantly criticized the star North Town players for being "lazy" and "too soft." Trujillo was on the proverbial coach's hot seat for all the classic, and for uniquely racial, reasons. He had the double jeopardy of being neither manly enough nor white nor brown enough to lead North Town youth into battle. He was constantly challenged to prove himself both to the Mexicano activists and to the more red neck Anglos.

Constructing New Race Relations: Telling Jokes and Homilies

As Coach Trujillo and I finished the first of several soul-searching talks about race, politics, and sports, the players began to arrive for the bus trip. This first out-of-town trip also proved to be revealing on the subject of race relations. The players took their seats as if some crusading Eastern liberal had written the script. All the Mexicano players quietly seated themselves at the back of the bus. Then all the Anglo players brashly seated themselves in the front of the bus with the coaching staff. At first, I was taken aback by this event, which seemed to be a sign dripping with Anglo racial dominance. Yet I wondered how such a seating arrangement could possibly signify subservience in a town full of politically assertive Mexicano adults.

Before we reached Larson City, at least ten racial jokes were hurled between the front and the back of the bus. One giant Anglo tackle, the son of the high school principal, cracked perhaps the best joke. He commented on the fact that the Mexicanos were in the back of the bus. He bellowed out: "Shewt, if we lose this game, *we* [the Anglos] are going to ride home in the back of the bus. This brought a nervous reply from Coach Trujillo that he might have to join them [the Anglos] there, too. Having just heard the story of his compromised political position with Mexicanos, I thought the comment was his way of downplaying the controversy over him. Or perhaps he was as subservient to Anglos as the Ciudadanos leaders claimed.

As we neared Larson City, to my great surprise, he cracked the following joke with the Anglo players: "We are going to have to take some of you boys to Boystown to show you how the *other half* lives." Anyone familiar with Texas border culture knows that the whore house sections of Mexican border towns are called "Boystown." The classic male rite of passage for South and West Texas males, which was beautifully portrayed in Peter Bogdanovich's *The Last Picture Show,* is to lose your virginity in one of these Boystowns. This embattled Mexicano coach was joking about Anglo males using Mexicana prostitutes. He was suggesting to the Anglo players that they were about to become men and friends with his race, if they would let him "make men out of them." Coach was evoking a common male bonding ritual and using humor to displace the racial tensions. He was also saying that they were all heading for "the border" of race relations in search of a new understanding.

Although this was a very clever use of male humor, I wondered if the young, more politicized Mexicano players sitting in the back of the bus were offended by this racial slur on their women. Their strong silence had evoked a number of nervous ethnic jokes from Anglos and the conciliatory humorous performance of Coach Trujillo. One could feel the powerful irony of their choosing to sit in the back. I saw this same quietly defiant behavior many times, and concluded that they were quite consciously inverting a popular American cultural symbol of discrimination. Riding in the back of the bus symbolized racial subordination and tension between the races, but Mexicanos were taking "their place" out of strength, not out of deference and fear.

The game with Larson City proved much easier than the coaching staff had anticipated. North Town's star players, two selected for pre-season state honors, had lackluster games, but the team performed ably and won easily. Throughout the game, I was able to prowl the sidelines with the team trainer/doctor. He was one of the original founders of the BGL, and had set for himself the task of convincing me what a splendid coach Trujillo was. He kept emphasizing how much racial unity the team had exhibited tonight. When I asked him about Coach Ryan, he gave the expected "He's a dumb red neck" response. Sensing that I apparently already knew about this controversy, he mentioned several racial incidents that Coach Trujillo had prevented.

The most important incident, by now an oft-told tale, concerned a fight between an Anglo and a Mexicano. Apparently the Anglo player, a big rawboned rancher's son, had punched out a rather unathletic Mexican American "band fag" for an off-color remark to a young Anglo woman. In retaliation, several friends of the Mexicano youth, who saw it as an unfair mismatch, ganged up on the Anglo in the school parking lot. Coach Trujillo called in the player and the two key members of this retaliatory Chicano strike force. According to the doctor, the coach properly chastised both sides—the Anglo boy for being too hot-headed, and the Mexicano boys for unfairly ganging up on one Anglo. During the recounting of this tale, the doctor evoked the classic ethnic stereotypes of the coura-geous, rugged, individualistic, fair-minded Anglos and the clannish, cowardly pack of maurading Mexican bandidos. More importantly, he underscored how a sensible Mexican coach was able to mete out the proper moral lesson to each offending side, thus racially reuniting North Towners.

Although the doctor's account of this incident turned out to be particu-larly fanciful, I ended up spending a great deal of time watching for examples of coaches serving as mediators of racial conflict, and at least one other coach, Coach Trujillo, did indeed take it upon himself to mediate racial attitudes and images. They directly intervened as peace-makers in at least two other incidents of conflict between players and students. More importantly, they often tried to redefine the reality of North Town race relations through telling a story or homily to their players. An excellent example of their role in redefining racial/ethnic relations was a story I overheard Coach Trujillo tell several Anglo players after practice one day.

Trujillo had just finished putting the boys through a brutal two-and-a-half hour full-pads scrimmage (a full-pads scrimmage is a simulation of actual game conditions with two complete teams trying to score and defend their goal). This scrimmage was taking place during the dog days of late September, and the temperature on the playing field was a least a hundred degrees Fahrenheit. The boys were exhausted and began joking and complaining about what a dictator the coach was. One quipped, "Man, I thought Hitler was a German."

Coach Trujillo read this ethnic reference as an invitation to launch into a racial treatise on the sense of equality and character of the Mexicano people, and himself in particular. Trujillo had been the first Mexicano player with a scholarship to play for a "lily-white" West Texas college. He then recounted his own version of the brutal two-a-day summer practice story that all football players tell. Usually this tale is told to illustrate one's pain threshold and ability to survive hot, sweaty practices. Often such practices do seem like the nightmarish inventions of a coach, who imag-ines himself as Rommel the desert fox on some forced desert march. Only "real men" survive these hot summer practices, and the worse they are, the better the telling of the tale. Young players usually recount these practices to older relatives and former players who hang out in local gas stations and restaurants.

Coach Trujillo created an interesting variant of this tale that also had a racial lesson. After the exhausted players returned to the locker room, one of the Anglo players apparently had the gall to toss the coach's equipment away from his locker, thus invading his hard-earned resting space. The coach confronted the offending locker mate and reminded him that they were all in it together. They were all survivors of the football wars; consequently, he was deserving of equal respect and space. With a twinkle in his eye the coach explained, "I was telling this guy in a nice way, 'Hey red neck, that's my space.'"

According to Coach Trujillo, this bold, honest confrontation of the Anglo, and by extension American society, brought instant respect from the uninvolved players sitting nearby. They could see that he was ready to fight for his rights, which he had earned "by the sweat of my brow." Seeing this hulking white monster of a lineman being cowed by this little brown bulldog was a new experience for his Anglo teammates. They purportedly responded with warmth and admiration, and this was the beginning of the coach's acceptance among his white teammates.

In a way, Coach Trujillo's story was much like the miraculous conversion tales that born-again Christians often tell. In a trying and difficult moment, he acted with courage and humility to be accepted as an equal. He risked everything and stood up for the ideal that the races should live together in harmony rather than discord. According to his tale, from that day forward, a new era of race relations began for his school and their football team. He relived his past to model what he wanted for his own players. No, he was no Hitler, nor were his people any different from Anglos. Moreover, he and his people were ready to fight for their rights. The coach told several homilies like this one. It is not clear how effective such moral lessons were, but this was how he dealt with the "race problem."

But, in the end, Coach Trujillo "threw in the towel." Despite a good season, second in the conference and a 7–4 record, he resigned and left his home town feeling "sick of the strife and the pressure on my family." The coach claimed that he had "lost a lotta friends" and had gotten an ulcer. He compared the South Texas racial situation unfavorably to other places he had been, such as Colorado and Michigan, and feared that North Town might never change. Being a real centrist, he had very little good to say about either political group:

My daddy wants out of the BGL. He can see that the Anglos just won't change. They just want to use him, and one or two Anglo board members still think I am just a Meskin. They'll never change. They always overreact to a Mexicano getting ahead. Look at the school elections. They handled the whole thing very poorly. Some kids were left off the ballot by mistake, and they should get rid of the rule that disqualified some of our best kids. They are just trying to protect their kids and hold us back. And the Anglos should not have quit the band trying to pressure the new Mexican American band director. I'm sick of the Raza Unida too. They use these pressure tactics and call people "vendidos" and shoot off their mouths. The indictments of voters is real bad, and the Anglos are pressuring to control the school board votes, but Raza Unida has gone too far. I believe they did try to steal the city election, and they did shoot a gun at the mayor's house.

Coach Trujillo had grown up in an earlier era of more restricted race relations, and it left a mark on him. He constantly referred to the problem of learning English. For him, his generation were made to feel ashamed about speaking Spanish to their parents. Coach lamented that red necks still felt superior, even though he was more educated than they were. When talking about interracial dating, he remembered Mexicano boys taking out Anglo girls in the following way: "I felt good about it, kind of like I won for a change, but also scared. I thought maybe they'll beat me up. Maybe my own people will call me a 'vendido.'"

As the coach reflected on his past, he came across as a man trapped in a painful process of cultural change. Unlike the new generation of kids, he was never a part of an aggressive civil rights movement and remained unsure how much to assert himself. The movement left him filled with a longing for change, but a certain fear about breaking the cultural rules he hated. In the end, Coach Trujillo decided the situation was impossible to change or live with, so he moved on, but not without a great deal of sadness.

The Cultural Role of a Coach in an American Community

The general public does not normally think of coaches as being racial philosophers or counseling psychologists, but Trujillo thought of himself as a peacemaker. In fact, coaches are often *the* key educators who socialize males into their gender role. As a result, young men are less likely to dismiss their moral lessons than those from male teachers considered "sissies." During extreme moments of physical sacrifice for the group or team, the players must face "moments of truth." The coaches are the caretakers of those moments when the young prove their masculinity. They, and military leaders, are the chief elders who guide young males through this rite of passage into the traditional American notion of manhood.

Nevertheless, these molders of manhood are mere mortals with college degrees who also grow fat and become bald. Coaches quickly lose their warrior status and become organization men, administrators of budgets, and public relations experts. These administrative minotaurs are half-man, half-bureaucrat. They must appease local factions, school boards, administrators, booster clubs, angry parents, and rebellious teenage youth. They must live within a budget set by others. At the high school level, they are paid a small extra sum of money for hundreds of hours of extra work. Many find it difficult to carry out the non-technical, more administrative parts of this role. Others are excellent public relations men because of the type of men they are and the "down home," rural life styles they lead.

The status of North Town coaches among fellow teachers was not particularly high. Dumb-coach jokes and stereotypes were exchanged behind their backs. On the other hand, a disproportionate number of "dumb coaches" became school principals and superintendents. Some teachers openly resented this fact. Old warriors, rather than fade away, tended to become school leaders, whereas teachers were mere purveyors of information. Coaches and ex-coaches were more likely to have side businesses, to hunt and fish, and to join local coffee cliques or Saturday morning quarterback groups. In short, they were "real men" who liked fraternizing with the entrepreneurs, politicians, and good old boys who actually ran the town.

North Town was the type of community in which male teachers who had athletic and coaching backgrounds were respected more than ordinary teachers. Locally elected board members, often male farmers and ranchers, rugged men of action, preferred their school leaders to be ex-coaches. The superintendent, himself an ex-coach, sported a fifties-style flat top and loved to hunt. The junior high principal, also a former coach, owned and ran a steak house. The high school principal was an ex-coach but lacked the capital for a business. Three of the present coaching staff had farming or small buy-and-sell businesses on the side. School board members invariably emphasized an ex-coach's ability to deal with the public and to discipline the youth. Coaches were men who who guarded and enhanced the community tradition of being a good "sports town" with strong, virile young males.

Prominent Citizens and Their Booster Club:
Reproducing Class Privileges

North Town was in many ways a typical "sports town." The town reportedly had a long history of Booster Club and school board interference into coaching the team. One of the coaches characterized North

Town in the following manner: "One of the toughest towns around to keep a job. Folks here take their football seriously. They are used to winning, not everything, not the state, but conference and maybe bidistrict, and someday even regional. They put a lot of pressure on you to win here.

The Booster Club, mainly composed of local merchants, farmers, and ranchers, had the all-important function of raising supplementary funds for improving the sports program and for holding a post-season awards banquet. The Club was the most direct, formal link that coaches had with the major North Town civic leaders. Some prominent merchants and ranchers were absent from these activities, because they disliked sports, or because they left it to those with more time and enthusiasm.

At this point in time, the Booster Club was run by a small clique of Anglos whom the BGL liberals considered "good old boys and red neck types." They became outspoken early in the season against their "weak Mexican coach." They fanned the fires of criticism in the coffee-drinking sessions over which of the two freshman quarterbacks should start, the "strong-armed Mexican boy" or the "all-around, smart Anglo boy." The Anglo boy was the son of a prominent car dealer and BGL and Booster Club activist. The Mexican boy was the son of a former migrant and small grocery store manager. The freshman coach, Jim Ryan, chose the Anglo boy, thus revealing his racial and class prejudice. In a similar vein, conflict also surfaced over the selection of the varsity quarterback. Coach Trujillo chose the son of an Anglo businessman, an underclassman, over a senior, the son of a less prominent Anglo. The less educated, more "common man" Anglo faction lambasted the coach for this decision, claiming he showed his preferences for the children of the more socially and politically prominent BGL-types.

One former player of this era, who later became a present-day coach and community political leader, eloquently recounted what "physical education courses never teach you" about coaching:

I will never forget Coach Bowman. He was a hard core sergeant type who didn't give a damn about pleasing the Booster Club. During a real rough practice the Smith kid got beat up pretty bad by a Hispanic kid and coach stopped starting him. His mother came in to the office one day to chew out Coach Bowman, and she caught him sitting there in his shorts with his legs up on the desk puffing away on this stogie. He told her that her son was a "goddamn sissy and didn't deserve to start." From then on, his days were numbered, and the Booster Club got him fired . . . and it works both ways. Hispanics do the same thing. When we had the big school board change and Coach Fuentes was brought in, he gave me a list of three kids, a quarterback, linebacker, and running back, who he wanted me to play on the freshman team. They were all the kids of school board members or buddies of the politicos. It was bad, man. I threatened to walk off the field and let him coach, so he finally gave in.

The coach went on to explain how local pressures and influences on coaches get played out. He advised me to watch who got invited to the parties after the games and to hunt on certain ranches:

> I'll tell you where you really see all this stuff, Doc. You never got invited to the parties, so you didn't see this. Every Friday night after the games, the prominent people in this town throw a barbecue and invite us coaches. The whole staff has gotta go and behave right if you wanna keep your job. That is where a coach can make or break himself . . . No there wasn't but one or two Mexicanos at these parties. It was all Anglos, until the Mexicano school board came in. Then everything changed. Nobody invited Coach Fuentes and his staff to these parties. They started going to parties on the other side held by the Mexicano politicos. Most Anglos also dropped out of the Booster Club at that time too . . . Really, there is no way that this town can have a good football program without a good mix of kids and the Anglo parents ramrodding the Booster Club. It is sad to say, but the Mexicanos will probably always be too divided to run the thing right. The Booster Club was in bad shape when they ran it . . . The other important thing is getting invited by the people who have got money to hunt bird or deer on their land. It is kinda of an honor for you to do this, and for them to have you. And if you've got good connections with star players and name coaches from the University or the pro ranks, then you bring them in to speak to the Booster Club. Local people like going hunting with a real sports celebrity even better. It's all part of the way it is down here, Doc. To survive, you gotta get along with certain people.

The pattern of community pressures observed in North Town was not particularly exceptional. A good deal of the public criticism and grumbling about choices of players had racial overtones. The debate over which white varsity quarterback to play also reflected community class differences among Anglos. North Town students and adults often expressed their fears and suspicion that racial and class prejudices were operating. Inded, class and racial bias crept into the managing of teams in many subtle, unintended ways.

It would be an exaggeration, however, to portray the North Town football team as rife with racial conflict and disunity. Nor was it filled with class prejudice. On a day-to-day basis there was considerable harmony and unity. Mexicanos and Anglos played side by side with few incidents. A number of working class Mexicano youths and a few low income Anglos were also members of the football program. At least in a general way, a surface harmony and equality seemed to prevail.

The only rupture of such public accommodations came when Coach Trujillo and Coach Ryan exchanged sharp words and nearly got into a fist-fight during practice. This led to Trujillo's making what many Mexicano political activists considered a humiliating public apology to Ryan. The two coaches were also severely reprimanded by the principal and superintendent. Ultimately everyone, especially the two feuding coaches, tried to downplay the conflict "for the good of the team." Powerful social pressures existed to control any public expression of racial disunity and class conflict on the team.

Observing all the political controversy that swirled around the selection of players evoked vivid memories of my own experiences with small-town sports. As I talked to the young, strong-armed Mexicano quarterback who was languishing on the bench, I could not help but identify with him. In my case, I was a farm boy who was unable to participate in sports until high school. Upon moving to town, I experienced my first taste of how sports perpetuates racial and class inequality. As a junior in high school, I had improved enough to gain a spot on the varsity basketball team. After several games, the coach took me aside and explained to me the facts of life and small town sports. I will never forget his this-is-good-for-the-team speech that relegated me to "riding the bench."

The coach started out his speech by recounting how much I had improved since moving from the farm to town and how much it hurt him to replace me with another player who was no better and a senior. But he felt he had to do it for the good of the team because several other senior players preferred my rival. His speech omitted the fact that the other player was part of a peer group of the sons of businessmen and doctors. Being an innocent "hick," I still did not understand that one could be technically but not socially good enough to play. I remember friends from "smoky row" (the poor section of town) explaining to me that I was a "nobody—like them," not someone who lived on "the hill" (the rich section of town).

Theoretically, school sports is the great social equalizer in American society. Talented non-white ethnic and working class youth are supposed to find social mobility through sports. There is some truth to this claim. The social mobility data in Chapter 5 show how well athletes do in the adult world of work. Given evidence of individual mobility, sports advocates are fond of arguing that sport always favors excellence and performance. Those players who are most skillful will always play, because the ultimate object of the game is winning. Coaches will select players objectively, without class or racial prejudices, because their personal interest, and the team's interest, is served by winning. Unfortunately, this free market view of sports is very a-historical and leaves out how sports actually functions in local communities.

Small-town coaches are generally subjected to enormous pressures to play everyone's child, regardless of social class and race. Success in sports was an important symbolic representation of familial social position. Adult males can reaffirm their claim of leadership and prominence through the success of their offspring. A son's athletic exploits relive and display the past physical and present social dominance of the father. In displaying past and present familial prominence, the son lays claim to his future potential. Every North Town coach lived and died by his ability to win games *and* his social competence to handle the competing status claims of the parents and their children.

Small-town sports becomes a pressure-cooker of familial and peer pressures. Socially prominent families, who want to maintain their social positions, promote their interests through Booster Clubs. The fathers of future community leaders spend more time talking and criticizing coaches in local coffee shops. These fathers are more likely to talk to the coaches privately. Coaches, who have ambitions to be socially prominent, are more likely to "network" with these sports-minded community leaders. A symbiotic relationship develops between coaches, especially homegrown ones, and the traditional community leaders. Preferential treatment of the sons of prominent community leaders flows from this web of friendships, hunting privileges, Saturday morning joking, and other such exchanges.

Moreover, as the subsequent discussion of student peer groups and classrooms will show, considerable pressure to favor the sons of prominent citizens comes from within the school as well. The school and its classrooms also become a primary social stage upon which students enact their social privilege. These youths establish themselves as leaders in academic, political, and social affairs, and teachers grant them a variety of privileges. This reinforces the influence of their parents in the Parent-Teachers Club, the Sports and Band Booster Clubs, and the school board. Both generations, in their own ways, advance the interests of the family on many fronts.

The Friendship Groups of Ex-players: Socializing Young Men

Another major aspect of the football ritual is how the spectators, the adult males in the community, socialize each new generation of players. Many fathers, uncles, cousins, and friends also played football, and the new generation of players came in contact with these ex-players in local pool halls, taco joints, drive-ins, and barber shops. During summers, the players often worked with or for these men. Conversations in the fields and produce sheds invariably turned to sports. Many players reported these conversations, and I observed several during "Saturday-morning-quarterback-sessions" in a local restaurant and gas station.

One Saturday morning after the all-important Harris game, two starters and good buddies came into the Cactus Bowl. One of the local rancher-businessmen shouted, "Hey, Chuck, Jimmie, get over here! I want to talk to you boys about that Harris game!" He then launched into a litany of mistakes each boy and the team had made. Others in the group chimed in and hurled jokes at the boys about "wearing skirts" and being "pussys." Meanwhile, the players stood slope-shouldered and "uh-huhed" their tormentors. One thing they had learned was never to argue back too vociferously. The players ridiculed these kinds of confrontations with "old-timers" privately, but the proper response from a "good kid" was tongue-biting deference. The whole scene reminded me of how we used to avoid the downtown area after a bad game. I wondered why Chuck and Jimmie were such gluttons for this barrage of criticism, why they had not anticipated and avoided it.

This sort of pressure on players began early in the week with various good-natured jests and comments. The most critical groups were the friendship cliques of ex-players who had recently graduated. Those that went off to college usually only came back a few weekends to watch games. If they continued to play, they returned as celebrities and tended to say very little. Being college players, they tended to be "above" any carping criticism of underclassmen who still played "high school ball." Usually, the more relentlessly critical groups were those ex-players who had never left town.

Some ex-players led the romanticized life of tough, brawling, womanizing young bachelors. These young men, while no longer kids, seemed suspended in a state of adolescence while avoiding becoming "responsible family men." They could openly do things that many of the players had to control or hide because of training rules. Many of these ex-players were also able physically to dominate the less mature high-school-aged players. But ex-players no longer had a stage upon which to perform heroics for the town. Consequently, they often reminded present-day players of their past exploits and the superiority of players and teams in their era. Present-day players had to learn from these tormentors and take their place in local sports history.

Older groups of middle-aged males with families and businesses were also influential in socializing the new generation of males. These types of males congregated in various restaurants for their morning coffee and conversation about business, politics, the weather, and sports. Particularly those leading citizens interested in sports could be found praising and criticizing "the boys." They took on a much more paternalistic, almost fatherly demeanor toward the players. Some hired the players and were inclined to give them special privileges. Athletes were more likely to get good paying jobs as road gang workers, machine operators, and crew leaders. Most players denied that they got any "favors," but they clearly had more prestige than other high school workers. Non-players complained that "jocks" got the good jobs. On the job sites the older males regaled players with stories of male conquests in sports, romance, and business.

The Homecoming Bonfire and Crowning: A Rite of Solidarity

During the football season other ceremonies like the homecoming bonfire rally and dance were also an important part of the football ritual. Ideally, North Town graduates returned on these occasions to reaffirm their support and commitment to the school and team. They came back to be honored and to honor the new generation presently upholding the name and tradition of the community. In reality, few ex-graduates actually attended the pre-game bonfire rally or post-game school dance. Typically, the game itself drew a larger crowd, and the local paper played up the homecoming game more. College-bound youth were noticeably present at the informal beer party after the game. Some townspeople were also at the pre-game bonfire rally, something that rarely happened during an ordinary school pep rally. Homecoming was a special ritual event that celebrated the continuity between generations of North Towners.

That afternoon, bands of Anglo males riding in pickup trucks began foraging for firewood. Other students not involved in hauling the wood gathered in the school parking lot. They wanted to watch what was brought for burning and shared stories about stolen outdoor wooden outhouses, sheds, posts, and packing crates. It was important to the onlookers which community members donated burnable objects, how cleverly objects were procured, and what outrageous objects were to be burnt this year. This was obviously a traditional event that entertained and bestowed status on both the procurers and donors of burnable objects.

Three groups of boys with pickup trucks eventually created a huge pile of scrap wood and donated burnable objects. The cheerleaders and band

and pep squad members then conducted the bonfire ceremonies. Several hundred people, approximately an equal number of Anglo and Mexicano students, showed up at the rally, along with a fair sprinkling of older people and non-high schoolers. Nearly all the leaders were Anglos, and they were complaining that not enough students supported the school or them. The cheerleaders led cheers and sang the school fight song after brief inspirational speeches from the coaches and players. Unlike the school pep rally, the police arrived to survey the fire. Rumors circulated that they were there to harass people because some crates might have been stolen from a local packing shed. It was also rumored that some of the football players were going to get drunk after the bonfire died down.

The huge blazing fire in the school parking lot made this pep rally special. The fire added to the festive mood, which seemed partly adolescent high jinks and partly serious communion with the town's traditions. The collective energy of the youth had broken a property law or two to stage this event. Adults present laughed about the "borrowed" packing crates and were pleased that others "donated" things from their stores and houses to feed the fire. The adults expressed no elaborate rationales for having a homecoming bonfire, which they considered "nice," "hot," and a "good way to fire up the team."

The "firing up the team" pun was actually a fairly good explanation of the bonfire. It was a kind of tribal fire around which the community war dance was held. The event was preparing these young warriors for battle, and the cheerleaders and band replaced the painted dancers and tom tom drums. In addition, the fire was a kind of community hearth. At least some people were literally returning to the "home fires" of their village and tribe. Gathering around the bonfire reunited all North Towners, past and present, for the special homecoming reunion and gridiron battle. Whatever the deeper symbolic meaning, those attending seemed to enjoy the pep rally. Several of the organizers and friends remained behind to watch the fire burn down. They gossiped about friends and acquaintances and told sports stories.

After the homecoming game, a school dance was held with a homecoming court complete with king and queen. The queen and her court and the king and his attendants, typically the most popular and attractive students, were elected by the student body. Ideally, they represented the most attractive, popular, successful youth. They were the best of a future generation of North Towners. Following tradition, the queen was crowned during half time at midfield as the band played and the crowd cheered. According to tradition, the lovely queen and her court were ceremoniously delivered to the crowning in convertibles. The king and his attendants, who were often football players, then came running from their half-time break to help the young women down from the convertibles. The players, all sweaty and dirty, escorted the young women, dressed in formal prom dresses, to their crowning. The king and his court lingered rather uneasily until the ceremony was over and then quickly returned to their team to rest and prepare for the second half.

On the particular occasion that I observed, the homecoming half-time ceremony took place as it always did, but with one major difference. The customary convertibles for the queen and her court were missing; consequently, the queen and her court, on this occasion all Mexicanas, had to walk to their crowning. This evoked numerous criticisms among Mexicano students and parents in attendance. Many felt it was a gringo plot to rob the Mexicanos of their chance to be leaders in the community. The *Chicano Times,* a radical San Antonio newspaper, screamed out headlines that accused the school officials of blatant discrimination. The administrators and teachers in charge of organizing the event denied these charges, but were left embarrassed and without any acceptable defense.

In this particular instance, this solidarity ritual became instead a source of divisiveness in North Town. The strong reaction of Mexicanos underscores the importance of this ceremony for marking community traditions and leadership. Those Mexicanos seeking to become integrated into and leaders of this community were not willing to be treated differently. They demanded that this ritual be enacted the way it had been in the past. They demanded that football and its homecoming ceremony serve its traditional purpose of creating continuity and unity. A number of BGL Anglos perceived the Mexicanos as "politicizing" the event and "causing trouble." Another way of interpreting their criticism was, however, as an attempt to preserve the pomp and splendor of the ceremony that marked the social status of future leaders. Mexicanos were trying to preserve a cultural tradition that would finally serve their children the way it had those of Anglos.

The Powder-Puff Football Game: A Rite of Gender Affirmation

Another ritual event, the powder-puff football game, although not as public and community-wide, also helped mark the importance of football and school sports. Anthropologists have come to call such curious practices "rituals of inversion" (Babcock 1978), specially marked moments when people radically reverse everyday cultural roles and cultural practices. During these events people break, or "humorously play with," their own cultural rules. Such reversals are possible without anyone's suffering any sanctions or loss of face. These moments are clearly marked so that no one familiar with the culture will misread such reversals as anything more than a momentary break in daily life. The powder-puff football game was a ritual of inversion that socialized North Town youth in important ways.

A powder-puff football game was traditionally held in North Town on a Friday afternoon before the seniors' final game. A number of the senior male football players dressed up as women and acted as cheerleaders for the game. A number of the female seniors dressed up as football players and formed a touch football team that played the junior women. The male football players served as coaches and referees, and comprised much of the audience as well. Perhaps a quarter of the student body, mainly the active, popular, successful students, drifted in and out to have a laugh over this event. More boys than girls, from both races, attended the game.

The striking thing about this ritual was the gender difference in expressive manner. Males took this occasion to act silly and outrageous. They pranced around in high heels, smeared their faces with lipstick, and flaunted their padded breasts and posteriors in a sexually provocative manner. Everything, including the cheers they led, was done in a very playful, exaggerated, and burlesque manner. In sharp contrast, the females donned the football jerseys and helmets of the players, sometimes those of their boy friends. They proceeded to huff and puff soberly up and down the field under the watchful eyes of the boys. They played their parts in the game as seriously as possible, blocking and shoving with considerable gusto. This farce went on for several scores, until one team was the clear winner, and until the young women were physically exhausted and the young men were satiated with acting ridiculous.

When asked why they had powder-puff football games, most male students could not articulate a very deep meaning for the event. Most said things like "It's good for a laugh . . . It's fun . . . It's a good break from school. School's boring." Others hinted at something more than recreation and teenage fun:

> I don't know, I guess it gives guys a chance to have a little fun with the girls . . . It makes the girls see how rough it is to play football . . . The guys get to let off a little steam, tease their girl friends a little, maybe show them who's the boss.

Some girls earnestly suggested the following meanings for the event:

> It gives us a chance to show the guys that we can compete too. We aren't sissies. We can take getting hit too . . . We can show them that football isn't just for

guys . . . Girls are athletic too. We can run and throw the ball pretty good, too. God, I don't know, just to have a break from sixth period . . . The guys get to have all the fun, why shouldn't we?

Teachers tended to look on the game as a silly, harmless event that helped build school spirit. One boldly suggested that maybe these big jocks were putting on bras because they secretly wanted to be girls. That tongue-in-cheek interpretation of footballers has already been seriously proposed by one prominent folklorist (Dundes 1978). Alan Dundes understands the butt-slapping and talk about "hitting holes" and "penetrating the other team's endzone" as a form of male combat that masks latent homosexuality. Such an interpretation would undoubtedly shock North Towners, who generally regarded this sort of thing as simply fun and silliness.

This interpretation also completely misses the cultural significance of such an event. Males used this moment of symbolic inversion to parody females in a burlesque and ridiculous manner. Males took great liberties with the female role through this humorous form of expression. The power of these young males to appropriate and play with female symbols of sexuality was a statement about males' social and physical dominance. Conversely, the females took few liberties with their expression of the male role. They tried to play a very serious game of football. The females tried earnestly to prove they were equal. Their lack of playfulness was a poignant testimony to their subordinate status in this small town.

This moment of gender role reversal was a reflection of sexual politics, not of sexual preference. A psychological interpretation overlooks the historical pattern of patriarchy in the entire football ritual. The powder-puff football game, although seemingly a minor event, was an important part of the total football ritual. This ritual socialized both sexes to assume their proper gender roles. As in their relationships with ex-players and elders, the powder-puff football game socialized the young males to believe they were socially and physically superior.

Generally, the women unwittingly participated in staging this expression of male dominance and privilege, but the assertive, serious way they played the game might also be teaching them some new lessons in competing with males. One could argue that the young women were also trying to invert this inversion ritual, thus turning young men into real rather than symbolic buffoons.

The community context of the football/school sports has been described in detail, but little has been said about how players see the game.

What do they like about it? Why do they play? What meaning does this sport have for them? No cultural description of an important ritual would be complete without the view of the participants themselves.

Players Talking About Their Sport: The Meaning of Football

The preceding portrayal of the community sports scene has already suggested what may be the major reason for playing football. Many young American males are willing to endure considerable physical pain and sacrifice to achieve social prominence in their community. Only a very small percentage are skilled enough to play college football, and only one North Towner has ever made a living playing professional football. The social rewards from playing football are, therefore, mainly local and cultural.

There are, however, other more immediate psychological rewards for playing football. When asked why they played football and why they liked it, young North Town males gave a variety of answers. A few openly admitted that football was a way for them to achieve some social status and prominence, to "become somebody in this town." Many said football was "fun, "or "made a man out of you," or "helped you get a cute chick." Others parroted a Chamber of Commerce view that it built character and trained them to have discipline, thus helping them be successes in life. Finally, many evoked patriotic motives, to beat rival towns and to "show others that South Texas played as good a football as East Texas."

Different kids gave different reasons for playing football, but these explicit statements do not reveal the psychological lessons learned in sports combat. In casual conversations, players used phrases that were particularly revealing. What players talked most about was "hitting" or "sticking" or "popping" someone. These were all things that coaches exhorted the players to do in practice. After a hard game, the supreme compliment was having a particular "lick" or "hit" singled out. Folkloric immortality, endless stories about that one great hit in the big game, was what players secretly strove for. For most coaches and players, really "laying a lick on" or "knocking somebody's can off" or "taking a real lick" was that quintessential football moment. Somebody who could "take it" was someone who could bounce up off the ground as if he had hardly been hit. The supreme compliment was, however to be called a "hitter" or "head-hunter." A hitter made bone-crushing tackles that knocked out or hurt his opponent.

Players that consistently gave out outstanding "hits" were called "animals," "studs," "bulls," "horses," and "gorillas." A "stud" was a

52

superior physical specimen who fearlessly dished out and took hits, who liked the physical contact, who could dominate other players physically. Other players idolized a "real stud," because he seemed fearless and indomitable on the field. Off the field a stud was also cool, or at least imagined to be cool, with girls. The image of a big powerful stallion captures the ideal of a true stud. He has his way with the mares, over-powers other stallions, and, though loyal, is almost too strong for his master. A strong coach, like a good horse trainer, knows how to handle his studs, how to give them their head, yet rein them in when needed. North Town players expected and wanted strong coaches and some studs to lead them into battle. They talked endlessly about who was a real stud and whether the coach "really kicks butt."

The point of being a hitter and stud was proving that you had enough courage to inflict and take physical pain. Pain was a badge of honor. Playing with pain proved you were a man. In conventional society, pain is a warning to protect your body, but the opposite ethic rules in football. Bandages and stitches and casts became medals worn proudly into battle. Players constantly told stories about overcoming injuries and "playing hurt." A truly brave man was one who could fight on, because pain and wounds challenged him to overcome greater obstacles. Scars were perma-nent traces of past battles won, or at the very least fought well. They became stories told to girlfriends and relatives.

The other, gentler, more social side of football was, of course, the emphasis on camaraderie, loyalty, friendship between players, and pulling together. Players also often mentioned how much fun it was to "hang out" with the guys. Some of them admitted to being "locker room and gym rats," guys that were always hanging around the fieldhouse and gym. They told stories of their miraculous goal line stands, of last-minute comebacks against all odds, and of tearful, gut-wrenching losses on cold muddy fields. Most of the players talked about the value of teamwork and how satisfying it was to achieve something together with other guys. Difficult, negative experiences were also shared. Long, grueling practices without water and shade, and painful injuries, were part of being team-mates. Only other football buddies who had been to the football wars could appreciate the sacrifice and physical courage demanded in practices and games.

There were also shining tales of good sportsmanship. Players told stories about being helped up and helped off the field by opponents. They also prided themselves in learning how to lose gracefully and be "good sports." At the high school level, winning was still the most important thing, and most coaches drilled that into their players. But if you could not win, the very least you could do was try as hard as possible, give all of yourself to the cause. The one cliché that North Town players constantly parroted back to me was "winners never quit, and quitters never win." Most North Town players prided themselves in giving their best effort. If they did not, the townspeople would lose respect for them and grumble, as they did during two conference losses. As the Chamber of Commerce claimed, North Town youth acquired their aggressive, competitive spirit on the town's athletic fields.

Another positive thing that most players mentioned was the emotional thrill of performing before large crowds of people. Many stories were told about "butterflies" and "getting the adrenalin pumping." High school players coming back to the bench were quite aware of the crowd. They threw down their helmets in exaggerated anger and disgust. They shouted at each other, slapped high-fives, and smashed each other's shoulder pads. Meanwhile, they cast furtive glances at girls in the pep squad or at older brothers prowling the sidelines. They constantly had to express their spirit and commitment to the game, even during sideline breaks. Others limped and ice-packed their injuries and grimaced broadly for all to see.

Many players, particularly the skilled ones, described what I would call their "aesthetic moments" as the most rewarding thing about football. Players sitting around reviewing a game always talked about themselves or others as "making a good cut" and "running a good route," or "trapping" and "blindsiding" someone. All these specific acts involved executing a particular type of body control and skill with perfection and excellence. Running backs made quick turns or "cuts" that left would-be tacklers grasping for thin air. Ends "ran routes" or a clever change of direction that freed them to leap into the air and catch a pass. Guards lay in wait for giant opposing linemen or aggressive linebackers to enter their territory recklessly, only to be "trapped" or "blindsided" by them. Each position had a variety of assignments or moments when players used their strength and intelligence to defeat their opponents. The way in which this was done was "beautiful" to a player who had spent years perfecting the body control and timing to execute the play. Players talked about "feeling" the game and the ball and the pressure from an opponent.

In the broadest cultural sense, one could argue that playing football was the American way of preparing its males for future wars. America does not need a draft and mandatory military service as long as school sports are organized in every hamlet, ghetto, and suburb in the country. Team sports, and especially American-style football, socialize males to be warriors. The young men of North Town were being socialized in the same way that my schoolmates and I were socialized in the fifties. We were taught to measure ourselves by our animal instincts and aggressiveness. Physicality, searching for pain, enduring pain, inflicting pain, knowing one's pain threshold emphasizes the biological, animal side of human beings. These are the instincts needed to work together and survive in military combat, and in corporate, academic, and industrial combat. The language used—"head-hunter," "stick 'em," and various aggressive animal symbols—conjures up visions of Wall Street stock brokers and real estate sharks chewing up their competition.

Other Males: Brains, Farm Kids, Nobodies, and Vatos

But what of those males who do not play high school football? Are they all simply categorized as effeminate "band fags"? To the contrary, several types of male students did not lose status for being unathletic. First, there were a small number of "brains" who were obviously not physically capable of being gridiron warriors. Some of them ended up playing other sports with less physical contact like basketball, tennis, track, or baseball. In this way, they still upheld the ideal of being involved in some form of sports. Others who were too slightly built, wore thick glasses, lacked hand-eye coordination, or ran and threw too poorly to play any sport sometimes ended up "hanging around" jocks or helping them with their school work. Others were loners who were labeled "nerds" and "weirdos."

Second, there were a relatively large number of "farm kids" or poor kids who did not participate in sports. These youth, like adult males active in their church or in jobs, had little time for sports. They were generally "homeboy types" who did not participate in many extracurricular school activities. Some of them had to work to support their families. Others had no transportation to attend practices. In the student peer groups, they were often part of the great silent majority called "the nobodies."

Third, there were also a number of Mexicano males who formed anti-school-oriented peer groups. They were into a "hip" drug-oriented lifestyle. These males, often called "vatos" (cool dudes) made it a point to be anti-sports, an activity they considered "straight." Although sometimes physically capable of playing, they rarely tried out for any type of team sports. They made excuses for not playing such as needing a job to support their car or van or pickup. They considered sports "kids' stuff," and their hip lifestyle more adult, cool, and fun.

For the vatos, sports events were, however, important moments when they could publicly display their lifestyle and establish their reputations.

A number of vatos always came to the games and even followed the team to other towns. They went to games to be "tough guys" and "enforcers" and to establish "reps" as fighters. The vatos also went to games to "hit on chicks from other towns." As the players battled on the field, they battled on the sidelines. They were another kind of warrior that established North Town's community identity and territoriality through the sport of fighting over and chasing young women.

Teachers assigned to crowd control knew most of these kids by their school reputations. The vice principal called them "thugs" and "little punks." I became friends with some of them in the auto mechanics shop. Most were in the vocational track, and they helped me rebuild my van engine. My rite of passage with them turned out to be having a piston dropped on my head. I lived through that to "rap" with them about drugs, girls, racism, school, and their future.

Perhaps my most memorable and fortunate experience with the vatos was riding with them to the Dobieville football game. I had missed the player bus and was complaining to one of the vatos who was still hanging out at the shop. He replied, "Hey man, why not go with us? Me and Jessie and Gordo and Paco are splitting for Dobieville around six-thirty. You wanna ride with us? Come on Doc, we'll show you how the other half flies!" Knowing a golden opportunity to play anthropologist when one lands on me, I said: "Sure, why not? That piece of junk you drive will get us there, won't it?" He shot back, " Eey ese [my friend, my man] con mucho gusto [with a lot of gusto], man, like a cold Schlitz! Aah!" So it was settled. The vatos had a gringo anthropologist riding shotgun for them to Dobieville.

The Sport of Working-Class Males: Hunting for and Fighting over Girls

On the way to Dobieville, I started up my queries: "So why do cool guys like you go to football games?"

I figured that would provoke some strong responses, and it did. Jessie said with an exasperated, incredulous look, "Why do you suppose, Doc?"

If you ask vatos a dumb (obvious) question, you will get a dumb (smart-assed) answer. Paco picked up on that challenge, "What else, man, CHICKS!"

Everyone laughed, and the conversation shifted to their "book" on. Dobieville "chicks." They mercilessly ran down a list of names, "too fat," "too big a pussy," "an ass that could kill," "a goodie-good," "beautiful but stuck up," "a gang-bang, like, she's always on her back, man," and on and on. The idea was to ride into Dobieville in their beautiful customized car and "steal" some of Dobieville's women. Taking their girls was somewhat like Cheyenne warriors taking coup, stealing something of value from another tribe and making fools of them. But unlike the Cheyenne, the vato warriors were more interested in dramatically confronting than in tricking their enemy. As they talked about going to the game, they emphasized a bold and dramatic entry: "Listen, when we get there Doc, we are going to stick together, come in fast and together. Right, carnal [brother]? You can come if you want, but . . . "

I interrupted them, sensing that I should volunteer to make myself scarce, "I asked coach if I could hang out with the players. I'm going to be heading for the player bench when I get there." Having clarified that I only wanted a ride and not membership in their "cool entry," they seemed to breathe a sigh of relief. Paco, usually the quiet one, cracked me up by saying, after a long, cool pause, "Ok, Doc, have it your way."

The vatos ended up walking into the game like a band of Huns arriving at the gates of the Roman Empire. After smoking two joints on the way, they swaggered in with cocky smiles plastered over their faces. The idea was definitely to attract attention, and possibly some young women, which might also attract some male protectors spoiling for a confrontation. Judging from their conversation, it was difficult to tell which was more important, stealing their women or provoking a fight. Clearly the women were the prize, but to risk danger and to test their courage to fight was also very important. Unlike stealing watermelons or apples from a neighbor, stealing girls was done openly and was a test of courage and honor. A man faced this danger in front of his buddies and under the eyes of the enemy.

This trip to Dobieville with the vatos made me flash back on a night when two carloads of us went to the Gladwin street dance. We were hunting for girls and were also ready for a fight. I remember us discussing if we had enough "firepower" [good fighters] to take on people we called, regrettably, "coons" [blacks] and "greasers" [white trash motorcycle hoods] from Marshalltown that showed up. There was no question that we could "cream those wimps from Gladwin," a tiny town. But Gladwin dances were known for their fights between the city kids from Marshalltown and the kids from Tama. Our town had the reputation of being a rough town with championship sports teams. We believed that we were the only small town that "had the balls to take on Marshalltown," either in sports or in street fights. Looking for "some action" in Gladwin or some other neighboring town was the most exciting thing you could do on a hot

Iowa summer night. I felt that same excitement riding in the car with the vatos to Dobieville.

The main difference between the vatos and us was that they were working class outlaws and we were all-American jock types. The same male ethos was there, but the vatos were outcasts using a respectable event, a football contest, to be disrespectful, rebellious, and cool. We would have never acted this way at a football game. A few working class whites went to the games to drink and chase women, but they were still conformist and supportive of the team. In North Town, working class Mexicano kids formed a counter-culture of males who were even more non-conformist and socially marginal than our "white trash" and "greasers." The vatos had the double jeopardy of being from the wrong class *and* race.

Ultimately, only one minor scuffle actually occurred at the Dobieville game. Some days after the game, I saw the vatos in shop class, and they told the same tales we used to tell after a foray into enemy territory. With great bravado, they recounted every unanswered slight and insult they hurled at "Dobieville geeks." They also gloried in their mythical conquests of Dobieville girls. Every coy nod, wink, and feigned disinterest was carefully recorded and pored over for meaning. For the vatos, the more the girls acted indifferently, the more these "chicks" longed for them.

At one point in this long, self-serving rap, I threw down the classic male taunt that I seriously doubted whether he had "scored." Jessie delighted in the challenge and launched into a long, slow, definitely cool reply:

Heeey, Doc, lemme explain how it is, maaan. Look, Doc, these things take T.I.M.E. . . . We were softening them up for the kill. You wait and see, me and Paco are going back there to visit Maggie, the cute one with long hair, did you see her, man, the one with the tight red dress, and her friend Juanita somethin'. You'll see, Doc. We got *something* going.

This sort of rhetoric flowed for some time. I realized that they were only trying to teach me how to read the signs. They wanted me to know when shyness and disinterest really meant the opposite. A cool guy was supposed to know how to read female behavior. Every male who grew up not knowing when to ask or when to put his machismo on the line knows this feeling. The vatos' whole identity was based on hustling women in a cool way. They spent much of their energy living up to a stereotype that Mexicanos seemed to believe, that "Latins make better lovers." This was one of those half serious ethnic jokes that the vatos hoped was true. Their public style, somewhat reminiscent of the "black rap," was radically different from the polite rap we used, and from the rap of the socially prominent North Town Anglos and Mexicanos. There was, however, this common aggressive male ethic of conquering the female.

For the vatos, fighting, smoking dope, and chasing girls was a far better sport than huffing and puffing around for "some fucking coach." These were males that jocks could call "troublemakers" and "lowlifes," but certainly not "fags." In some ways they enacted the brawling, drinking, girl-chasing ideals of young single males better than the more conformist jocks. This contradiction, as well as racial and class differences, kept these two groups of North Town males socially distant. A kind of uneasy detente existed between the vatos and the jocks. Each one "had their own thing," yet each one criticized the other for being too "straight" or for being "hip" in the wrong way.

In a very real way, this antagonistic relationship between "hip vatos" and "straight jocks" reaffirmed, for the jocks, their social prominence and superiority. They saw themselves as getting the women, *and* the social approval of their elders. The jocks actually established their social prominence by conforming far less to training rules than their "all-American" public image suggests. How players handled being "in training" illustrates nicely how many "straight" jocks established their "hipness" with their peers. It also illustrates how jocks from prominent families enacted and solidified their public positions of social prominence.

Being in Training: A Cultural Contradiction for American Males

Young North Town male athletes were thrust into a real dilemma when their coaches demanded that they sacrifice various pleasures of the flesh. Ideally, being in training meant no drugs, alcohol, tobacco, or pot. It also meant eating well-balanced meals, getting at least eight hours of sleep, and not wasting your emotional and physical energy chasing women. These dictates were extremely difficult to follow in a culture where dangerous drugs are used regularly, and where sexual conquest and/or romantic love are popular cultural ideals. Add the overwhelming use of sex and women's bodies to sell commodities, and you have an environment not particularly conducive to making sacrifices for the coach and the team. Young North Town athletes envied the young bachelors who drank, smoked dope, and chased women late into the night. If they wanted to be males, American culture dictated that they break the rigid, unnatural training rules set for them.

Contrary to the vatos' caricature of jocks as "straight" and conformist, many North Town footballers actually broke their training rules. They often drank and smoked dope at private teen parties. Unlike the rebellious vatos, who publicly flaunted their drinking and dope smoking, jocks avoided drinking in public. By acting like "all-American boys," jocks won adult praise for their conformity. Many publicly pretended to be sacrificing and denying themselves pleasure. They told the old-timers stories about their "rough practices" and "commitment to conditioning." Consequently, if jocks got caught breaking training, adult males tended to overlook these infractions as "slips" or "temptations." In short, "cool jocks" knew how to manage their public image as conformists and hide their private practices of non-conformity.

One incident, when two of the players were caught drinking at a school livestock show, illustrates how many adults preferred to handle this cultural contradiction. Roddy, a senior tackle, and Bob, a senior linebacker, were suspended from school for this incident. Since football season was over, this only jeopardized their graduation, not winning the conference championship. Both youths were from ranching families, and according to the liberal white board members, they had the "good old boy," "red neck crowd" supporting them. The main line of argument made on their behalf was that "boys will be boys" and "these are good kids." This is, of course, the classic defense often used to condone the drinking and vandalism of privileged college fraternity kids.

Fathers who had experienced this contradiction made the boys-will-be-boys argument on behalf of their sons. They gave their sons and other players stern lectures about keeping in shape, *but* they were the first to chuckle at the heroic stories of playing with a hangover. They told these same stories about teammates or themselves over a cup of coffee or a beer. As a result, unless their youth were outrageously indiscreet—for example, passing out drunk on the main street or in class, getting a "trashy girl" pregnant—a "little drinking and screwing around" was overlooked. They simply wanted the school board to stop being hypocritical and acknowledge that drinking was a part of growing up to be a prominent male.

In the small sports world of North Town, real jocks actually enhance their public image of being in shape by occasionally being boozers or dopers. Indeed, one of the most common genre of stories that jocks told was the "I-played-while-drunk/stoned, or the "I-got-drunk/stoned-the-night-before-the-game" tale. The stories we told in the fifties were still being told today in North Town. Olmo, a big bruising guard, who had become a hard-living, hard-drinking bachelor, told me a classic version of this tale before the homecoming game:

Last night we really went out and hung one on. Me and Jaime and Arturo drank a six-pack apiece in a couple of hours. We were cruising around Daly City checking out the action. It was real dead. We didn't see nobody we knew except Arturo's cousin. We stopped at his place and drank some more and listened to some music. We stayed there till his old lady [mom] told us to go home. We got home pretty late, but before the sun come up, 'cause we're in training, ha ha.

Olmo told this story with a twinkle in his eye, especially the part about being in training. I asked him how it was possible to play well, if he had "hung one on" the night before. This launched him into the story that he wanted to tell about drinking before, and even during, games. He told these stories often, because other players told this same story to me. Olmo was a legend the way that Duffy, a hard drinking, rugged linebacker, was when I played. We non-drinkers marveled at how much Duffy could hold and "sweat out" during the game. In addition, we always speculated about how much his long, passionate rendezvous at the motel drained him. Stories of players' sexual exploits were recounted in the same vein that drinking stories were. A real man could be in shape because his extraordinary prowess overcame these allegedly debilitating vices. A real man could have it all and become complete through drugs, sex, violence, and glory.

Most players secretly, often openly, admired these sorts of rule breaking behaviors. Olmo and Duffy were models of ideal male behavior. To lesser degrees, other players who were "cool" emulated these behaviors. "Homeboys," the farm kids, and "goodie-goodies" rarely broke training, but the pressures on them to do so were enormous. Drinking parties, like North Town's post-homecoming bash, drew a number of the players. This celebration made celebrities out of the players. Their willingness to "bend an elbow" and "take a toke" was, in some ways, the highlight of the party. Kids clustered around the bonfire and various pickups and shared beer and pot with their warriors who had beaten the enemy. This post-homecoming bash was a rural, adolescent version of the party scene from the movie *North Dallas Forty,* an inside look at the life style of professional football players.

A Summing Up: Some Contradictions in American Culture

American society prides itself on promoting social equality, but one of our major popular or leisure culture practices, sports, does not always promote this ideal. At the community level, football was a complex ritual that socialized North Town youth to become males and females. The local sports scene was an important school activity that also staged the prominence of selected families and their children. At times, the selection of players and coaches became class issues. At other times, it became a racial issue. Sports, and football in particular, may have many virtues, but one of its more undesirable and unintended consequences is to promote or reproduce various forms of social inequality.

The football scene in North Town also reflected a general contradiction of values or lifestyles that other observers of American culture have noted (Poster 1981; Henry 1965). These social critics have argued that American culture increasingly emphasizes new ideals of consumption, impulse release, and hedonism. Mass media advertising has developed to extol the virtues of unrestrained consumption. Over the years, a new, more consumption-oriented American society has emerged. These cultural changes leave most American communities in a state of flux and contradiction. Life in North Town constantly reflected these two contradictory norms of consumption/hedonism and asceticism/delayed gratification.

Those youths who aspired to be socially prominent had to master this cultural contradiction. In response, they learned to live dual public and private lives and skillfully manage their public image. They put on a different performance for a different audience. On the one hand, the "cool players" were paragons of discipline and conformity for the adults. In public, they acted like the community's "straight" future leaders. They were more sober, work-oriented, and restrained. The socially prominent youth, like their parents, had to be public guardians of the old virtues and values.

On the other hand, these same players were clever "tricksters" who indulged in the private play and hedonism that other "cool" kids idealized. These youth also had to be practitioners of the new consumer-oriented popular culture. Like their successful parents, they worked hard and earned their right to play hard. But unlike the rebellious, deviant kids, who also "played hard," they were better at convincing adults, as the rebels said, with their "goodie-goodie acts." Such conformity to older public values of restraint and sobriety solidified their position of social prominence.

The socially prominent youth were impression management experts in other youth scenes as well. The next chapter describes how the friendship and dating practices of student status identity groups staged class and gender roles in ways reminiscent of the great American football ritual.

THREE

Finding an Identity in the Social Status Scene

North Town youth partied as hard as they played football. Having fun meant "getting plastered" or "getting stoned." They constantly talked about letting off some steam after a long, boring week of classes. Drinking parties were festivals to celebrate the harvest of another weekend free of teachers and parents. These parties were strictly segregated by race, and I attended only those held by Anglo youth. These parties were usually held in an open field about three miles outside town. The field was owned by a local doctor, who apparently allowed his son, a college student, to use the land if he "cooled it on dope" and "cleaned up the place afterwards." A large bonfire and the headlights of various pickup trucks lit the party area. The center of action was two kegs of beer spiked with "Everclear" (180 proof alcohol). I discovered the Everclear at the first party I attended when I felt woozy after one glass and naively asked, "Jesus, that is pretty potent beer. What's in it?" My naiveté delighted everyone in earshot, and was followed by a torrent of how-much-liquor-I-can-hold tales. A longish conversation ensued about the glories of drinking and evading parents and teachers.

Meanwhile, knots and clusters of kids were drifting off to pickup trucks. Boys were hustling and "grab-assing girls," and girls were being coquettish about these "crude" public advances. Onlooking buddies in-spired the aggressors with choruses of teasing and laughter. Several se-niors said laughingly that they were "breaking in" the underclassmen. Some serious drinking was indeed being orchestrated by the "school leaders." Some serious coupling and petting was also going on, but most of it was too self-conscious to rival the debauchery of an adult party. North Town youth reminded me of the fun-loving youth idealized in American summer movies about frat and beach parties.

As people got progressively drunker, I discovered one reason I may have been invited. The daughter of a prominent BGL leader came at me in a drunken rage:

> What the hell are you doin' here? Are you gonna write a book about how Anglos discriminate against Meskins? Why were you in Crystal City last year? Are you a friend of Ramirez's, that sorry son of a bitch? I want to tell you something to put into your damn book. We are the ones who are getting discriminated against! Did you see what happened in the school elections? Do you see what happens in the halls to us ? Those Raza Unida are a sorry bunch of bastards! Do you know what they want to do? They want to take away all the Anglos' property and kick them out! They want to give Texas back to Mexico, some damn place called Aztlan. Do you know what Mr. Alonzo made us do in junior high? He made us watch the American flag burn! That isn't right, *you* know *that*! He also beat up two old ladies once just to keep them from voting! They are all a sorry bunch of traitors. There are a lot of good Meskins, but these are some sorry goddamn Meskins.

Several others crowded around to watch the confrontation between this feisty fifteen-year-old orator and the cowering anthropological snoop. Others echoed their agreement, but I said very little in response, hoping not to provoke them. Eventually a peacemaker suggested we have another beer, and I agreed saying that the conversation was a little too hot for me. This outburst of criticism, which only lasted a few minutes, seemed to relieve a great deal of tension, but I then found myself the target of some coquettish, sexual play.

I had drifted away from the confrontation towards a conversation among several senior girls. They were talking about going to college, a topic I assumed was quite safe. I sat up on the car fender near one of them to chip in a comment or two, and suddenly she draped her leg over mine. She looked at me in an amused, somewhat defiant way. Her drunken boyfriend, a college student, had just come up to "cop a feel" and steal a kiss. Much to my discomfort, he was nearby "shooting the bull" with some of the guys. As she placed her leg on mine, she seemed to be saying, "Ok, sucker, your move." I quickly removed her leg and continued talking about the virtues of going to the University of Texas. In response, she put her leg over mine again, so I asked her not to get me in trouble with her boyfriend. She threw back her hair victoriously, smiled, and tossed me an "Ok, Doc."

The boyfriend and his buddies, having scrutinized us from a distance, staggered back and seemed to accept my olive branch. Rather than fight, they wanted to argue about how much better Texas A & M was than the University of Texas, and how the Aggies were going to "gig" (beat) that bunch of "tea sips" (snobbish wimps) next year. Meanwhile, the rock music played on, and the boys were busy trying to lure giggling girls into their pickups. A couple of them talked about "turning on some girls" with "a little weed" and having fun. You could smell the sweet fumes of pot, but the main event still seemed to be getting drunk on spiked beer.

Several of the football team led the drinking, and most of the kids identified as the school "leaders" or "most popular" were there celebrating. It reminded me of my own high school and college parties, with very little serious conversation and lots of bravado about sex, booze, and raising hell. Experts who write about generation gaps and adolescents as distinct, rebellious counter-cultures sometimes forget how much teenagers long to be adults. They want to do exactly the same things adults do for fun and pleasure, *before* adults think they are ready for such "mature" carnal pursuits. This party and its expressive style seemed like a caricature of how adults party. Such parties provided the socially prominent kids endless status-enhancing stories for their "straight" classmates.

Many of the kids had apparently lied to their parents about coming to the party, but they claimed that their parents knew about "after-the-game blasts." Partying after football games was a long-standing North Town tradition for adults and youth. According to the kids, parents grudgingly accepted these drinking parties—if that kept their kids from using other drugs. The party-goers also believed that the police and county sheriff would look the other way. Lawmen were not supposed to arrest prominent people's children for "having a little fun." Adults interviewed about teenage drinking did express relief that the kids may be "going back to beer," which they considered less harmful than pot.

Most parents condemned, however, the idea of public drunkenness and disorderliness. They usually talked a hard line about kids abstaining. Typically, parents portrayed themselves as intolerant of dope and fairly strict on drinking. But parents who were not strict Baptists, especially the males, also had a "kids-will-be-kids" attitude. They accepted a little discreet merrymaking as part of growing up. Many youth perceived this contradiction between a public hard line on drinking and tolerance toward discreet private drinking. The kids felt that this gave them a right to "live it up a little." That was part of being young. They claimed that their parents had done the same thing, and they minimized their pious denials.

The issue of drinking and drunkenness was also a source of much gossip and many stories that marked ethnic relations and stereotypes. Anglos tended to portray the Mexicano community as having too many cantinas (bars) and a problem with drunkenness. To my surprise, a number of Anglos attributed these problems to the moral laxness of Catholics. Various social workers, educators, and religious leaders from both races also expressed fears about a growing Mexicano "drinking problem." Several older Mexicano community leaders organized campaigns against a local night club, and a neighborhood liquor store run by prominent Mexicano political leaders. Mexicanos often cited drinking in cantinas and the lure of "cantineras" (prostitutes) as the cause of an increasing number of female-run households. In response to these Anglo criticisms, the new Mexicano leaders tended to portray Anglos as hypocritical about drinking. They delighted in telling stories about prominent Anglos who avoided drinking in public but who were were heavy "home drinkers" (Foley et al.1988).

The majority of "straight" North Town youth (the "goodie-goodies," "homeboys," "nerds," and "religious freaks") actually did far less drinking and hell raising. They lived a lifestyle very similar to their parents'. By the time they were seniors, perhaps 75 to 80 percent of the kids had experimented with drinking. But perhaps 50 percent of North Town youth were the quiet, non-drinker types. Despite all the rhetoric about drinking and hell-raising, North Town was basically a conservative, family-oriented community of sober, hard-working people. North Town adults generally portrayed their town as "not too Bible belt" and "not too wild." Most adult parties I attended had liquor, and drinking was hardly a taboo subject among the community leaders and townspeople. The cultural rule was to be discreet and in control when drinking in public. Loud, aggressive, drunken behavior was looked upon as ill-mannered and irresponsible.

The dominant cultural ethic was to work hard and be successful, which earned you the right to some serious fun and recreation. This cultural ideal was, of course, practiced discreetly, while also being a good family man/woman. For many North Towners, there was no contradiction between working hard and playing hard. The socially prominent families worked hard to create successful farms and businesses. Their youth worked hard to get good grades and to lead the school to football and band victories. These accomplishments earned both the right to party hard on weekends and after the games. There was nothing particularly rebellious or deviant about their drinking and partying. They were simply being good Americans and following the values of North Town adults.

Dating and Friendship Among North Town Youth

But what else did the youth of North Town do for fun and recreation? According to them, North Town was a very boring place to grow up. Driving around in cars, hanging out at the Dairy Queen, picnics on the river, and dances and movies in other towns were the main "things to do." Many claimed to be "sick of the town" and the other kids, whom they had known since first grade. Most longed to escape to the cities and to college where there were new people, movies, night clubs, and more "action." They fantasized about how exciting the outside world was. I was constantly asked whether Austin was as swinging a place as everybody claimed. Several kids at the party said their parents would not let them go there, because they were afraid they would get into trouble with drugs. Returning college kids fed the fantasies of these high schoolers with endless stories about their sexual and drinking adventures. North Town high school kids were, therefore, left plotting their escape to urban America.

In this small town setting, the car became all-important for living a more autonomous, hip lifestyle. Most males did not have their own cars, except those who worked or lived in the country. The others borrowed their parents' cars on weekends. Males with cars quickly formed roving bands like the one I accompanied to the Dobieville football game. Having a car and gas allowed one to search for action in nearby towns and in San Antonio. You could also "cruise around" to the local hangouts, "pick up chicks," tease pedestrians, and, most important, find private places for drinking, smoking dope, and necking. On foot, the kids were resigned to hanging out at the local Dairy Queen and Taco Bar, or staying at home.

The way North Town youth chose their friends and lovers and conducted intimate relationships revealed a great deal about our cultural values. This study extends and revises a number of earlier studies on American youth. Jules Henry, a particularly critical portrayer of American youth and schools, emphasizes the emotionally superficial, lonely quality of adolescent friendships and romances (Henry 1965). Henry characterizes Americans as searching for psychological release from the relentless pressures of competition, production, and consumption. North Town youth said and did many of the same things, but I have characterized their social organization and adaptation somewhat differently from Henry.

What struck me as important about the stories of many North Town youth was the matter-of-fact way they defined friendship. Friendship generally seemed to mean "hanging out" with someone. Kids who were "cool" rarely talked about being friends as an emotional, intimate relationship. One of the more articulate athletes, when asked about his best friends and "girl friend," put it particularly well:

> I don't really have any best friend. Most guys I know don't have that close a guy friends. I have lots of guys I hang around with. We go out on dates together. We talk. We ride around in my truck, drink together, you know, have some fun. But I'm not that tight with them like I am my girl. If you have a steady girl friend, yah, I guess ya spill your guts to her . . . I mean you tell her lots of personal stuff that you couldn't tell the guys . . . Because you would be afraid that they might blab it to somebody else and make a fool outta you . . . As a guy gets older, mostly juniors and seniors, you get more mature and start looking to go steady. You got a car and you are getting more serious, maybe even thinking of getting married. Most everybody has a group he belongs to, but that group isn't always your best friend.

These same themes came up in conversations with many other students. One popular Mexicana, the daughter of a professional, said that "everybody has a group" and added that girls needed a group more that boys. Mexicanas had greater difficulty getting their parents to allow solo dates or attending football games. The "cool" Mexicanos frequently complained about how conservative Mexicanas and their families were. The young women often needed a "hanging out group" to be allowed to go out in the evenings. A gang of ex-slumber party mates made unchaperoned outings much easier. Parents were also much more likely to accept group dates that included these same neighborhood girls.

Girls reported a view of friendship that also paralleled Henry's findings. Girls frequently said that other girls were very "untrustworthy" and "always gossiping" about each other. They claimed that it was hard to have best friends, and perceived boys as getting along much better. The main reason cited for so much gossip and conflict was competition over boys. The competition to attract and keep males was fierce, and the burden of keeping the male loyal fell upon the females. It was accepted that males were less sincere and loyal and would tend to chase other females, if given a chance. Other females were often perceived as "always trying to steal your boy friend."

The competition among males most frequently mentioned was over sports, friends, and summer jobs. Males talked about "getting" the same females, but they went to considerable lengths to minimize such competition with other North Town males. Guys used elaborate spying methods to determine if a female was "somebody else's chick." Fighting over a female invariably ended up being a question of honor and reputation. When you lost a fight to a local, that defeat followed you around forever. There were, therefore, powerful social pressures to minimize competition over females that led to fistfights and a loss of face.

In short, the politics of dating tended to pit females against each other much more than it did males. This difference may partially explain why females reported less trust and friendship bonding than males did. Females, being objects of exchange among males, were pressured into strong competition to attract and hold the most desirable males. They gained their gender status through winning a male's attention and loyalty and through domesticating a sexually restless, domineering male.

Males did compete relentlessly over females, but as the trip to Dobieville suggested, they tended to tribalize this competition into "raids" on other towns' females. If fights occurred out of town with an "enemy," that left a very different set of stories to tell. If an outside female snubbed you, or an enemy male beat you up, your buddies could tell a very different story to townmates. The beauty of "fighting with" or "hustling" outsiders was that it left few witnesses to contradict your account. Even if one's buddies told contradictory tales about one's exploits, there was room for ambiguity and face-saving denials. If a group of males really did hang out together, the least they did for each other was invent and preserve their images as fighters and lovers.

Both males and females said they preferred dating outsiders. Relating to outsiders fulfilled fantasies about the more exciting outside world, *and* it greatly curtailed the competition and gossip that constantly threatened these youths' reputations. All of this sounded extraordinarily similiar to dating in the fifties. There were signs, however, that the women's movement was influencing ideas about gender roles. According to the home economics teachers and the young women I interviewed, this new generation of North Town women was more interested in careers, marrying later, and smaller families. Nevertheless, I was surprised that the feminist movement had not influenced the girls more. These young women had no feminist consciousness about being objects of possession and exchange in a male-dominated dating game.

Dating and Going Steady: The Social and Emotional Bases of Friendship

Males and females from both racial groups made the distinction between who you hang out with and who you really "let your hair down with" or "spill your guts to." These expressions suggest that many youth were afraid to be open and vulnerable with each other. You "hang with" your group, but you "confide" in the person with whom you are romantically involved. When you do confide, it is thought of as "spilling your guts." According to many youths, being too open and talkative about feelings was difficult and dangerous. Yet, when the pressures of life got too unbearable, these kids had to turn to someone. Typically, the "school leaders" said that they could only be vulnerable and talk about their hopes and fears with their steady girl- or boyfriend. Only someone who claimed to "love you" could be trusted. A lover would not betray your fears and weaknesses to your competitors for social, athletic, and academic honors.

There were several reasons why only a romance and steady girl- or boyfriend could create enough vulnerability for an intimate, emotional relationship. In North Town, if a girlfriend slept with you, she risked everything socially. If abandoned, she could lose her reputation and become a "slut." If a boyfriend slept with you, he risked his social reputation as well. If he became "henpecked" or "got dumped," he could gain a reputation of being a weak, unattractive, unhip male. Going steady was a very risky affair in the swirl of local gossip and fragile gender reputations. Nevertheless, the stakes—an emotional haven, pre-marital sex, and enormous status enhancement—were high enough to take the risk. As a result, "going steady" took on the connotation of planning to get married and becoming an adult member of the community.

This view of going steady was similar to what one investigator of a traditional Mexicano community (Horowitz 1983) has called a "bonded sexuality." Going steady was a carefully worked out exchange relationship between the sexes. This idea of a "bonded sexuality" that legitimates pre-marital sex in a traditional cultural setting also applied to both Mexicanos and Anglos in North Town. This exchange relationship between males and females was not necessarily egalitarian, however. Each sex made rather different concessions for the advantages gained.

The main way a North Town "cool" female could have an intimate relationship with a "cool" young male was to give in to his sexual demands. The only way she could do this and not lose her reputation, however, was to demand that he was "serious." Being "serious" meant giving her a ring, locket, letter jacket, or other items that signaled to peers they were "going steady." The male also had to be willing to trade time "hanging out" with the guys for attending to a girlfriend. He had to meet her between classes, carry her books, take her home after school, and call and date her. He had to do this in a manner that was not too servile and dependent, however, or his buddies would call him "pussy-whipped" and "henpecked." But since his buddies believed he was "getting it," the ultimate expression of masculinity, his dutiful demeanor was a small price to pay for steady sex.

A female, on the other hand, had to make a number of demands for the young male's attention, or she would risk strong criticism from her girl friends. She had to play the role of a coquette who was dependent and in need of constant attention. She had to gain his attention and monopolize the time he formerly spent with buddies. She then took care of his sexual, emotional, and social status needs. In return, she got a strong protector and companion, and at least in theory, a promissory note for a future husband. Ultimately, the woman had to be subordinate to her man.

From my view, males from both races got the best of the bargain, but young North Town women were beginning to criticize the male privilege inherent in these "going steady" exchanges. A number of girls interviewed complained about boys always getting what they wanted (sex) or "dropping you." Growing numbers also reported less interest in early marriage and large families, which made them less willing to put up with males who reneged on going steady exchanges. Nevertheless, their attitudes about and acquiescence to male dating preferences sounded like the 1950s. North Town was still very much a man's world when it came to dating practices. Once any of these males got into a steady relationship, the intimacy and emotional dependency may well have developed as the need for public bravado receded. Most of the school leaders and jocks admitted that their girlfriends were close to them.

Judging the emotional depth of these relationships from conversations was very difficult. These private discourses about romance and sex were also always public performances of idealized gender roles. Boys invariably talked about romance in terms of sexual conquest. Girls invariably talked about romance in terms of love and marriage. Getting people to talk about their romances in very intimate, personal ways was difficult. What they might say to friends on a slumber party or while cruising around was not what they would say to an outsider.

In many cases, the males expressed uncertainty about their feelings toward their girlfriends. When the conversations shifted to emotional matters, most of these males became very inarticulate. This behavior may have reflected lack of feelings, or simply a reluctance to admit to another male their intimate, vulnerable feelings for a female. Conversely, females were much more willing to talk about their feelings for boyfriends, and they often worried about guys "just wanting sex and not really caring."

Adolescent males had little difficulty, however, in expressing how they felt about a woman's physicality. Being good looking and sexy was mentioned much more often than character, intelligence, and personality. Generally, North Town youths rated each other socially much like youth in other American towns. Looks, athletic ability, dress style, and drug use ultimately determined how kids labeled and classified each other as "hip" or "straight." A person's style of expressing his or her social identity became, therefore, an important marker of status. This often set boundaries for who could socialize with and date whom. Before exploring the dating scene fully, I will describe the identity labels that North Town youth claimed marked their style and status. What identity label one had was crucial for determining who could date whom.

Identity Labels Among North Town Youth: Town Kids,
Kickers, and Vatos

The major social identity labels North Town students used were very similar to those of the student status groups found in earlier studies (Hollingshead 1949; Coleman 1961; Schwarz and Merton 1967; Cusick 1973; Brake 1980; Varenne 1982; Canaan 1987). Typically, the great divide between youth groups has always been social class. The earlier studies tried to document this with socio-economic measures (income, education, residence) of the youths' families. There was always a high status group, which kids labeled "socies," "BMOC/BWOC s," "preppies," and "stars," who came from middle or upper income familes. There was also always a low status group, which kids labeled "greasers," "hoods," and "white trash," who came from low income, poorly educated families.

In North Town, unique ethnic/racial factors were also operating; consequently, the lowest status group was the Mexicano vatos. These people were clearly working class, so they were low in status because of their poverty *and* their race. The vatos had elements of a distinct dress style that were borrowed from the expressive traditions of the Mexican American pachucos (hipsters) and from the hippies. They wore their hair long, talked constantly about dope, listened to acid rock music, and occasionally donned the bib overalls of farmers. In addition, they occasionally wore black patent leather shoes called "Staceys" and black short-billed soft cotton hats not unlike those of a chauffeur. Their ideal set of "wheels" was a classic 1955 to 1957 Chevy painted a flashy color. As indicated in Chapter 2, the vatos saw themselves as "fighters" and "lovers." The school authorities had their own labels for the vatos. They called them various derogatory names such as "punks," "delinquents," and "troublemakers." In response, the vatos developed their own distinct counter-culture against the school and constantly battled school officials.

In between these social class extremes fell the majority of students, who were variously labeled "nobodies," "nerds," "homeboys/homegirls," and "geeks." To complicate matters, none of these labels distinguished exclusively among economic classes. General social status among youth was also based on one's expressive life style as either "hip" and non-conforming or "straight" and conforming. These two factors, family wealth and expressive style, were not related in any simple way. Kids from prominent families occasionally fell into these middle groups that had lower status. Some well-off youths were "nerds" about dressing, dating, drug use, and subtle forms of non-conformity. Conversely, some low income kids gained a measure of social prominence by excelling in conformist school activities such as sports and band. Students who were considered "cool" and "hip" typically had money, but achieving a high social status in the youth scene was also a matter of style and personality.

Moreover, the advent of new expressive counter-cultural styles such as "freaks," "dopers," "long-hairs," and more recently "punks," "new wavers," and "punk heads" has further complicated the student status group rankings. Some suburban studies showed "freaks," "long-hairs," and "punks" (in the punk-rocker sense) as unconventional intellectual and artistic student leaders who tended to have a relatively high social status. This status was based on wealth, but not entirely. The unconventional intellectual types distinguished themselves from more conformist "preppie" or "rah-rah" types. The conformists included "jocks," "band-freaks," and the "cheerleader/pep squad crowd." North Town had a few Anglo and Mexicano kids who were labeled "hippies" or non-conventional intellectual types, but in much smaller numbers than those found in studies of suburban schools. In rural North Town these non-conformists generally had a lower social status, and some were even perceived as social outcasts.

North Towners also noted a major stylistic difference not mentioned in urban studies of American youth. North Town youth distinguished between a "town" and "country" style. The North Town label most analogous to farmer was "homeboy/girl," although that label was neither entirely negative nor used exclusively for rural kids. In North Town, being "country" referred to a Western, cowboy style and was was held in greater esteem, because it connoted a strong regional culture. The Western ranching way of life has generated its own regional culture of popular music, cowboy folklore, rodeo festivals, and a distinct dress, food, and dance.

American popular culture, and particularly Texas, has made this into a popular rural, regional form of expressive culture. The American romance with the cowboy lifestyle has been endlessly canonized and mythologized in nineteenth-century penny novels and twentieth-century movies and TV shows. Many North Town businessmen and professionals owned land and identified with and emulated this Western country lifestyle to a degree. The status difference between the town and country kids of socially prominent families was, therefore, often very minor.

This Western country style idealized the rugged, physical "workin' men," who were often called "kickers." A "kicker" or "shit kicker" was a rough-tough cowboy/cowgirl rodeo type who wore boots, dipped snuff, guzzled lots of beer, and "kicked ass" when offended. Jokingly, some kids called others who affected the rodeo cowboy style "Rexall Rangers" or "drugstore cowboys." A few middle class adults and kids adopted a very toned-down version of this Western "workin' man" style. They thought of kickers as being more working class. Some town kids thought dipping snuff was "gross" and that the kickers could be loud and crude.

In addition, being a kicker also had strong racial connotations for some North Towners. Quite often, being a kicker meant being a "red neck," someone prejudiced toward non-whites. Most Mexicano student activists used the term "kicker" as synonymous with "Anglo red neck." This was a person who was prejudiced toward Mexicanos and called them "Meskins." There were, however, rural Mexicanos who affected a kicker style, and for them the term had no negative racial connotations. Their view was very similar to that of other Anglos, who used the term kicker and shit kicker to connote their expressive cultural style.

Finally, Anglo youth made the distinction between a traditional kicker and what might be called a "hip kicker." Hip kickers liked rock and roll music and drugs, and they tended to be less "red neck" toward Mexicanos. A number of "progressive country" musicians from Austin, Texas such as Jerry Jeff Walker, Willie Nelson, Wayland Jennings, and Doug Sahms idealized this cultural fusion of country and long-haired hippie expressive styles. Various music experts have labeled this style "cosmic cowboy," "red neck rock," "outlaw country," and "pissing-in-the-wind music." North Town youths invented their own "hip kicker" style with little reference to or interest in the Austin music scene.

My best informant on hip kickers and other groups was Tara, a fifteen-year-old girl who called herself "a white trash kicker." She was a free-spirited, dope-smoking, sexually active young woman who had run away from her parents. She lived in an apartment in my neighborhood, and was waiting out the mandatory school age for dropping out. The principal called her "wild" and "an underachiever," which he considered a compliment. Tara had been through soul-searching discussions with her counselor, threats from the infamous vice principal, and fatherly jokes from the principal. Her parents called her a "little bitch" and had told her to "get out." In short, she was less than a model student, but definitely street-wise and very sensitive to student status groups.

One day she saw me walking by her place, so she invited me in for a beer. She told me about her family problems and her "honey" (boyfriend) who "shot blanks" (was infertile) *but* was a real "pussyman" (good lover). Gradually, I got her talking about the groups at school. She confirmed what many less colorful students had told me, but I placed a special value on her account. Tara saw herself as an "outsider" who was already grown up and on her way to a "real life." She spoke without a trace of resentment and with a good deal of wry humor about friendship, dating, and peer groups in her town:

> The biggest difference between the Anglo kids is between what I call the "too goods" who look down on you and a "low girl" like me. They look down on us, and I am a slut because I might go out with a Mexican. *But,* if one of these rich kids went out with me, they wouldn't tell anybody, because they'd git laughed at. If they banged a rich girl like them, they tell everybody, but they'd be hypocrites about wanting to bang me . . . I know the ones who do dope on the sly. I know the ones who say they hate Mexicans but are always wishing they could do it with the pretty ones. They are always trying to be goodie-goodie, but they drink and raise hell, too. A couple of them are always sneaking over here when my honey is working the rigs and trying to get what I got. I know all their bull . . . Ya, it's mostly the jocks and the kids with ranches and stores and farms, the ones with some money. The girls are mostly in the band and some of those goodie-goodies on the volleyball team. They like to act like I'm a slut, and that they don't ball their pussy-whipped boyfriends.

One familiar term she used, "pussy-whipped," jumped out, and I could not resist playing dumb and asking her what it meant. According to other males, that was one of the worst insults you could hurl at another male. She sensed that I was putting her on a little, but seemed to play along with me and said:

> I mean that the cute rich girls who the big tough jocks chase, they wrap these guys around their little fingers. Don't you see how they boss them around? Jesus, it is sickening! They act so pure and fucking sweet I wanna puke. We know who the little bitches are, though.

Tara went on for several hours classifying who were the "rich bitches" and "goodie-goodies" and "studs" and "all-American boys." She was amused by their feigned conformity, which allowed them to manipulate teachers. But most of all she disliked their pretensions, or "airs," as she called it. All she wanted from them was a little honesty about who they were. Tara characterized the quality of their personal relationships by saying that most of them "were too busy trying to impress each other to be good friends." It wasn't "cool" to be too "chummy" with others if you wanted to get ahead because you never knew who might "lay you low with some kinda dirt." She added that they were also afraid someone might gossip that they were "lesbos" or "fags." Tara was convinced that the "stars" could not have fun, because they always had to keep up a good front. She, on the other hand, had nothing to lose (socially). She could "get stoned" and "get laid" without worrying about it. For her, being a "kicker" and white trash was a more honest, less restricted, better way to live.

I then asked her how she got along with Mexicanos, and she said "there were good ones and bad ones, like gringos." She described how she and a couple of other "kicker friends" hung out with the vatos. She had no precise term for them, but said:

> You know, the ones that Mr. Big Dick (the vice principal) thinks are "trouble-makers." These are the Mexican kids I think are cool. They don't take any shit from him or anybody else. Did you hear about them breaking his windshield out after the game? It served him right. He treats people like shit.

Tara said that Mexicans also had their "big shots," but she did not know many of them personally. She assured me that it was "obvious" who they were. They were the jocks, the class officers, and the leaders of the school who were in the advanced classes with the Anglos. The Mexicano kids she felt most comfortable with were the vatos, and she and two friends "smoked dope and played grab ass with them in Chato's van." She was convinced that Mexicanos were "cooler about dope," and that more of the "better Mexicans" smoked dope than the "better Anglos." For her, Mexicano kids generally tended to be less straight than Anglo kids, mainly because they had less money and fewer pretensions.

Tara's perspective suggested to me some new ways of looking at the identity labels and the meaning of student groups. Ultimately, I adopted a "cultural performance" view of these identity labels for large groups of youth. I contrasted these large, public groups for displaying one's social identity to smaller, more intimate dyadic relationships.

Student Groups as Identity Performances: The Social Class Divide

As several of the youth studies have pointed out (Varenne 1982; Canaan 1987), student status groups often seem rather "flexible" or "loosely knit." Students invariably disagree about who is in what group, and whether there are actually "groups." The studies of student groups have never shown that student peer groups are corporate groups in the classic sense. In most theories of social organization, a number of people become an organized, functional group when two basic criteria are met. First, a group must develop a scheme for solving life problems—social, economic, and political. These obligations and practices create a pattern of reciprocity and rules among the members. Second, some sense of shared identity—often based on shared expressive cultural practices such as food, dress, music, dance, folklore, and language—marks membership in a functioning, problem-solving corporate group.

These large, flexible student groups partly fulfill the second criterion for a corporate group, and they should be thought of as "situational identity groups." The group labels represented different styles or social identities that were periodically displayed or performed publicly. These student groups were primarily for "hanging out together." Who a student publically hung out with expressed his or her social status. The performance of these social status identities occurred constantly in extracurricular activities and in classroom games. Such groups developed, therefore, a limited sense of a shared social identity. Their identity was marked by some distinct language and expressive (dress, music, dance) cultural styles that students adopted or invented. Students thought of themselves as "members" of such social identity groups, but such groups required few reciprocal obligations or bonds and provided no comprehensive scheme for solving one's life problems.

Relatively large groups of loosely organized youths, who identified themselves as "kickers," "jocks," and "vatos," actually hung out together in both large and small numbers. Their comportment, language, and dress tended to follow a particular expressive style. Even when they were not hanging out with other kickers, some students were known for their kicker style. The same was true of jocks and vatos. The precise size of these various identity groups was difficult to determine, since being a member only meant having a certain expressive style and occasionally hanging out together publicly. Any attempts to quantify the groups precisely would be difficult. Investigators who have been preoccupied with classifying kids into these "groups" miss the point that these are largely symbolic labels that the kids invent. The symbolic quality of these groups does not, however, diminish their importance or reality. It simply makes them harder to "see" consistently walking down the halls or to count precisely.

For males, these groups centered around those who had a car and hung together outside of school. For females, these groups centered more around school activities such as band and pep squad or church youth groups. Nothing excluded some kids from being labeled several ways, or from momentarily hanging out with kids identified with other identity groups. Not infrequently, teenagers denied that they belonged to any identity group. Some investigators have taken such denials of group membership as evidence that such groups only exist in discourse (Varenne 1982). I took this "talk" seriously and looked for other ways that the students who rejected labels organized their social relationships.

Student Groups as Intimate Relationships: The Great Silent Majority

In contrast to the visible, large high and low status groups that "hung together" in public, the majority of North Town youths did not consistently belong to a group that constantly displayed their social identity. Such youth were typically classified in lower or mixed social identity categories such as "nobodies," "nerds," and "homeboys/girls." Having been labeled negatively by others, they tended to deny rather than display their status identity through "hanging out." At other times, they sought to hang momentarily with youths who had a positive identity. Some kids flirted in and out of these groups, as if they had visitation privileges. Generally, the youths who were supposedly nobodies and nerds tended to relate to each other in much smaller, more intimate dyadic relationships of two or three.

These North Town youth more frequently reported having intimate friendships with peers of the same sex. They also consistently reported less intense feelings of competition with other youth. Because they often lacked money, personal looks, athletic ability, and/or family connections, they were excluded from what the prominent kids called "the rat-race to be popular and successful." "Nobodies" and "homeboys/girls" were freer to develop intimate friendships than the more success-oriented kids were. They tended to bond together in response to the negative labeling they experienced. Their friendship dyads were a haven from the relentless social climbing and competition among the upwardly mobile youths.

This general pattern of relatively impersonal, large status display groups that hung out together and of smaller, intimate dyadic friendships cut across both races. Some socially prominent youths in both races reported having intimate dyadic friendships, but "nobodies" and "homeboys/girls" were more likely to develop same-sex friends who were considered intimate. On the other hand, the socially prominent youths were more likely to develop their intimate dyadic friendships with the opposite sex. These youths tended to be less shy and more advanced socially; consequently, they were oriented toward earlier dating and sexual play. Socially prominent youth had much greater social pressures to "go steady," and thus to fulfill the mainstream ideals for gender and class roles. Since the "nobodies" were not going to inherit community positions of social prominence, they were free, as one put it so eloquently, to do many things:

I think maybe kids like me, you know, a "nobody," are freer to just be who we are. We don't have to go around wearing a mask. I'm not always trying to be better than somebody else. Nobody cares what I do. I can't get the good-looking girls, but there are some ok-ones I get along with. Mostly I hang out with Pancho. We have lots of fun together . . . Yeh, I tell him things about my feelings. We talk about problems we have with school and our parents.

In contrast, the jock cited earlier felt that everyone needed both a group of people to pass time with *and* a girlfriend who shared his hopes and fears. He and many other socially prominent youths defined friendship as "hanging out" with someone. They often reported having no close same-sex friendships. Many did, however, have girl/boyfriends. Not all were "going steady," but that was the ideal intimate relationship. The socially prominent youths invariably hoped to be going steady by their junior or senior year. Getting a good-looking, socially successful girl/boyfriend greatly enhanced one's status with his or her "hanging out" buddies. Dating became, therefore, the search for the intimacy that was missing in their "hanging out" friendships. If they were not going steady, they tended to lead rather lonely, competitive social lives filled with drinking and horsing around together.

Friendship and Dating Across an Old Racial Divide

Much has been said about the general social life and friendship among North Town youth, but what about friendship and dating between Anglos and Mexicanos? One of the first things a visitor to North Town High would notice was how territorial each ethnic/racial group acted. These invisible "territories" were most apparent when a new kid arrived in school and was learning his or her place. The first incident I observed involved a Nebraska boy. During the first few days of class, he hung out with the vatos near the administration building. He had not yet learned that except for the homeboy-type rural kids, who ate in the school cafeteria, most Anglos ate lunch at home or in local restaurants. Consequently, the Nebraska boy found himself on the school grounds with either "cool" vatos or "square" country kids.

Being a "cool" jock type himself, he quite naturally gravitated toward "cool" Mexicanos. For him, the cool vato style was still not associated with a lower class and race. When Anglos arrived on campus before classes, they typically congregated in front of the academic building. Initially, the Anglos made no effort to rescue this high status Anglo jock from the vatos' hanging out territory. After three days, a new Anglo football buddy physically led him out of the Mexicano group into the Anglo group. He never hung out again with the vatos, although he frequently greeted them in the halls and in classes. He quickly learned that hanging with the wrong people would leave him in a social "no-man's land."

Another revealing occasion occurred when a new Mexicana transfer student chose the wrong bench. During her first day in school, she sat down on the Anglos' benches in front of the main academic area. When the Anglo football players arrived, they were surprised to see this diminutive brown intruder on their bench. At first, they stood behind her talking and joking loudly. They began scuffling in mock anger, and one pushed the other down on the ground in front of the girl. She tried to avoid the falling bodies and began looking around. She surveyed the white footballers, then the clusters of Mexicanos in front of the gym. Suddenly something seemed to click in her head. She quickly got up and moved to a Mexicano bench, and she never made the same mistake again.

This territoriality carried over to the toilets and hallways as well. Many Anglos disliked going into the toilets alone, because they feared being "hassled" by a gang of vatos. Anglo girls dreaded walking down the halls alone, especially after most kids had entered their classes. Groups of Mexicanos often shoved, whistled, and made catcalls at them. Mexicanos, especially the vatos, controlled the halls and toilet areas, and they enjoyed "blowing the gringos some shit." Anglos generally preferred avoiding these confrontations, which delighted the vatos. Since they could not cruise in their cars, they liked "cruising" the hallways for a little action.

Yet, having characterized these territories and tensions, some qualifications must be made. Very little violence and few racial confrontations actually occurred in the hallways of North Town high. The kids had worked out their territories, and rather strict rules of public etiquette. These unspoken rules helped them avoid racial confrontations. Predictably, the school board took credit for calming racial tensions. They constantly pointed to their new discipline-oriented principal and his "firm but fair" discipline system. From my perspective in the trenches, it was the youth who made the school run smoothly. Anglo and Mexicano students got along remarkably well, considering the past they had inherited and the present political hostilities among adults. In addition, the role of the teachers, described in Chapter 4, was also important.

Anglo Views of Race Relations

Despite the relative calm, there were many bitter feelings on both sides. One Anglo girl's ideas on relating to the Mexicano kids illustrates a widespread feeling among Anglo students. She responded to my questions about being friends with Mexicanos in the following manner:

> It's real hard to be friends with Meskins because they are always picking on you. One day a Mexican girl, who I thought was my friend, raised up my skirt so all the Mexican boys could see me. She just did it to get in with the bullies so they wouldn't pick on her . . . Sometimes they start speaking Spanish and laughing at you when you can't understand. They don't want to be friends. They call us gringos and always stick together. The boys are taught to use knives, and the girls have so many sisters that they are always fighting. They fight so much, because they are brought up that way. Sometimes the real tough guys pick fights with whites. It isn't fair the way they fight. Whites are always fighting with them.

What she meant by fighting was teasing, arguing, and joking. What bothered her most was the "clannishness" of Mexicanos. She simply did not trust them to treat her as an individual. This girl went on to attribute much of the Mexicanos' aggressive, clannish attitude to the La Raza movement, which she and her dad hated. Another Anglo boy added several cultural reasons why racial conflicts and misunderstandings happened:

> They have a very different culture like food and the way they joke around. They are always teasing me at work about my girl friend, my mother, my father, my dick, you know, very personal things. They do it with each other all the time and never get hacked off, but sometimes this kind of stuff really pisses whites off.

These cultural differences have been called "ritual insults." Several classic studies of black male teenagers portray them testing each other through this sort of verbal dueling (Baugh 1983; Labov 1972). Somewhat analogous forms of Chicano humor apparently became a source of racial conflict between Anglos and Mexicanos.

The most commonly mentioned irritant for Anglos was, however, the academic performance of Mexicanos in the classrooms. The following excepts come from a conversation with several Anglos during a break from playing tennis. Most of these youth were college-bound students, and three of the five were among the school leader, "town kid" crowd:

> God they are so dumb. I hate being in that math class with them. They don't even know how to read and talk . . . They don't get ahead in school because some of them don't want to become American, don't want to learn English. I think American is better than Mexican. No, I guess I shouldn't say that. That is biased . . . Hey, maybe we better not say anything, this racket is probably bugged. We'll probably get mugged . . . Only a few of them are La Raza leaders. The rest of them just follow like sheep . . . School elections are a farce. We don't have a chance for anything anymore. They have got it rigged so only they win . . . Classes with Mexicans are a drag. They are so dumb they can't understand or speak English . . . They live like pigs. Only Meskins can get welfare. I've got a grandmother who can't. It makes me sick to see them lined up to get commodities and food stamps . . . And they just keep having kids like crazy. That's why they are so poor. They are like gypsies, some of them; they always have to leave and go north to make some money . . . Why can't they stay around here and work hard and support themselves?

These Anglo kids expressed the same stereotypes that many of their parents expressed about the dumb, lazy, welfare-cheating Mexicano. This mixture of racial and class prejudices has been consistently reported in other race relations studies. Many Anglo kids resented being in classes with Mexicanos, who, they claimed, "held them back." Several prominent Anglo families had placed their children in private schools in San Antonio, and there were constant rumors and threats that more Anglos were likely to follow suit. In fact, few did, but the most common criticism of the local schools was their low academic standard, which was often attributed to "too many poor, dumb Mexicans."

Not all Anglo kids expressed fears about going into the hallways and toilets alone, or hostility about "dumb Mexicans." There were Anglo kids who had a more live-and-let-live or liberal attitude. Mexicanos perceived many subtle distinctions between red necks and Anglos who were "ok." One group of Anglos considered "ok" were the "homeboys/ homegirls." They were mainly a group of mild-mannered, non-aggressive country kids. These kids were, as Coach Trujillo put it, "good old" kids who don't wish anybody any harm." The other Anglos judged non-racist were not easily clustered into a group. First, there were a handful of pot-smoking, working class kicker girls who hung out with the vatos. Many students called them "sluts" and "whorey-types." Second, there were a few kids who had long hair and a hippie style. Several played in the band and Mexicanos thought they were liberal on the race issue. Third, there was a group of socially prominent girls who secretly dated several Mexicano football players. The Anglo red neck boys called them "Latin lovers" and tried to discourage these secret liaisons.

One liberal Anglo girl, Mary, a top student and active in the band, expressed attitudes quite different from those labeled "red necks." She was much less sure that La Raza was evil, and generally had non-stereotypic views of Mexicanos. (Today, Mary is a professional who lives in San Antonio.) Several other Anglo youths who were "good old farm kids" and a few of the band kids shared these views:

> My father says they will take over and kick us all out. I don't know, really. I guess they did that in Crystal City. I guess they hate Anglos for what we did in the past. But we haven't had it so bad here. Some of the Anglos here overreacted to the salute thing in the band. Some Anglo kids just wanted to quit. They never told their parents the truth about what the band salute really meant. It wasn't political at all and some of them knew it, because the band director explained it to us. Some were just red necks. They didn't like the new band director, who was Chicano. They still wanted an Anglo in charge, so they got mad and quit, but it wasn't right . . . Lots of Mexicano kids are for the Raza Unida, but they don't really seem to know much about it. My dad says they want to create a separate state and kick us out, but I don't think most of these kids have that idea. They are for their race and for having things better. That is all. And you can't blame them . . . I've lost some friends over this thing, because I think people on both sides are exaggerating about all this stuff.

A long-haired Anglo band member, Brian, had the reputation for smoking dope and hanging out with the vatos. Brian wanted to go to New Orleans and start his own rock and roll band. Most of the vatos thought Brian was a "mellow dude." (Today, Brian is married to the daughter of a prominent Anglo rancher, the type who shunned him then, and he runs his father's produce shed.) He had this to say about the racial situation:

> The Latins are for change. They dig it, are looser, not so uptight. There is lots of discrimination here, because most white parents put pressure on us to stay away from Mexicans. I've seen them get some pretty bad treatment around here. I saw one guy stripped naked and frisked at the gas station. I don't think

he did anything, but the cops just wanted to hassle him. They love to hassle us about dope too, if they can. They kinda assume that the Mexicans are doing it but not the "goodie-goodie" Anglos. Last year, when they busted all those guys [Anglos], it was a real shocker to lots of Anglos. Now the Anglos who dig dope are mostly the nobodies, but some of the footballers do it too . . . The straight Anglo girls, the volleyball teamers, wouldn't go out with me. I have a bad rep for hanging out with these "locos" too much. [He and a couple of the vatos listening exchanged insults and all laughed it up.]

I became fascinated with why some Anglo youths in a self-proclaimed "red neck town" grew up being liberal on the race issue. They had been raised on prejudices and stereotypes, had heard strong criticisms of La Raza at home, and had faced strong peer pressures at school—yet they remained open-minded. The main thing which seemed to set them off from others was their social marginality. All were good students, but they were not usually the most popular, attractive standard-bearers for the school. Some were in the band and other school activities, but they were not the high status Anglo kids. Many of them saw themselves as less conforming and conventional than their peers. They were all oriented toward going into some profession and moving away from small-town life. None of these youth saw themselves settling down and running North Town's businesses, ranches, and public institutions. Although native North Towners, they felt a little like outsiders in their own town. They expressed more ambivalent, open attitudes toward what was happening politically and socially.

Mexicano Views of Race Relations: The Activists

Mexicano attitudes toward Anglos also ranged from negative to very accepting. Those Mexicano youth most negative tended to be those who were the most politicized. They were more involved in the Raza Unida. The following youth, Jacinto, the son of a prominent Raza Unida leader illustrates a more assertive view toward Anglos and race relations:

Lots of the gringos put on a nice face now. They are scared because it is hard to put us down anymore. We and our parents can really harass them. But they are still down on us and still favor the Anglos. It is really obvious, anybody can see it. These fucking gringos just can't stand to see us be equal to them. They wouldn't let Pablo be the mayor. Shit, what could Pablo do? They had the council, but this is the way they are. They had to kick the shit out of the Mexicans. Pablo is a good man. He would have helped everybody. We are going to have to beat their asses. They will never change. They can never accept a Mexican over them. They've always been on top, so now they can't stand to lose, but we are going to beat their ass in the elections and run this fucking town. We can run it better than those conservative bastards who have run it for years and haven't done anything for our people.

Commenting on the schools and his educational experience, this same fourteen-year-old, who became a practicing civil rights lawyer, had this to say:

School is a place where you find out you are dumb and that the gringos are better than you are. They always get all the breaks. They never do anything wrong. The Mexicans are always the ones who get in trouble. After a while Mexican kids get so they don't care. They just give up. You know, man, it just gets to be a drag. You are always at the bottom. It seems like you have to work harder than the damn gringos to do anything right. I'm in the top sections now, but I started out at the bottom. I flunked one year and stayed in the Mexican school while some of the rich Mexicans went to the Anglo school. I eventually worked my way up to the top in junior high, but I remember lots of times the teachers used to tell Mexicanitos to go to the board. Then we'd go up there and couldn't work the problems. They'd say, "you can't work the problems, go sit down." Then the gringos would laugh and you'd feel real stupid. The teachers used to use a lot of big words that I couldn't understand. You know, not such big words, I mean I know them now, but then they were big for me. They expected you to know what they were talking about, and most of us didn't. Eventually they break your spirit, man. You just feel like you have to take too much shit for nothing, so you check it in, man, *some of us* check it in, Doc.

This young activist was a top student, football player, and class president. He was disciplined, serious, and a clean cut, all-American boy. Jacinto was publicly very critical of Anglos, and many of them saw him as a "brown neck" toward them. Privately, however, he often distinguished between local Anglos whom he considered uncompromising "red necks" and those who were "ok."

A number of the other more politicized Mexicano students expressed similar views to Jacinto's, although perhaps not so forcefully. They often expressed bitterness about the discrimination they had experienced, but most did not dislike or hate Anglos. They were always quick to distinguish between "red necks" and "ok-Anglos." Nor did they have a set of stereotypes about Anglos that were as negative as the red neck Anglos had about them. Politically active Mexicano kids were critical of Anglos, and they were sometimes bitter, but they were also willing to relate to Anglos who treated them with respect. There were, as some Anglos claimed, a few "brown necks," and the rough cultural equivalent to the Anglo kickers were the Mexicano vatos.

Mexicano Views of Race Relations: The Rebellious Vatos

The other group of Mexicano kids that were more hostile towards Anglos was the vatos. The following comments were collected during a rap session with four kids in the auto mechanics class. We had just finished tearing down the engine of my van, and I offered to buy everyone a cold drink. After much pleading for "cold ones" (a six pack of beer) they settled for cokes. This spirited conversation ranged over many topics, but the essence of what was said about gringos was the following:

> We don't like gringos, man. They act like they are superior. They ain't no better than we are . . . Ya, they always fucking get their way in school. They get whatever they want, like getting out of class, or detention, or something. They always got an excuse that the teachers buy. I get tired of them [he enacted a kind of whimpering, whining behavior] getting the breaks . . . They don't like us either. Most of them just put up with us . . . The chicks, most of the chicks aren't very friendly, either. They won't go out with you. Up north Anglo chicks will go out with Mexicans. Here very few will . . . If you drink at the Dairy Queen, Anglos will give you shit, shoot you the bird [give you the finger]. But if they come over to Hector's, we don't say nothing. . . . Naw, not many come over. We go to the Dairy Queen a lot more than they come to Hectors . . . Shit, man, they are afraid they'll get their asses kicked, if they come over to Mexican Town. It's better, really, if we each have our own place.

The vatos' attitudes were not entirely negative toward Anglos, however. As indicated, they occasionally hung out and smoked dope with several kicker girls. Several of the more liberal, long-haired Anglo "hippie types" also joked around with the vatos. When talking about hating and disliking gringos, vatos always made exceptions for those gringos that they considered "hip." The vatos often evoked the rhetoric of "Chicano power" for their racial feelings, but most were uninterested in electoral politics. Generally, the vatos avoided competing with the Anglos for school honors, placement in advanced classes, and a spot on the teams. They resented the Anglos' class privileges and their elitist attitudes in much the same way that Tara, the "hip kicker" girl, did. Like Tara, they too were social outcasts and had little interest in being successful conformists. They preferred the freedom that being an outcast afforded them.

Their attitude toward school and the teachers was also very negative. All said that school "sucks" and that the teachers were "shit." They were particularly angry at the school board's dress code rules, and were constantly harassed about the length of their hair and style of clothes. The administration often suspended them for cutting classes and insubordination as well. One day in mechanics class, Gilberto arrived with a big grin on his face. He announced that he had been suspended for two weeks because they had caught him sleeping in his car. It was his birthday, so he had decided he owed himself a little relief from classes.

Most vatos were simply waiting out the mandatory drop-out age. They needed to work to support their cars and their hip lifestyle. They were glad when summer came, because most picked up extra money working in the melon harvests. Several joked that they wanted to go into the service to "see the world" and "make a man out of myself." When being serious, they only half believed those clichés, but in reality they had few better options. The military often seemed better than staying in North Town and picking melons or sorting tomatos. Going to college was "too hard" and "cost too much money." Most aspired to working class jobs like their fathers', such as driving a tractor, trucking melons, fixing cars, setting irrigation rigs, and working in packing sheds. Some wanted to be carpenters and bricklayers, or work for the highway road crews.

Being able to survive on a blacktopping crew during the summer heat was considered a very prestigious job. They thought about hard, physical labor exactly the way we did as youths growing up in rural Iowa. A road gang or railroad gang was the rural equivalent of working in a factory foundry. It was dangerous, dirty, heavy work that only "real men" did. It was a true test of a young man's body and character. The vatos preferred the same rough, physical work we did. They considered working with their hands honorable, a test of your strength and manliness.

In contrast, school work was seen as boring, sissy stuff. Teachers who constantly harped on doing homework were like nagging parents. Some were disparagingly called wimps and fags. Others were so sober and serious about their lessons, they were simply "nerds." There were notable exceptions such as "Mr. Roach-clip," rumored to have been a doper in Vietnam, and Coach Sergio Zapata, a fast-talking, street-wise San Antonian. In general, the vatos considered school the smart, rich kids' domain. They saw themselves as good fighters, rappers, lovers, and laborers, but not as students or bookworms.

The number one school authority on the vatos' hit list was Brad Jones, the vice principal. Jones was a young, athletic-looking native of the area who walked in a very erect, reserved manner. He was righteously open about his duty to punish the "punks" and "troublemakers" who sought to disrupt the school. He took his job very seriously, and thus quickly became unpopular, which he took as a sign of his effectiveness. The vatos hated being sent to him, because they felt that he always talked down to them. He used his "file" of previous offenses as "evidence" to prove that the offender had a chronic, perhaps fatal criminal flaw. He liked rubbing in one's past failures to conform to the school rules.

The following was a discipline session that I eavesdropped on from the teachers' lounge. It reminded me of Captain Queeg's classic strawberries incident in *The Caine Mutiny*. Warren Williams, a very unpopular, "nerdy" teacher, had sent three boys to Jones for playing with a balloon in class. The following is the inquisition over the balloon incident:

"What have you been up to, son, whose balloon was that? Why were you playing with balloons in Mr. Williams' class?"

Francisco replied in a very subdued voice, "It was Benito's. I was just picking it up. It wasn't mine."

Jones then ordered him to get "Ben" in here. When Benito arrived, he asked him if he was "into it again," but as he began to answer Jones became agitated and said, "You talk when I tell to you, boy! Now listen up!"

Jones then started his usual degradation ritual of reading the prisoner his previous record of offenses from his file. He spent two or three minutes rubbing in two other detentions and one suspension for misbehavior. Meanwhile, Benito sat in silence as Jones deplored his record. Then he launched into a series of cutting questions:

"What kind of grades do you get, F's? Are you going to make anything out of yourself? Don't give me that stuff? Don't sit there and tell me the balloon isn't yours? Whose is it, if it isn't yours? You're a little troublemaker, so you might as well admit it now. You are not going to get away with this."

Ultimately, a third boy admitted that the balloon was his. They were all given two weeks of detention for the incident, to be served either in the morning or after school. Mr. Jones said that he could not "take up my lunch hour for your mistakes!" I saw the three boys file out of the office, heads bowed and silent. Jones came into the teachers' lounge with a quiet, self-assured smile on his face. Two of the other teachers chuckled, and one asked if he had had more trouble with "the punks." Jones replied, "Not really." and went about his hall patrolling duties. My anthropological imagination flashed on Clint Eastwood, and I saw him holster his six-shooter and throw back his poncho as he mounted his horse and rode down the school halls.

A few weeks later, however, Jones, as a couple of the vatos said, "got his." I was attending my first after-the-game dance in the high school gym. It was a curious affair with many youths sitting in the bleachers. Almost no one was dancing to the records that the local D.J., a jive-talking high schooler called "Ratonini" (the rat-man), churned out. Ratonini played a curious mixture of rock, country western, and con junto music. Each different style of music would lure two or three different couples onto the vast gym floor, but no more.

At one point, there was a minor altercation at the entrance. Jones and Billy Parsons, the social studies teacher, were taking tickets at the door. Several vatos were hanging around the door trying to see who was at the dance, and possibly crash the gate. Jones finally became irritated with their rubbernecking and cajoling. He told them either to pay and come in or get out. They backed off a little but still did not leave. They were lurking around waiting for something.

Suddenly a couple of clean-cut students ran up and breathlessly announced to Jones that someone had smashed out the windshield of his car. He became furious and rushed outside to see what had happened. Paco, one of the guys hanging out at the door waiting to see Jones's reaction, gave me a defiant look and nodded his head skyward, as if to say, "See what's happening, Doc? Put that in your book, man!"

Without saying anything, the group of vatos at the door followed Jones to the scene of the crime. No one could prove who smashed the windshield in, but everyone in school knew it was the vatos' revenge on Mr. Jones. The incident immediately acquired folkloric immortality, and to this day is probably still told in the halls of North Town High.

On the surface, the vatos were an angry, defiant lot. The smashing of Jones's windshield was vintage vato guerrilla warfare. It was the kind of daring, rebellious act that everyone associated with these "dudes." If, however, you could penetrate their defenses, most vatos deeply resented being semiliterate. They exhibited all the "hidden injuries of class" that Richard Sennett and Jonathan Cobb (1972) document brilliantly. They considered themselves smart—at least about life and practical things. But many of them had been convinced that they were dumb about books and learning standard English. Years of failure had taught them to publicly reject, but privately internalize, the criticism of teachers.

The Views of Mainstream Mexicanos

The majority of Mexicano youths fell somewhere between the activists and the vatos. Most were not strongly anti-Anglo or anti-school. They were very much like their Anglo counterparts, who were considered "homeboys/girls" and "nobodies." They were obedient, non-aggressive conformists who did not particularly like school but felt it was less boring than "staying home" or "working in the fields." They filled the practical classes and were not particularly good students. Most dutifully supported the teams, voted for the prominent kids as their leaders, stayed out of trouble with teachers, seldom dated, and hung out with one or two close friends. Since most of these youths came from low income families, they did not plan to go to college. High school would be their terminal degree and, like the vatos, they aspired to working class jobs. Those with better school records aspired to white collar working class jobs in offices. In short, these youth would become the future silent majority of American society. They would quietly marry, produce several children, and go to work in a low paying job that someone had to do.

I generally found Mexicano racial attitudes toward Anglos remarkably generous and non-vengeful. A classroom discussion observed on the topic of the "school's race problem" illustrates what many Mexicano youths told me in private. This was one of the few times that I observed an honest classroom discussion about race relations. As indicated earlier, teachers generally avoided such conversations for fear of creating racial misunderstandings. Ironically, this discussion was held in the social studies class of a very red neck Anglo teacher.

The conversation started out slowly, but the Anglo kids broke the ice. They began criticizing Mexicanos for getting too many "free handouts" like food stamps and free lunches. The Mexicanos countered that many poor Mexicanos could not find work, because they lacked an education and had few skills. One Mexicano boy then made a conciliatory comment that Mexicanos "try hard to be good citizens." He asked the Anglos to understand that his people were doing their best. The Mexicano youths were generally asking for understanding. Initially, they avoided criticizing the Anglos about racial discrimination against Mexicanos.

An Anglo girl then shifted the conversation and asked why so many Mexicanos flunked in school. Several Mexicanos responded that most kids spoke Spanish in their houses. They explained how difficult it was to start school without any knowledge of English. Others complained about getting behind or getting bad grades and ultimately losing hope. Many blamed themselves for not trying hard enough. Another said that she thought Anglos were real smart in school and got good grades. She added that Mexicanos resented Anglos because they "always got their own way, like getting out of class or detention." This brought strong denials from Anglos, and one conciliatory "that's not always true." Mexicanos countered that Anglos sometimes "act superior," as if they were "better than Mexicans." One Mexicana retorted that "Mexicanos are just as good as Anglos." Anglos complained that they no longer had a chance in the school elections, because Mexicanos bloc voted against them. The Mexicanos defended this practice by saying they wanted to show the Anglos that they were not "just sitting there" and that they "could beat them, if they wanted to."

Nothing said during the discussion varied from what these youth told me in private. What struck me as interesting about the conversation was its open, reasonable tone. This entire exchange was generally devoid of harsh denunciations and accusations. Even more surprising, the Mexicano response was very conciliatory in tone. At the time, they reminded me how Gregorio, a big standout tackle, saw his abilities and race relations. He was in the practical sections, and was reading at approximately a sixth grade level. When asked why he did not do very well in school he replied:

> I guess I am dumb. I am in the slow classes because I am dumber than the Anglos, I guess. I can't speak English so good, and I can't read very well. I never have done good in school. The teachers go too fast. I wanna be better. My parents want me to go to college. I try real hard, but I can't get it 'cause I must be dumb.

When asked why so many Mexicano kids seemed to be failing, he gave a widely held "folk belief" among low achieving Mexicano students. These kids blamed neither the system nor the gringos:

> Too many Mexicano kids goof off. They don't care. They don't try hard enough. They just don't pay attention. They like to raise too much hell . . . Naw, most of the teachers don't discriminate very much. Most of them give you a break. Some don't. Some talk bad. Some favor the Anglos. It used to be bad. We all had separate schools. Now we don't. It was pretty bad in grade school. The old Anglo teachers didn't like us very much. They thought we were stupid and dirty. I remember one sending kids home because she said they had lice. Roberto's mom got real pissed off when he came home crying about having lice. I don't think it is like that anymore in grade school. My brothers and sisters never say stuff like that. They like school and their teachers.

Gregorio was generally a very likeable, gregarious teddy bear of a kid. He talked and moved slowly and with little self-assurance. He expressed no bitterness toward Anglos for "holding him down." When I asked him what he thought of Anglos he replied, "Aw, they're ok, most of them are pretty friendly."

His father was a migrant worker who had high hopes for his son, who he considered a "good football player." The mother was a shy woman who stayed in their modest home and cared for their seven children. Gregorio felt the enormous pressure of being the eldest. He had to carry the family banner for his younger siblings. Every summer he worked the melons and, like many working class Mexicanos, put his money into the family coffers. He received only an allowance from his wages. His parents described him as a "good boy," because he neither smoked nor drank and was not rebellious. He was a humble, hard-working lad who believed himself to be too thick to be good in school. He hoped to go off to the service and someday study under the G.I. Bill. He believed that being in the service would somehow improve his educational skills.

One must be careful to not turn Gregorio into a stereotype of the smiling, good-hearted, humble Mexicano. For me he symbolizes those kids often labeled "nobodies" or "quiet types." Many of these kids were apolitical and relatively unaggressive about race relations. Some Chicano militants accused these quiet nobodies of having a "colonial mentality." Gregorio did not exactly accept his subordination, but he *did* have rather low expectations for himself and was apolitical:

> I don't go along with all that Chicano stuff. I don't care about the election thing. It's ok if some of the Anglos win, and most of my friends feel the same way. Some of the most active Raza kids won't talk to me, but I talk to all of them. I make them say hi, even if they get uptight. I try not to fight with anybody, Mexicano or gringo. We all gotta get along. It's better that way.

Unfortunately, most of the Anglo kids knew very little about, and appreciated even less, the Gregorios of North Town. The Mexicanos they came in contact with were the upwardly mobile, academically advanced students. They tended to stereotype low achieving Mexicanos as being "dumb" rebellious vatos or nobodies. Mexicano youth such as Gregorio were actually very similar to the rural Anglo kids of modest academic ability and social aspirations. These kids good-heartedly followed the real movers and shakers of the school regardless of race, and they had learned not to expect to inherit the earth.

Gregorio's story was not unlike the stories of several outcast "white trash" kids. They had all been psychologically beaten down in similar ways. The main difference was that Gregorio and others like him ascribed "dumbness" more to being Mexican than to being poor. They tended to see themselves in racial rather than class terms. In contrast, Tara saw herself in very strong class terms. The low achieving Mexicano youths invariably had the double burden of race and class to overcome.

Interracial Dating: Longings, Secret Rendezvous, and Vigilantes

One of the most interesting facets of race relations among North Town youth was the stirrings of interracial dating. Despite the adult restrictions on interracial dating, a minority of youth from both ethnic groups wanted to date each other. Many youth reported pressure from their parents to date only youth of their race. The social worker, who lived next door, described two incidents of child-beating that resulted from interracial dating. In both cases, the sheriff and he were called to a house to prevent an Anglo father from beating his daughter. Their daughters had been caught secretly dating Mexicanos.

In addition, one Anglo girl, who was dating a popular Mexican American football player, became pregnant and dropped out of school. She reported losing most of her friends and being very isolated. A Mexicana, the daughter of a prominent Ciudadanos leader, also married the son of a prominent BGL leader. North Towners appreciated the irony of this alliance, but the couple felt relatively isolated from each other's group. As in the case of three other mixed marriages, such couples reported strong pressures from both sides and were very isolated socially.

Despite such pressures, many North Town youth expressed a certain fascination with dating kids from "the other group." Considerable gossip marked certain kids as longing to break the unspoken rule of segregated dating. Approximately eight or ten Anglo boys, all athletes and mostly country or "kicker" types, were rumored to be "hot to date Mexicans." Ironically, two of these boys were part of a "vigilante" group organized to protect white girls. These self-appointed vigilantes patrolled the Anglo neighborhood in their pickups. They tried to intimidate Mexicanos who visited Anglo girls. On two different occasions, a Mexicano football player reported being chased upon leaving an Anglo girl's house. On one occasion, a pickup load of kicker types passed by the tennis court and boasted about "running Carlos off." Apparently, he was on foot and allegedly "ran like a jackrabbit" to a "safe" gas station.

Several of the Anglo girls, derisively called "Latin lovers," complained about the vigilantes' admonitions. These white protectors thought that "dating Meskins" would "stretch them" (their sexual organ) and ruin their reputations. The girls were both flattered and irritated over the vigilantes' efforts to protect them, and they disliked being called "Latin lovers." They thought that the Anglo boys were overreacting and were being somewhat hypocritical. The Anglo girls pointed out that their "protectors" were also interested in Mexicanas. These Anglo girls confided that some Mexicano boys were "smart" and "nice" and "more interesting." They liked the "respectful" and "romantic" way these boys talked to them. Moreover, they were "tired of most of the Anglo boys," whom they had known since first grade. Whenever I suggested that maybe the "grass was greener on the other side of the fence," the Anglo girls usually laughed coyly and said "maybe."

It must be noted that prominent Anglo girls responded to only the most successful Mexicano student-athletes. The eight or ten Mexicano boys who consistently "hung out" with Anglos were from the college-bound Mexicano middle class. The one exception was an unusually good-looking jock who lacked the grades to go to college. In sharp contrast, none of the upwardly mobile Mexican American girls were dating local Anglo boys. There were two or three Mexicanas, including Tina the cheerleader, who dated Anglo boys from other towns. The reason for this gender difference became apparent as North Town youths explained the pressures they felt.

Mexican American girls were far less likely to date Anglo boys, even from prominent families, for several reasons. First, Mexicano parents supervised their daughters more closely than Anglo parents. Traditional Mexican practices of chaperones and formal visits to the house had disappeared, but Mexicano girls generally had stricter evening hours and often were simply forbidden to go out on dates. Second, going out with an Anglo male had strong connotations of being a whore or concubine. Many stories circulated in the Mexicano community about Anglo patrones and lawmen who had Mexicana mistresses. Most Mexicanos believed that an Anglo would not marry a Mexicana, and thus lose status among his own people; consequently, most Mexicanos reasoned that the only thing Anglos must be after was sex. If a Mexicana dated an Anglo, it was assumed that she was sleeping with him. These perceptions made it very difficult for a Mexican American girl to risk her reputation by dating an Anglo. Finally, Anglo males, being on top of this patriarchal racist social order, had the most to lose by dating Mexicanas. The status-enhancing female prizes were the rich, cute Anglos, not the Mexicanas.

In sharp contrast, Mexican American males had enormous pressure on them to date Anglo females. A number of the Mexicanos talked about dating Anglos as if it was a political victory for their race. It was an important way of showing Anglo males that Mexicano males were as good as they were. To be able to date and seduce an Anglo female was considered a sign of power and status. One of the football players put it this way:

Any guys who are good in sports can get the girls, it don't matter what race. Some of us are getting it on with the gringas, because we know how to talk. We can feed them a line better than the Anglos. Some of those kickers are dumb with girls. The Anglo girls like us because we are different, but some of us get good grades and are as good as they are now . . . No, the Anglo guys are afraid to go out with Chicanas. Lewt [an Anglo football buddy] always says he doesn't really like Beatrice, but I know he writes her secret love letters all the time; but he's afraid to take her out. I don't know why. Maybe he thinks some of us will gang up on him. I told him we wouldn't, but he didn't say anything.

Even the more politicized activists joked about "getting a gringa." They were always plotting how to approach them, and endless sexual teasing and joking occurred in the advanced academic classes. The most successful, aggressive Mexicano boys were constantly flirting, touching, joking, and teasing the prominent Anglo girls. Almost daily, they enacted their repressed, unrequited desires towards Anglo girls. Several socially prominent Mexicanas expressed disgust over Mexicanos who fawned over the "gringas," and called them "vendidos."

The racially mixed advanced academic classes included the best students from each race. These youth tended to compete with each other academically the way the adults competed politically. One social studies class, taught by a young Mexicano teacher, promoted this kind of interracial interaction. Mr. Silva admitted being delighted and envious of the changes in race relations. The new assertiveness of the Mexicano boys towards the Anglo girls intrigued him, and his advanced freshman class was a laboratory of unrequited sexual curiosity. The following is a scene observed in Silva's classroom.

The morning class started in the usual way. Several couples lingered in the hallways for some last-minute caresses. Ricardo, a curly-haired, light-skinned, handsome halfback, and Mandy, a freshman Anglo cheerleader, were leaning on the wall near the doorway. Their classmates tossed knowing looks, raised eyebrows, and taunts as they filed by the couple. Ricardo and Mandy were oblivious to the teasing, and they continued to bump and rub each other. Silva came to the door and said in a coy, teasing tone of voice, "Ok, break it up, you lovebirds."

The "lovebirds" reluctantly took their seats, and Silva, still smiling devilishly, orchestrated a round of comments from the proverbial peanut gallery of onlookers. "What were you guys doing out there?" "Are you coming up for air?" "Ricardo's got a girl, nah nah nah!"

Silva's reaction was amusement, and after fielding and commenting on these teasing remarks, he continued asking coy, provocative questions like, "Are all of you going to the game tomorrow?" He said this with such sly anticipation that the kids read his question as an invitation to talk about what happens *after* the game. Several little brushfires of gossip ignited about who was going with whom to the game. All of this speculation led back to Ricardo and Mandy. They gave the obligatory denials, which provoked knowing nods and grins. Meanwhile Ricardo's football buddies were drawn into the act. Lupe, another Mexicano with an Anglo surname, was innocently sitting behind Mandy's best friend, Jennifer. Someone conjured up Lupe and Jennifer as a couple and joked that "It looks like a double! " To which Mr. Silva said coyly, "¡a ver!" (let's see!).

This pulled Reggie, a tall, beak-nosed, dark, high-strung footballer, into the teasing game. He was a "hanging out" friend of Lupe's and Ricardo's, but they were not "that tight." Sitting across from Jennifer, he leaned over and touched her arm and whispered in dead seriousness, "What about me? Wanna go to the game with me?"

Jennifer jerked her arm away quickly and ignored Reggie with a look of total disgust. Her agitated, haughty response was filled with the hope that no one had heard Reggie's audacious request. She whispered to Mandy, "Oh, God! " and Reggie got the message. I knew he was hurt, so affecting my best innocent face, I asked him later if he was going to ask her out. To that he replied, "That stuck up bitch will never go out with a Mexican like me, Doc. I probably scare her. She thinks the La Raza want to kill all the gringos."

At that time, I was not sure what he meant by "a Mexican like me," but I kept watching these flirting exchanges, and eventually the pattern became obvious. Reggie was "just a Mexican," but Ricardo and Lupe were going to be school leaders. They were from good families, were college bound, and, perhaps more importantly, were good-looking "studs." Reggie was a tall, dark, gangly kid from a poor family. He was a nobody socially, despite the fact that he was a pretty fair football player. He knew he had virtually no chance of getting a socially prominent white girl, but his machismo made him try. To protect himself, he explained his own unattractiveness to the gringa as political. In fact, he was never really involved in the movement.

I saw this same scene repeated on other occasions, but this particular incident took on a special meaning for me. When I returned to North Town years later to update the fieldwork, I ran into Reggie. With that long, sad face, he recounted his drug problem and his difficulty in finding a good job. As we talked, I saw the same hurt in his face that I had seen ten years earlier. I felt compelled to ask him about Ricardo. He no longer saw much of Ricardo, but Ricardo had not been enough of a "stud" to play football in college. He had gotten a degree, and moved away. Reggie wasn't sure, but he had heard that he was "a pencil pusher in some office."

Interracial Dating: Some Class Differences in Communicative Styles

This incident poignantly represented the great class divide that dictated interracial dating. The door was open for the new, promising Mexicanos, and they were quick to come in. But the vatos and other working class Mexicanos, even those who had made it through sports, were still just "dumb Mexicans." They lacked the manners, the light skin color, the clothes, and the ambitions of a Ricardo or Lupe. As the Mexicano footballers dating Anglos claimed, they knew how to "bullshit" the gringas with their suave "Latin lover" raps. They also knew how to "bullshit" teachers and get ahead in school. Getting ahead in school went hand in hand with getting the girls, who liked winners not losers. These upwardly mobile Mexicanos were polished and debonair compared to the rough, dirty vatos or to Reggie.

The vatos, unlike Reggie, had no social aspirations. They knew that only the "wild" pot-smoking "whory" kicker girls would go out with them. The vatos understood that their style of hipness was too rough and rebellious to "score with the rich bitches." Being good guerrilla fighters, the vatos enjoyed what they could get from the kicker girls, while the "Reggies" were left with their frustrations. Of course, the real winners in social status terms were the "Ricardos." They were aggressively Mexicano, and they still got the Anglo girls. They were a new bicultural middle class that wanted to combine the best of both worlds.

This difference in "rap" also became apparent when these boys discussed how they courted girls and their families. It was widely disputed among the kids whether "going steady" really led to marriage, or was just a male ploy to "get laid." The general male view was well expressed by the following "cool" Mexicano ladies' man:

> You almost gotta go steady to get it around here. The girls are afraid that you are going to blab about them and ruin their rep. You don't ruin a good thing, unless you are messed up in the head. It takes quite a while, too, even if you're going steady, but most girls will, if you feed them a line of shit. You can get in their pants. They really want to, but they have to think you love them and want to marry them before they give in. Besides, lots of guys don't want to wait too long to get married. All the good looking chicks will be gone and nothing will be left but the ugly bitches, the whorey ones who give it to everybody just trying to get married.

As this vivid male testimony indicates, males generally had a very instrumental view of going steady. Most actually did see it as a manipulative ploy for "getting into a chick's pants." They were able to give elaborate, objective descriptions of their "dutiful demeanor" and the "lines they fed their chicks." They prided themselves on being able to "talk their way out of trouble" over being late, looking at other females, forgetting birthdays—all the important signs of attentiveness. The following testimony from a "hip kicker" football player on his rapping ability illustrates the art of male deception and impression management:

> My chick is always getting pissed off, if I don't pick her up after band practice. So I tell her the coach kept us late, or I had to do some chores for dad, or something. You gotta do this like you are real sorry, you know, hang your head a little, talk in a low voice, give her a hug or two. You have to let her know you did wrong, even if you didn't. I usually feed her some bull about how much I love her, too. Girls really like that soft, gentle stuff . . . No, everybody doesn't have the same rap. I think lots of guys act like animals. They just want it, so they go for it. I think the guys from better families have better sense. They aren't as crude, you know. I'd never dip on a date. Most girls don't like that, especially the ones from good families. I'd never get too loud in public either . . . You gotta stay on the good side of her parents and teachers, too. If word gets around that you are too wild, they are gonna forbid her to see you. You gotta be a little wild, be a "guzzler" and party, so you balance it out, play the game.

Such feelings do not rule out sincerity, in the beginning or later, but nearly all "cool" males talked about sexual conquests as the art of deceit. Further, most socially prominent males aggressively pursued sex for the pleasure and the gender status it bestowed. They invariably described their courtship style as playing the conformist all-American boy for adults, and the dutiful, attentive lover for the girl. In addition, they also had to balance such conformist behavior with a little "wildness." The most frequent metaphor used was "play the game," which meant pleasing everyone from adults to their "guzzling buddies." On such matters, the success-oriented males from both racial groups agreed.

In sharp contrast, the more rebellious working class vatos claimed that they had a very different, less "pussy-whipped" style of dealing with their "chicks." They placed far less emphasis on the little civilities and concessions, and were always boasting about "letting a chick have it," or "letting her know where she stands." They also expressed very little interest in appeasing parents and teachers. Their idea of how to conduct social relations was to do as you please and say what you feel. This showed people that you were free and better than they thought you were. How much of this talk was macho bravado was difficult to say. At least in the case of the "kicker" girls, they often publicly acted in a brash, outspoken, rough manner, and the girls seemed to respond to it.

A Summing Up: The Youth Scene and the Interplay of Class, Race, and Gender

The North Town youth scene strongly reflected a number of American popular culture practices and ideals. Loosely knit status display groups invariably had great social significance. They were symbolic groups that constantly displayed important class and gender differences among North Town youths. The kids "caught in the rat-race" were indeed the trend setters. They definitely enacted the popular culture ideals of a swinging adult life style of power, physical attractiveness, social popularity, sex, drinking, and material success. They enacted or performed these mainstream cultural ideals and behavior through their school leadership in sports and academics, and through their personal drinking, friendship, and dating practices.

The majority, who had negative or no particular group social identities, became the audience for the stars who enacted American popular culture ideals. Some of the conformist-oriented "nobodies" and "nerds" aspired to imitate the "somebodies," but many others did not actually enact the ideals of the status-seeking youth. They tended to conduct their social relationships in a less competitive, more intimate manner. They learned to take their place as followers in the lower echelons of the status hierarchy. They learned to live quiet, discreet social lives that would prepare them for the hard-working, straight, great silent majority.

It is important to restate how patriarchal and male-dominated the football and social scenes were. All males, regardless of class and race, engaged in these cultural practices, and North Town females tended to acquiesce and play subordinate, supporting roles. Moreover, class privilege was also a general feature of the football and social scene. These findings were consistent with many other studies of the American youth scene. The new story, however, was the Mexicano challenge to the old system of racial privilege. Class and gender practices circumscribed or mediated this ethnic challenge in complex ways. As a result, only some Mexicanos gained new privileges. Only middle class Mexicano males gained the same privileges that Anglo males had in the world of student status groups and dating. This suggests the continuing importance of class.

Conversely, Mexicanas tended to have fewer new privileges, because they were still less valued as objects of exchange and possession. This suggests the continuing importance of gender. Further, Mexicano males who were nobodies and vatos were left behind for *both* class and racial reasons. The vatos gained a peculiar, ephemeral kind of status as rebels and outlaws, but their class and race greatly minimized their gender privilege. They were not able to attain the socially prominent white females, who were the prize in this patriarchal world. Finally, Mexicanas who were nobodies or rebels were left even further behind for class, racial, *and* gender reasons.

In short, North Town's "adolescent society" was varied, changing, and inherently filled with contradictions. The socially prominent youths, in spite of controlling the stage, were never a model that everyone willingly or uniformly emulated. The racial barrier was breaking down, but at different rates depending on class and gender factors. At least in this setting, gender and class privileges still seemed to be intact. The civil rights struggle of Mexicanos to create a new positive identity had begun to erode the old structure of racial privilege. The erosion of racial privilege was limited, however, by the continuing importance of class and gender. This suggests that, if civil rights advocates also attack class and gender privileges, these forms of inequality might also be transformed.

Finally, differences in communicative style between vatos and the upwardly mobile kids of both races were apparent in dating and social relationships. All males treated females like objects and related in very instrumental, manipulative ways. The middle class males of both races were generally better at impression management, however. The suave middle class Mexicanos were far more successful with prominent Anglo females than the rough, crude vatos. Each social class group extolled the virtue of their "raps" with females, but the vatos lacked the ability to convince parents that they were decent and responsible. They were too open about their drinking, dope smoking, and cruising around to be reassuring. In contrast, the all-American types managed their images better with parents and hid their "unstraight" drinking and dope smoking.

FOUR

Working and Playing Around in the Classroom

Life in North Town High School was very much like that in other small town American schools. Going to class occupied most of the students' time, and they were constantly and continuously evaluated. Students endlessly talked about "big assignments" and "killer tests" and "pop quizzes." Rarely, however, did you hear students talking about any exciting new information or ideas. There was little talk about academics, except among those odd students called "brains." These gifted academic students tended to be thought of as "study freaks" and "bookworms." Students disliked the students who took studying and learning too seriously. Many of their comments about those students and teachers who "thought they were brains" were strongly anti-intellectual in tone. Most students came to school for extracurricular activities and for the social scene. School was football games, band practice, flirting with girls/boys, hassling teachers, and hanging out with friends. It was also boring lessons, scary tests, and "nerdy," "picky," "know-it-all" teachers.

The first thing an outside observer might notice was that classes were ability grouped. Students were divided into "advanced," "average," and "practical" based on test scores, grades, and teacher recommendations. To be in the practical sections, especially if you were an Anglo, had very negative connotations. The "practicals" were the "dumbies" and "losers." Most teachers considered these groups very difficult to teach, because of their limited academic skills and low motivation. These students were simply waiting to turn sixteen, the age at which they could legally drop out of school. Conversely, the advanced classes were full of collegebound students, and the emphasis was on academics. These classes were comprised of the Anglos, the new Mexicano middle class, and a few highly motivated, talented working class Mexicano students.

This characterization is based on how students and teachers talked about these ability groups and on a follow up survey done ten years later.

The survey showed that students rated high academically came from upper middle class (business and professional) (32%) or lower middle class families (small business, trade, technical, and low level office workers) (46%). In sharp contrast, students in the low sections came from blue collar 80%) or lower middle class families (18%). In this survey "high" was being on the honor roll, "average" was being in the advanced academic sections, and "low" was being in the practical classes. Other national studies (Oakes 1985) have found similar patterns in many other American schools.

The practice of grouping students by ability was a sore point with some Mexican American parents. Most teachers agreed that the academic level of practical classes was approximately fifth or sixth grade. At times, the reading level for the textbooks was even lower. The racial composition of these classes was almost 100 percent Mexicano. More than 60 percent of all Mexicano students were in the practical sections, while only a handful of Anglo students were assigned to these classes. Mexicano political activists were fond of saying that Anglos had to be retarded before they were placed in the practical sections.

Race Relations and Racism in the Classroom

Distinct racial territories existed in all classrooms, even the racially mixed ones. When free to do so, students tended to cluster together along student status group lines. The prominent Anglos tended to sit in the center and front. Prominent Mexicanos tended to sit on the sides and in the back. Vatos almost always sat in the rear of classes. During student council, election, and yearbook staff meetings, these racial separations were even more apparent. On such occasions, the socially prominent kids from each group competed actively for the school leadership positions. These competitions were similar to the political competition among adults.

Teachers generally made few attempts to alter the racial and class segregation in classrooms and in student activities. Many teachers felt like they were "walking on eggshells" to avoid racial issues. As the racial joking in sports indicated, the race issue was unavoidable. Kids also made ethnic jokes in classrooms about their lessons. For example, a discussion in history class about the "brown bomber," Joe Louis, sparked "brown power" joking. A comment about "Tex-Mex" in Spanish class led to a brief argument about "Chicano dialect." A discussion of the band in speech class led to charges that Anglos had unfairly walked out on the new

Chicano band director. Between the teachers' silence and the kids' joking, you could feel a constant tension over the race issue.

Teachers' views of the "race problem" varied, and a few still used rather dated and derogatory ethnic labels such as "Latin." These teachers cited various reasons why the low achieving Mexicano kids "did not care," and were "never serious about school." Their theories ranged from the home economics teacher's argument that Mexican food was protein deficient to the English teacher's argument that Catholicism encouraged lax moral values. A number of teachers felt that Mexican American families were too permissive. Parents were criticized for failing to supervise and discipline their children adequately.

Most of the more traditional teachers had views similar to those found in a northern California study reported by John Ogbu (1974). The study portrayed teachers and prominent citizens, "the taxpayers," as having a set of negative myths about low income people. Ghetto dwellers of all races supposedly had disorganized, fatherless family systems and were welfare loafers uninterested in the schools and education. North Town teachers also blamed poverty, family breakdown, and low educational aspirations for the high incidence of academic failure among Mexican American students. The image most frequently evoked was the single parent welfare mother with unsupervised, dirty, poorly clothed children.

Unlike Anglo youths, Anglo teachers did not openly express racial prejudices in casual conversations or interviews. They claimed that Mexicanos failed because they grew up as ignorant, dependent migrant farm laborers. As a result, Mexican Americans generally had very low levels of education and a limited knowledge of English. These cultural deficits purportedly resulted in low aspirations, family breakdown, alcoholism, and a fatalistic attitude toward the future. In the traditional Anglo teacher's view, Mexicanos clung to their old culture and language. Anglos frequently told stories about successful Mexican immigrants who had quickly Americanized. In addition, successful Mexicano youths were thought to come from the "better families" who had established businesses, learned English, and integrated into the society.

Their pro-acculturationist views led many Anglo teachers to view the "Latins" as their wards. Many of the more dedicated Anglo teachers tended to see themselves as uplifting this downtrodden race and class of peones. Their attitudes were more paternalistic than hateful and racist. The follow derogatory comment came from one of the more popular, professional Anglo teachers:

I don't mean to say anything bad or derogatory, but the Latin kids, some of them are about one step above an animal when it comes to learning. Some of these slow learners just don't have it upstairs. They seem to be more skilled and talented with their hands. For some reason they do better in vocational skilled type work. But it is too bad that some people think vocational work is for dummies and lower type people. People seem to prefer white collar work. They don't want to work and get their hands dirty, but really, skilled labor is paid more. We need more vocational curriculum for the Latins. Too many of them will never be able to cut it in an academic curriculum.

This teacher was the first to admit that "some Latins" were doing well and "could compete with the Anglos," but the overall view was very paternalistic. Like Booker T. Washington, a paternalistic nineteenth-century black educational leader, this teacher relegated most "Latins" to being "hewers of wood and haulers of water." Their academic deficiency was a product of their limited cultural and historical development. As a people, only a portion of this race were ready to compete with the superior Anglos. In the meantime, the schools needed to give them a practical education that prepared them to fit into working class jobs.

Given such views, I expected to see a great deal of racial prejudice expressed and practiced in North Town classrooms. A social science literature that is self-consciously "liberal" suggests that low income public schools are rampantly racist. A series of passionate ethnographies done in the sixties have described the horrors of urban ghetto schools (Rist 1973; Rosenfeld 1971; Leacock 1969; Eddy 1967). Subsequently, other accounts have presented a more complex, varied portrayal of race relations in desegregating schools (Johnson 1985; Schofield 1983; Lightfoot and Carew 1979; Metz 1978).

To my surprise, some Anglo teachers who privately expressed racist views were not perceived as "red necks." Since I considered the kids a better judge of Anglo prejudice than I was, this apparent contradiction puzzled me. After much observation of these teachers, I realized that they appeared to treat Mexicano and Anglo kids in the advanced sections more or less the same. Their expectations for Mexicanos in the practical sections were much lower, however. Nevertheless, I observed few blatant incidents of racism, and Mexicano students thought most of their Anglo teachers were "ok." I came to agree with their assessment.

These teachers performed their public role without being openly racist for several reasons. First and foremost, the existence of the Chicano movement greatly heightened everyone's sensitivities and consciousness about racial discrimination. Anglo teachers were forced to scrutinize their behavior and be careful about expressing anti-Mexicano views. A growing number of Mexicano parents were willing to complain publicly about teachers. A number of Mexicano community activists maintained a vigil to find discrimination in the schools.

Nevertheless, teachers' classroom pedagogical practices were never put on trial the way the BGL school board's policies were. As indicated, some kids joked with teachers about "getting La Raza after you," but very few actual incidents occurred. Teachers had to handle spontaneous ethnic joking and ethnic tensions on a daily basis, but only a very small number of formal complaints were lodged against teachers. Even during the most serious incidents, such as the homecoming car fiasco, students mainly criticized the teachers in charge for their incompetence. Similar criticism occurred during the hotly contested school elections. Rhetoric flowed about the teachers' rigging the school elections and denying Chicano kids positions, but ultimately the kids accepted the fact that some Mexicanos were disqualified because of low grades. The town and the school were frequently full of loose talk about racists and reverse racists, but when heated moments passed, few of the teachers were actually singled out for criticism.

A second reason that Anglo teachers rarely expressed their private racial views was a strong local belief against "letting politics into the schools." Teachers were pressured to avoid taking sides on the racial issue, because people felt that "racial politics would ruin the quality of education." On the philosophical side, many teachers genuinely believed that avoiding racial and political issues led to a better educational environment. Other research on American schools shows this to be a common attitude among teachers and community members (Ziegler 1966). On the more pragmatic side, they also feared that the school board was trying to appease Chicano militants. They worried that the board might make sacrificial lambs out of them if a controversy arose.

Third, beyond the social and political pressures of the moment, the role of a teacher has some built-in restrictions that help control blatant personal bias. Most public school teachers believe that they have a public trust to be fair and impartial. It is true that countless studies of teacher expectations, interaction styles, and attitudes show that they have often failed to uphold these professional ethics. Not infrequently, teachers have been described as classist, racist, and sexist in their classrooms. Most American teachers remain committed, however, to the ideal of an egalitarian, democratic public school system. In a situation where the minority community is vigilant, teachers will try harder to live up to the public trust placed in them.

It is easy for outsiders to take racial incidents out of context. I did, however, observe two teachers who blatantly violated the rights of Mexi-cano children. The following vignettes will illustrate why many Mexicano kids felt that these teachers were "real red necks."

In the first incident I observed, the lesson of the day started with a discussion of current events. The class jumped from the oil crisis to Watergate to several gruesome murders. The teacher was tossing ques-tions at the "good students" in the front rows. The Anglo kids were playing up to him and asking questions that placed an exaggerated stress on sophisticated-sounding adverbs. Using this style of speech signaled to the other kids that they were actually mocking the teacher. After the teacher finished explaining what Nixon said, one student chimed in, "He certainly was right to say that." That mocking response brought smirks from several classmates.

Meanwhile, the vatos in the back of the room were being flagrantly indifferent. One was sleeping. Another was gazing out the window. A third was doodling low-rider cars on his notebook. The teacher rebuffed the vatos by yelling at them: "What do some of you people think this class is? a welfare line? You can't just come in here and get something for nothing! You've got to work in here, so pay attention and participate!"

The contrast between the teacher's favorites sitting up front asking phony questions and the vatos dozing off in the back drew a racial line through this scene. The teacher sat with his face directed away from the Mexicanos. He generally ignored them, except for insulting reprimands. He rarely looked at them, and he mainly interacted with the Anglos. When he became frustrated with his class, he would lash out at the slower Mexicano students. On another day he said: "Some of you kids are too slow to be in school. You need to be out in the fields doing something useful. The results of this pop quiz make me sick. I've gotta get me some students in here to replace you brown deadbeats."

Such comments, which implied that "dumb, lazy, welfare-cheating Mexicans" ought to "shape up or get out," were not uncommon. Accord-ing to both Mexicano and Anglo kids, my six observations of this teacher were typical. He was an arch-conservative who hated La Raza and thought "judges turned criminals loose faster than they get in." He re-ferred to blacks as "niggers" when he criticized the civil rights movement, which he considered "a communist plot." His view of international affairs was that "the Europeans are trying to hog Middle Eastern oil," and that "giving aid to the third world was just throwing money down a rat hole."

Another example of blatant prejudice was observed in the classroom of an older practical arts teacher. Students also rated this teacher as "very red neck." She told the following story in her class one day:

Mr. Davis told me about this Mexican boy who came here. He was fifteen and he couldn't even tie his shoes, because servants always did it. Now we (you Mexicans) don't want to be that helpless do we? Eventually he learned English very fast and got so he could compete with Americans. He became so comfortable here that he never wanted to go back to Mexico. You see, it is possible to be a success if you work hard and learn to get along. Eventually this boy got his own business going, and he is a real success today. He dresses nicely and has a cute little house and a nice family. I think many of you could be like him if you had his dream.

During this story, which is a variant of the classic Horatio Alger myth, she looked pointedly at the Mexicanas in class. The classroom had only two tables. All the Anglo females sat around the teacher's table, and all the Mexicanas sat around the other table. During the story, she had to look across the room and talk at the Mexicanas. Meanwhile, the Anglo females sat smugly listening and nodding in agreement. The Mexicanas sat quietly with eyes downcast, as if to listen with great humility and reverence. She told the story with an air of gravity, as if a seminal idea was being delivered to a lump of groveling humanity.

The class then shifted to the regular lesson, and she conducted a chatty conversation with Charlene and Janie, two dutiful charmers who were experts at making her lessons successful. The contrast in behavior between the two tables was so marked that it seemed as if a Chicano militant had scripted it. The teacher and the Anglo table laughed, told stories, discussed the lesson, and generally acted as if the Mexicana table did not exist. Not a single Mexicana asked a question, gave an answer, or made a move to participate in any way. They were very quiet, and only spoke when the teacher asked them to read a passage from the book or to answer a question. They spoke and read with great reluctance and difficulty. This invariably brought impatient responses from the teacher and the Anglo students, who giggled at their mistakes. This scene had a smug, colonial character, and the Anglo teacher was bent on Americanizing her meek brown subjects. Such a scene was not typical, but similar incidents did occur in other classes

Mexicano teachers consistently reported one practice that they considered racist. The administration rated six or eight native born Anglo teachers of prominent familes as the master teachers. As a result, these teachers were given what their critics considered preferential assignments. This group of elementary and junior high teachers always taught the advanced academic sessions, but their Mexicano critics were quick to dispute their claim as the best teachers. Whether these teachers were given preferential treatment was impossible to determine. Systematic observation of the top Anglo teachers in the elementary schools found these teachers to vary considerably in racial attitude and teaching style (Meadowcroft and Foley 1977).

The Academic Level of Work in North Town High

The following comment illustrates a typical student view of school and academic work in North Town High:

> School is really boring, but it's better than being at home. There is nothing to do at home. If I stay there, my parents make me work and get on my case. I come to school to see my friends. I like going to the games . . . My classes? They are a drag. It's the same old stuff year after year. We don't ever learn anything new. We get tested over the same things.

Hundreds of students said virtually the same thing. They constantly told my-class-was-more-boring-than-yours stories. Most said they could hardly wait to get out of high school and find a job. The top third of the students were anxious to graduate and go to college or university. Those headed for college, particularly the Anglo students, often expressed the following views of their school:

> I know that when I go off to college, I will be way behind kids from big city schools. We don't ever do much of anything here. Everybody I know who is in college says it takes a year or two to adjust to the extra work they give you. We aren't getting prepared here to compete. Too many of the teachers don't care. They are just in it for the paycheck. Part of the problem is the school has too many dumb Mexican kids who can barely read. They bring down the level for everyone. My dad is thinking of sending me to a private school in San Antonio.

The national achievement test scores rated the overall academic level of North Town High School below the state average. I was not allowed access to the school records and these achievement test scores, but the principal reported that North Town students scored in only the thirtieth percentile of Texas schools. Most teachers and parents felt that North Town schools were below average. Two high school counselors estimated that approximately 35 percent of the graduating seniors pursued some type of higher education. Our follow-up survey twelve years later revealed that 37 percent of the students had gone to college and 19 percent earned a four year degree. In short, North Town High School had the profile of a working class school with relatively small numbers of collegebound middle income students.

The actual academic level of work being done in the more advanced classrooms was difficult to characterize. North Town High generally seemed very weak academically. Returning North Town university students told tales about how poorly prepared they were for university-level academic work. I was continually surprised at how little intellectual content was actually demanded in most of the academic classes. Advanced Spanish, English, government, bookkeeping, and biology seemed very rudimentary for college preparatory courses. For example, my junior American history class in a top academic school read fifteen college-level paperbacks during the year. In North Town, students struggled to finish one superficial textbook that was barely on a high school reading level. My students also wrote a fifteen-page research paper each semester. In North Town, students struggled to finish a five-page research paper for the year.

The most striking quality about lessons in all subject matter areas was, however, what I would call their pedagogical formalism. Almost without exception, classes were geared to the textbooks. This meant that students marched through the textbooks at a very predictable, slow pace. Typically, students would read a few pages of textbook on Monday through Wednesday and have discussions of this material. These discussions consisted largely of memorizing new terminology and writing the answers to the chapter questions. On Thursday, they would take practice exams, and prepare for their Friday quiz.

This general approach to the subject matter generated a great deal of busy work answering chapter questions and taking practice tests or "pop quizzes," but very little reflection or independent work. Most students copied the answers to the dreaded chapter questions from classmates. Not infrequently, the role of the "class brain" was to provide others with the correct answers. Most students avoided these exercises, because they considered them boring, unnecessary work. In short, the classes organized around the textbook made all subject matter into a very predictable work routine. There were, of course, notable exceptions. Some teachers, who will be characterized in greater detail later, consistently "played with" this academic work routine. About half the teachers observed occasionally opened up the textbook-driven routine with outside materials.

Generally North Town High School teachers taught five classes with up to 150 different students. They relied, therefore, on the simplifying technology of a canned textbook. This study confirmed the findings of recent studies that have stressed what a controlling technology textbooks have become (Apple 1982). These watered-down, bland versions of history, literature, and science afforded the teachers helped control the pace of work. Textbooks also made difficult content choices of subject matter and evaluation procedures much easier. As some textbook publishers have bragged, their textbooks were "teacher proof."

The second striking quality of pedagogical formalism was the pedantic manner in which many teachers presented subject matter. In addition to relying heavily on textbooks, North Town teachers generally recycled the classification systems that they learned from university professors. For example, English classes busily learned the difference between literary forms such as romanticism and realism. Biology classes feverishly memorized the various plant and animal phyla. History classes catalogued the conventional caricatures of great leaders and memorized dates, events, and chronologies. Spanish classes learned the idiom and grammatical style of speech used in Spain.

Day after day, I watched teenagers memorize hundreds of abstract terms that undoubtedly would have made sense to biologists, historians, and literary critics. Such academic specialists make their living finding subtle distinctions among plant, animal, literary, cultural, and historical forms and events. The collegebound students assumed that they would get more of the same at the university; therefore, memorizing the experts' classification systems made sense. Those not going to college had little reason to remember anything about phyla, algebraic and chemical formulas, historical chronology, and literary forms. Such pedantry undoubtedly increased student boredom as much as the routinized schedule of work geared to textbooks.

The overwhelmingly anti-intellectual attitude of most students surprised me, and I initially explained it as a rebellious reaction to the boring, routinized, pedantic character of their work. After a year in North Town, however, I came to see that the school simply reflected the general conservatism of the community. The town's social and political environment did not demand or encourage a highly open, imaginative, critical curriculum. North Towners did not want their children reading avant-garde literature or critiques of corporation polluters or revisionist accounts of President Johnson's political corruption. They wanted their schools to discipline and mold their children into hard-working, family-oriented, patriotic, mainstream citizens. The schools were supposed to be relatively devoid of the controversy and intellectual ferment that one tends to find in the university.

The reasons for this conservatism were similar to those found in other studies. Many previous investigators have shown how enduringly conformist and mainstream most school boards are (Kirst 1985; Counts

1969). Typically, upper class businesspersons and members of "high status" professions, such as doctors, lawyers, and technical people, have dominated school governance. Moreover, middle class people were much more likely to vote in school board elections and to intervene in school affairs through the PTA, parent-teacher conferences, and general lobbying of schools. As in other parts of the country, the "better people" of North Town tended to run and to influence the schools. In recent years, that group has begun to include the responsible Mexicano middle classes as well.

In this case, the "mainstreamers" from the two races strongly disagreed over many fundamental electoral and government policies such as district apportionment, voting rights, affirmative action, and a variety of federally sponsored programs for low income citizens. Nevertheless, mainstreamers from both races aspired to build the same type of society. They all advocated the basic American values of individualism, competition, hard work, and a consumption-oriented life style; consequently, most of the new ethnic reformers had no radically different ideas of what schools should teach.

The teachers, some quite competent in their subject matter areas, generally adapted their conceptions of academic work to the local attitudes of students and parents. Some teachers would talk privately in animated, informed ways about new plays and novels, world historical events, and recent scientific discoveries. Some were well educated, intelligent, intellectually oriented people. What went on in their classrooms was markedly different from what went on over their kitchen tables. Some of the younger, well-educated teachers were interested in ideas and their subject matter, but publicly they were unable to risk being too passionate about presenting new ideas.

North Town teachers generally feared parental complaints and school board sanctions in the same way that teachers in Waller's classic study (1960) did. They sensed that they lived in a "fishbowl" and had to be very proper and conventional socially and intellectually. The school's "maverick intellectual" reported being reprimanded for discussing controversial subjects in class. Several single teachers reported receiving "informal advice" about their love lives. The teachers, and especially the coaches, were subjected to what seemed like malicious, unfair community gossip. My fieldnotes were full of comments about teachers being closet "fags," "drunkards," and "dope addicts." Given such community pressure, teachers lowered their academic expectations and endlessly negotiated over the amount of work and grades given.

The Negotiation of Academic Work: The Making Out Game

Recent ethnographies of schools have explored more extensively the general nature of academic work (Garza-Lubeck 1987; Borman and Reisman 1984). Some critics suggest that academic work is inherently alienating because schools have adopted scientific management techniques of controlling students. These new forms of managerial control "deskill" teachers and students and evoke rebellious responses to these degradating forms of work (McNeil 1986). In contrast, I became fascinated with recording how students "fiddled" with, resisted, slowed down, avoided, and redefined academic work tasks, rather than how teachers controlled student-workers. I was drawn to how both teachers and students humanized the dry textbooks, constant testing, pedantic lessons, and predictable pedagogical routines.

In searching for ways to characterize these negotiations over academic work, Michael Burawoy's (1979) study of factory workers provided a useful though partial analogy. Burawoy found workers playing what he called "making out games" in their struggles to resist and manipulate their work tasks and the wage rates. A making out game is simply the way that workers collaborate with each other to make the work task easier, thereby achieving the same or higher pay rates for less work, or the same work in less time. Ultimately, workers always try to get the best pay for the least amount of work. Conversely, managers always try to get the most work for the least amount of pay. This is, of course, the fundamental principle on which all capitalist production systems are organized. There is always an inherent contradiction between the interest of the workers and of those who own and manage the means of production. There is always a need for owners and managers to mediate or minimize this class conflict of different interests.

Burawoy goes on to point out that shop floor work tasks are designed to be neither too hard nor too easy. The work tasks have to have a built-in quality of indeterminacy and unpredictability. Making the rate set for a task has to be somewhat challenging. Workers then use alliances, shortcuts, and work slowdowns to achieve their production rates. In the end, these engrossing games actually generate more non-material gains than wage gains. Workers gain a great deal of personal psychological satisfaction from outwitting management. It is in this sense that the making out games "manufacture consent." Workers are kept busy playing this satisfying game and actually producing the desired rates of work rather than rebelling.

Like factory work, academic work or school lessons are also notoriously ambiguous; therefore, lessons engender many different, engaging types of making out games. The key similarity between schools and factories is that academic work can be as boring and alienating as industrial work. Schoolwork often does not challenge academic workers to be creative and develop their human potential. Academic workers, therefore, enjoy outwitting teachers and slowing down the boring routines of pedagogical formalism. North Town's academic workers had basically the same goal as the industrial workers. The making out games students played with teachers usually had the objective of getting the best grades possible for the least amount of work.

In response, most North Town teachers tried to demand or cajole the most academic work for the lowest grades. They functioned much like lower level managers in a factory. They allowed a certain amount of chiseling, gold bricking, and manipulation of the work tasks and grading procedures rather than impose rigid work rules on their academic workers. Those teachers skilled at communication understood that making out games were a way of getting students to work. Those skillful at colluding with students created and used these games to minimize serious disruptions of academic production. Those lacking skills in negotiating and mediating worker demands were plagued with more potentially disruptive making out games. As in the factory, most classroom making out games became a subtle form of worker entertainment and control.

Burawoy goes on to argue that factory making out games on the shop floor are one of several mechanisms that help "manufacture consent" or blunt worker rebellion at the point of production. These everyday games on the institutional level ultimately contribute to the preservation of the class structure on the societal level. This suggests that small everyday events like students' getting out of work may also have larger implications. Classroom making out games may also be perpetuating the class structure of the larger society. Indeed, schools are more of a microcosom of society than factories are. To a much higher degree than factories, schools reflect the class, race, and gender differences of the larger society.

The analogy between academic and industrial work is not, therefore, a simple, clear-cut one. Unlike factories, schools do not produce commodities for sale and profit. School "owners" or "managers" are not a capitalist class that makes personal profits from producing productive laborers. Schools do socialize the youth to be good workers and citizens. In the general sense, schools produce the most important commodity in a free market system: laborers for the labor market.

Schools must, therefore, socialize students to be good workers who are punctual, disciplined and loyal, and who finish tasks on time. They must also teach workers to put up with the boring routine of many industrial and office jobs. Schools must also teach some academic workers to strive for leadership roles and others to resign themselves to being followers. An important part of being a leader and active citizen is learning a number of communication skills such as how to manage one's public image to get ahead.

The making out games that teachers and students mutually construct transmit many important cultural lessons. Nothing is more typical of American high school classrooms than these highly stylized, everyday speech performances. The kind of making out games played varies with the teacher's pedagogical style. This account uses the students' views to characterize the different teachers' performance lines and styles of communication. All students participate in these games, but, as the examples will suggest, not all play the same role. Some students perform different roles, thus achieving different relationships with teachers and gaining different rewards for their performances. This account presents a general model of this classroom ritual that covers the variety of teacher preformances and making out games.

Playful, Mutually Constructed Classroom Making Out Games

Perhaps the most common making out game is the group parody of the lesson. Parodies of lessons usually start with one student's making fun of some aspect of a lesson or of him or herself. On other occasions, the teacher may parody the lessons and students respond. If the parody is clever, other members in the group spontaneously join in. At that point, the parody of a lesson becomes a well-orchestrated effort that enlivens and slows down the lesson for the day. The first example of a parody of a lesson is taken from an advanced junior English class.

The teacher, David Read, was a young Viet Nam veteran with a master's degree. He had grown up in a medium sized city in the Midwest. He was a popular teacher, considered "a cool dude" who "joked a lot" and was "pretty liberal." He was called Mr. Roach-clip, and rumor had it that he had done dope in Nam and probably still did, which explained his impish smile and occasional far-away look. He was liked by virtually every type of student, although some of the top students noted that he lacked the experience that several other "good" teachers had.

Read dreamed about teaching in a junior college with older students who appreciated literature. He loved literature and enjoyed getting people to read anything. He thought the curriculum and school lacked interesting, more mature reading materials. He wanted students to read more critical, contemporary books than classics like *Silas Marner*. He disliked the administration, considered the BGL school board reactionary, and was generally liberal on the race issue. Nevertheless, he was unsure of how evil La Raza was and continually pumped me for information on them. Having grown up in a less tense racial environment, the antagonisms he experienced between Mexicano and Anglo students puzzled him. He had very few stereotypic views of Mexicanos, and assumed that poverty and poor English explained their high rates of academic failure.

The making out game chosen came from a lesson on American literature. Read began class with a review of famous American short-story writers. He mentioned a number of names and tried to get the class to recall stories they had read by O Henry, Twain, Harte, and Dickinson. They quickly zeroed in on classifying the stories as examples of natural realism. As the teacher began to lecture and illustrate his classification scheme, the class began shifting the high-minded, academic tone of the discussion. Read commented that Emily Dickinson wrote simple, expressive stories. Charlene, an attractive, popular girl, fired the first salvo by whispering to those around her: "Emily Dickinson was simple. She was simple-minded in her realism."

This provoked Charlene's hanging-out pal Janie to ask Mr. Read, "Wait! Wait Mr. Read! You are going too fast! What is realism, again? What is the difference between realism and romanticism? I thought Emily Dickinson was a romantic."

Most of the kids groaned at Janie's question. They knew Read would take it seriously, because he often took Janie more seriously than she actually took her studies. She and Charlene had been reading a movie magazine and doing their nails during the opening lecture. But her show of "interest" would provoke a long, serious lecture on the difference between realism and romanticism. Curtis, a friendly jock sitting next to me, felt compelled to point out the girls' routine: "Oh god Doc! Here we go again! I'm getting sick of those two playing the dumb blonde routine with Roach-clip! They are always getting his attention. Yah, they really care about Emily Dumbikinson."

After seeing these two pull this routine several other times, I had to agree they were slowing down a boring classification exercise and getting the floor as "interested students." Curtis's only complaint was that Charlene and Janie were no more interesting than naturalism! Nevertheless, most of the class played along with other "dumb" but "meaningful" questions from Charlene. She had obviously initiated a game, and her classmates joined in with various put-downs. One of the boys accused

Charlene of "messing around," however. That drew mock indignation from Charlene and a friendly reprimand from Read for arguing with a fellow student.

This challenge from the teacher gave both Charlene and Janie the floor for a series of "I-did-not-talk-yes-you-did-talk" exchanges with poor Read. This was all done in a good-natured way, but in the meantime, Emily Dickinson and realism had been put on hold. Once this brushfire was extinguished, Read went back to the lesson, but the seed had been planted for a small group of jocks to kick into action. Paul, the quarterback, had been languishing through Charlene and Janie's disruptive routine, but the jocks had been inspired to improve upon the girls' performance. Paul used a different tack, one that only high status students could do with any success. He blurted out in as blunt a manner as possible: "I can't read this stuff. Why do we have to read anything by Emily Dickinson? I think she's weird."

Several other boys read this as a challenge to Read, and they tittered in anticipation to see how he would handle Paul. Now it was the jocks' turn, and they quietly egged on Paul, their leader. One whispered encouragement, "All right, baby!" "Ya Paulie! ya!" Read did not initially overreact to Paul's rather sharp comment, because Paul was neither a troublemaker nor a poor student. Paul was being somewhat aggressive, but he was playing the I-don't-get-it routine, which can be read as trying to be serious rather than disruptive. Read gave an earnest reply on the importance of Dickinson's writings as Paul feigned interest.

Paul had succeeded in stealing the girls' scene, which delighted the jocks. A flow of banter passed between the girls and the jocks as Read slogged through his appeasement of Paul. They quietly teased each other in a mutual competition for best-con-artists-of-the-day. Neither the girls nor the jocks actually cared who had the stage as long as more was going on than a discussion of realism. They were actually allies rather than competitors or rivals in this particular work slow-down. The undercurrent of banter between the jocks and these girls was allowed, because it was part of keeping the lesson lively and entertaining. Read generally enjoyed such playful conversations, as long as he could shift the conversation when he liked. More often than not, he was able to humor students back to work.

Meanwhile, the majority of the class sat passively enjoying the scene that the girls had initiated and the jocks had transformed. Kate and Elsa, two serious students, occasionally interjected questions into this discussion of naturalism and Dickinson, but they were bit players in this particular making out game, which lasted approximately twenty minutes.

Charlene and Janie had framed their questions as ridicule of Read and his "serious" lesson. The jocks picked up on and extended their "dumb blonde" routine with a "confused student" routine. Both routines were completely misread by the teacher, because he did not share their view that this particular lesson needed to be parodied. There were times when Read did roll his eyes skyward and parody his own "dumb" questions or tedious grammar assigments. But today was not one of those days.

Later in the lesson, Dale, a skinny kicker kid and bit player in most making out games, made his move. Just before the class was to adjourn, he jumped the bell and put his cowboy hat on. Read, who had been thoroughly diverted from his lesson, was wearing thin. Normally, he would have bantered with Dale, but this time he demanded that he remove his hat or, he threatened, "it's off to detention hall for your hat and you." Read needed to assert his authority. He had concluded the short story discussion with a set of technical words for definition and spelling. He then threatened the class with a pop quiz on the short stories to reassert that "this was a serious lesson." Too many students had broken his frame of performance. Read needed to repair his image, so Dale was made into a sacrificial lamb.

In the spirit of the parody that had transpired, Dale responded with perhaps the most clever self-parody I saw during that school year. In his defense, Dale pleaded in a wry, droll Texas style: "Aw come on, Mr. Read, I can't take my hat off. This is a part of my cultural heritage. I would feel naked without it. You can't destroy my culture. You are destroying my Texas culture, if I have to take this hat off."

Not only had Dale actively joined the making out game, he had been able to get in an ethnic joke as well! Being a hard-core red neck, he had gotten in a jibe at the La Raza movement. He was so effective that he disarmed Read, who usually allowed him very little room, but as the bell rang he chuckled and granted Dale a reprieve with a dismissive "just cut the bull and get out of here."

The real winners were Charlene, Janie, and Paul and his buddies. They had successfully derailed the lesson while convincing Read that they were the real workers in the class. They had helped the teacher perform his role through their feigned interest and phony questions. For their passive classmates, they had transformed the lesson into something more enjoyable. As they had done so many times before, these kids were the leaders of classroom discussions, and these performances established their social prominence.

I ultimately came to see these "disruptions" as mutually agreed upon and constructed moments of play, or "coffee breaks" from academic work. Not infrequently, both students and teachers sought ways to avoid or make work enjoyable. Good teachers like Read were often able to read the performance "frame" of student behavior. In this case, a "frame" is some subtle non-verbal or verbal set of cues that tells a teacher not to take a given set of actions literally as "rebellion" or "disrespect." The main way that students framed their behavior in classrooms was through humor. Students did all sorts of parodies and self-parodies that signaled that "I am only kidding. I am not challenging your authority." Such humorous framing of their actions and comments signaled the difference between "willful work disruptions" and "playful work breaks."

Teachers who understood the communicative "frame" were able to negotiate the shifts between work and play with confidence and ease. In such classrooms the inevitable making out game did not deteriorate into aggressive confrontations of teacher authority. Teachers with this skill conveyed to the students that they had sense of reciprocity and the ability to negotiate over their authority and the work norms. Such teachers and their kids created continually shifting, lively, open classes. Read, who was considered a fairly "hip" teacher, had some of these skills. So did other teachers with radically different styles.

Straight Teaching Performances: The Good Old Boy/Girl Style

The successful performance styles of teachers ranged from what kids called "good old boys/girls" to "street-wise dudes." A good old boy/girl style of teaching was perhaps the most common performance that North Town teachers enacted. My favorite good old boy was Buford Roy, the senior English teacher. Roy, who was studying for his Ph.D., was a native of West Texas. He dressed in Western style shirts and boots and talked in a slow country drawl. His manner was as slow and deliberate as his drawl, and he was fatherly toward his students. He possessed a dry, matter-of-fact sense of humor that poked fun at situations and the absurdities of people and their bureaucratic rules. Roy lived on the "Mexican side of town" and generally stuck to himself socially. He was not particularly popular with fellow teachers but was enormously popular with students. They expected the school board to fire him for his unconventionality and frankness about political and racial issues. His political beliefs were liberal by local standards.

On the other hand, he considered himself a conservative on many social and political issues. He was definitely a "square" or old-fashioned on many of the social practices such as smoking pot, protesting the war, and open marriages. He did not like the nihilist writers of the lost generation or stream of consciousness writing, which he thought confused the kids. What set him apart was not his political ideology or values, however. Roy exuded the aura of a man who was too forthright and straightforward for his own good. He simply told it like he saw it. He was, as one school bureaucrat put it, "a little too unvarnished."

His views on Mexicanos, whom he called "Latins," initially seemed rather biased and uninformed. He felt that the Latins had become too sensitive to disciplining and too quick to see Anglo racism. He held the La Raza movement partly responsible and claimed that the *Chicano Times* printed half-truths comparable to Nazi and communist papers. In his view, Latin kids were generally more easy-going, more sexually mature, and less likely to succeed in school. He blamed some of this on poor family life and home discipline. He lived on the Mexican side of town because he saw himself and his family as a model for them. He frequently made comments about helping them lift themselves by their boot straps, and was very committed to making a difference in the lives of these youth.

His teaching style was a mixture of lecture and discussions. Like the other English teachers, he taught the classification systems for literary criticism and a formidable technical jargon for analyzing poems and fiction. He required students to do several research papers of five pages using multiple references. In addition, he held a number of discussions about current events, particularly in the extemporaneous speech units and in his speech class. These discussions impressed his students that Mr. Roy was different from other teachers. During one class period, the students made impromptu speeches about what they disliked about school. They talked about football being too favored and important, the lack of necessity for a vice principal, girls being restricted from auto mechanics, the need for the school marching band to be racially united, and the poor cafeteria food. Mr. Roy expressed his opinion and let them express theirs on all these topics.

On the other hand, he also spent a good deal of class time teaching the kids to memorize sayings, authors' names, and information useful on the SAT exams. He demanded that the kids learn how to take class notes and remember names, dates, and characterizations for exams. For those students who needed it, he gave practice tests and emphasized test-taking skills. A great deal of class time was spent learning how to take tests and write formal, footnoted short research papers. He constantly reassured students that these types of activities were good preparation for college.

Roy's general line of self-presentation was that he was an "old pro." He was the "gatekeeper" who taught what you needed to make it in college.

He rarely varied from this portrayal of himself and his role. This led him to be rather formal, and he never clowned or joked around with the students. He did, however, frequently tell stories about different writers' private lives, and he made dry, sarcastic remarks about various famous people and politicians. At his best, he was a poor man's Will Rogers who made the kids laugh about people's pretensions and foibles. He never turned this folksy, down-to-earth wit on himself or the kids, however, and he tended to treat them as a kindly, paternalistic father would.

In response, students rarely confronted him or openly disrupted work. Instead, they frequently whispered to each other, "disattended" if the lectures became boring, and openly negotiated for "breaks" on the test, free time to play cards, and other little privileges. The college-oriented students were particularly dominant in his class, because Roy had convinced them that he held the key to their success in college. They generally matched his high-minded seriousness with serious work behavior. These students conformed to his demands and worked hard, but they also expected him to give them quiet time or card playing time at the end of a successful lesson. The same principle of reciprocity was operating as in Read's class, but periodic free time rather than sporadic "playful time" or breaks from lessons was granted. Mr. Roy asked them to work hard, and in return they were occasionally allowed a few minutes to socialize and play cards.

Making out games were less playful in Mr. Roy's class, therefore, because he was all business. Neither he nor his students made fun of the lesson and performance he was putting on. Nevertheless, students, typically the socially prominent students, often performed the same routines of feigned interest that they did in Mr. Read's class. The jocks and cheerleaders and top band kids still asked phony questions and played I-don't-get-it routines to slow down and derail lessons. The following excerpts were taken from one of his senior English classes.

Class started with Mr. Roy going over the book report topics. Chuck, a burly football player, reported that he was reading a book about the Ku Klux Klan. I glanced at Rudy, a teammate of his, and he nodded his head in one of those quick, a-hah-you-see-that quips that only a cool stud could make. Chuck was known for staying aloof from Mexicanos, so Rudy considered the KKK report a revealing choice. The reports continued and Sandy, an attractive, college-bound Mexicana, said she was studying the idea of life and death in nihilist writers. This brought a frown and vacant stares from several students. Mr. Roy then went into a speech criticizing nihilist writers.

Meanwhile several pep squad girls were quietly talking to Don, the team's best player, and Rudy, a tough little linebacker, about the game, Halloween parties, throwing water balloons, and getting drunk. Rudy interrupted their social patter by asking me about my van and whether I went camping in it. When Mr. Roy noticed me being drawn into the conversation, he finally stopped the whispering with a question to Don, who replied: "Huh? I dunno nothing about nilists [sic]. Uh, ask Sandy. You tell him for me, Sandy, ok?"

This brazen admission of indifference piqued Mr. Roy somewhat. Don was one of his favorite students, an all-American boy from a decent family. He rarely showed any disrespect for teachers, even though he confided to me that school was "real dry" and "pretty bad." He always had a smile on and always seemed attentive. But Sandy quickly rescued the stars and recounted what she knew about "crazy nihilists who hated everything." A buddy of Don's, Jeff, the son of a local merchant and noted "slick dresser," asked a "meaningful" clarification question designed to keep Mr. Roy busy: "I don't get it, Mr. Roy, why did these guys hate everything?"

Rudy and I exchanged knowing smiles. He approved of Jeff's performance, which was as cool as his dress style. Everyone knew that he had punched Mr. Roy's favorite "broken record," and people could settle back into some "down time." The strategy in Mr. Roy's class was to use his intensity against him. When he was moralizing about a topic, which he tended to do, he became absolutely glassy-eyed. He rarely saw any of the note-passing, whispering, flirtatious looks, and well-moderated "unseriousness." The kids were getting some relief from their "serious student line" to accommodate Mr. Roy, the resident intellectual. This sort of passive resistance to a teacher's deadly seriousness was another kind of making out game. Mr. Roy's otherwise orderly, well disciplined, reasonably interesting classes were routinely punctuated by such "mental vacations," which were done very unobtrusively.

There were a number of other good old boy/girl types in North Town High. Two other competent "old pros" who played gatekeeper included a popular math and science teacher. They were often mentioned as good, strict, no-nonsense teachers who "really knew their subject." They also tended to run their classes in a similar paternalistic and professional manner. They were far less colorful and witty than Mr. Roy, however, and lacked his reputation as a maverick intellectual. They taught and communicated in a relatively humorless, business-like manner and only occasionally played with students or the lessons. The making out games in their classes ranged from the openly assertive put-ons typical of Mr. Read's class to the passive, clever put-ons of Mr. Roy's class.

Finally, there were several good old boy/girl teachers who were much more authoritarian, less flexible, and significantly less popular. They shared a very common view of why so many kids were failing. According to these teachers, modern kids were a reflection of modern society. They no longer strove to excel and be the best and simply lacked pride. As a result, they wanted to be "entertained"and "spoon-fed." This widespread apathy was attributed to disruptive politics, drugs, the war, hippies, what was generally happening in America. The teachers labeled much of this "immaturity." To them immaturity meant not conforming to the goals of mainstream society and losing pride in America and oneself.

These teachers often had a Western style of dress and speech. They all exuded a more macho style of interaction and discipline. They frequently threatened kids with "licks" (paddling), made many moralistic speeches about working harder, and refused to give too many films, which they considered a sign of laziness. They generally tried to maintain the fiction that the boring work they assigned was interesting and refused to play with the lessons. These teachers developed reciprocal relationships with youth that made fewer concessions toward student humor, parodying of lessons, and playful work. They clearly distinguished between serious work and free time. If students worked hard on the assigned lesson, they would get the last twenty minutes to do quiet seat work or to chat with friends. This exchange was a pragmatic business deal where work time is traded for free time. These classes had fewer of the controlled work disruptions than Mr. Read's classes, which gave frequent playful breaks for relatively steady work.

Aggressive Making Out Games: The Vatos' Revolt

These more traditional, authoritarian, and paternalistic teachers often provoked stronger, more angry, and openly aggressive reactions from some students. In their classes, especially in the practical sections, the proud, angry vatos took center stage and often initiated the making out games. These games took on a more confrontational, combative turn, which occasionally led to detentions and expulsions. Some of the more popular good old boys were able to manage the vatos reasonably well. On the other hand, those traditional good old boys who relied primarily on force and intimidation simply created battlefields full of guerrilla warriors.

The following incident took place in a freshman science class taught by Mr. Cain. He was a no-nonsense, South Texas teacher who wore boots and a cowboy hat and dipped snuff. He was rather stern and humorless and prided himself on being very knowledgeable about his subject matter. He was generally respected as a "hard teacher," but not particularly well liked. He started the class by asking about the difference between acids and bases. This topic had been covered the previous week, so students were particularly vocal about doing yet another review. Mr. Cain eyed his students and asked questions that increasingly irritated them: "What are you writing? Where are your chapter questions? What are you laughing at? Who said that? Who has the correct answer?" His manner was inquisitional and threatening, and he talked in a loud voice and hovered over offenders' desks. Since he was a fairly husky, athletic-looking man, he used his voice and body to intimidate the "slackers" and "deadbeats." He spoke in a sarcastic manner that conveyed a self-confidence bordering on arrogance. The class was not responding, however, so he picked out two vegetating students who were literally crouching down in their seats, as if to hide. Mr. Cain asked sarcastically : "Ok, let's try an easy one, what is H-2-O, Ricardo?"

Ricardo, a quiet, conforming "nobody" said timidly, "I don't know, sir."

Mr. Cain roared back, "Well, look at your notes!"

Ricardo came back, "I don't have it in my notes, sir."

Mr. Cain countered, "Ricardo, what day did I give that to you?"

Ricardo replied, "I'm not sure, sir, maybe the first?"

Mr. Cain said emphatically and rather triumphantly: "Two weeks ago! I gave that to you two weeks ago! You people have the memory of a mosquito! I'm running out of gas with you people! This is too much work. You people have been chewing on these definitions and formulas for two weeks. There is no excuse for this!"

Having lectured them, Mr. Cain said they were all in "big trouble" with him. Juan, a hard core vato, rose to the defense of everyone and retorted defiantly that nobody could figure out what he was talking about. Mr. Cain, somewhat flushed from Juan's brazen honesty, took up the challenge by sending him to the board. He pointedly showed Juan that he knew nothing, at which Juan slouched in bored indifference. Mr. Cain then began sending other kids up to the board to do formulas. He proceeded to turn Juan's inquisition into a formal degradation ritual for the entire class. A series of "nobodies," who were not particularly good students, marched to the board. None of them could do a single problem. This gave Mr. Cain the opportunity ask embarrassing questions, chide halting responses, give the correct answers, and then banish the offenders to their seats with a curt, "Now go sit down!"

During this sequence of psychological browbeating, he also called upon Jack, the class brain, to come forward and smugly work the problem. After Jack played his loyalist role, Jill, a "perky" "terminally cute" volleyball player, also showed up the "dumbies." Meanwhile, Mr. Cain continued to be sarcastic, which encouraged some of the conformists in class to carp and criticize those at the board. A few students were obliging, while the rest of the audience grew increasingly sullen. Only the threat that all these questions were going to be on "tomorrow's test" seemed to keep the troops in line.

Then, like one of those sudden showers that come up in dry South Texas rangeland, Jim and Charles initiated a little comic relief. They were two of the better students in the class. Jim walked over to the wastepaper basket and nonchalantly crunched up some paper and tossed it in, muttering, "So much for my questions." Charles, as if connected to Jim with an invisible trip wire, repeated the same routine without saying anything. This got Mr. Cain's attention and interrupted his inquisition at the board.

Mr. Cain was not sure, however, if he should gloat or be suspicious. Normally, the paper-in-the-trash and the sharpen-the-pencil routines were dodges to get out of or disrupt work. In this case, however, Charles and Jim had been extremely clever. Their cowering manner, and Jim's muttering to himself about being wrong, suggested conformity to Mr. Cain's degradation ritual. Since they were very good students, it was possible that this was a sign of humility rather than arrogance. Charles then pushed it to the limit and asked, "Can I please go to the restroom?" As he left, he snickered at Jim, who then asked if he could get a drink. Mr. Cain, sensing that a floodtide of requests would surely follow, said "no" and told him to wait until after class. Their requests for restroom and drink privileges signaled their classmates that a teacher con was on, and Mr. Cain had been had.

Meanwhile, several of the vatos had grown sullen. Their heads were down on the desks, and Carlos began openly talking to Juan about "looking for some chicks tonight." Mr. Cain swooped down on Carlos and demanded to know if he had finished the study questions on acids and bases. Carlos played along and asked which ones they had to do. Mr. Cain then used a rather classic teacher's ploy of colluding with the class "brain." He asked Jack to play ventriloquist's dummy and explain the assignment to the "real dummies." Carlos was more than ready, however, to meet Mr. Cain's challenge.

Carlos got out his book and asked in a deadpan voice, "Do we have to do this one?" Mr. Cain walked back to his desk, took the book from him, looked at where his finger was still precariously pointed, and said quite definitively, "Yes." With great aplomb and anticipation Carlos replied, "I've already got that one done."

This got a ripple of laughter and a challenge from Juan, who said proudly, "I'm not going to do that one." Juan had decided that it was time to take on Mr. Cain directly. Mr. Cain said everyone was going to do every problem, to which Juan repeated, "I'm not." Juan now had the stage, and, upon request, he defiantly explained why he deserved special compensation. He confided to an impatient Cain that he had to run errands for his mother, and there was no time for homework. He added that maybe he could just copy the answers like everybody else did. This was a particularly irritating comment to Mr. Cain, because it implied that his "good students" were no different from the vatos. Mr. Cain threatened that anyone caught copying would flunk the test.

When I asked Juan later about copying he replied, "Shit, man, copying is what school is all about!" The other students generally felt it was their right to copy boring stupid questions. They treated chapter questions like the busy-work they were. Consequently, Juan's irreverence and openness delighted the conformists in class. He was saying something that they lacked the courage to say.

The whispering and bantering and bragging continued intermittently as Cain tried to finish his mini-lecture on the definitions of base and acid. At one point, he flashed and threatened Juan with detention. Juan pleaded innocence, but Carlos egged him on. Mr. Cain then wrote both of their names on the board for detention and threatened worse, if they continued "horsing around." As on many other occasions, the vatos were, as they put it, "nailed" for being disrespectful and uncooperative.

In contrast, Charles and Jim had pulled a potentially disruptive routine that was interpreted as showing penitence. When it became clear that they had actually deceived the teacher, Mr. Cain merely disattended to being made a fool. On the other hand, when the vatos made a fool of him in confrontations, he made an example of them, and they were given detention. One disruption was rewarded, and the other one punished. The students clearly recognized both cases as making out games to shift Mr. Cain away from the dreaded routine at the board. The vatos were particularly interested in ending that game, because they and the nobodies were the big losers. Jack, Charles, Jill, and Jim were the big winners, because they collaborated in Mr. Cain's performance as a "tough disciplinarian." They played their supporting roles when called upon to help punish and put down the rebellious, disrespectful vatos.

Much later, Carlos and Juan explained that Mr. Cain was a "real asshole" who loved to try and embarrass them, which is why they loved to confront him. They considered getting detention from him a small price to pay for "standing up to him." For them, this was a character contest for saving face. They were primarily interested in disrupting Mr. Cain's performance as a "tough disciplinarian." On days when he chose to underscore that image, they felt obliged to challenge him. Challenging him was strictly a question of honor. These "troublemakers" and "punks" had to show the world that they were courageous and proud of who they were. They also gained a certain satisfaction out of entertaining the other kids and taking over the class from the "goodie-goodies."

Other Aggressive Making Out Games: The Teacher as Nerd

Students also called teachers "nerds" and "creeps," and these teachers were far less respected and liked. As a result, they evoked even more aggressive making out games than humorless, authoritarian teachers. Three teachers were singled out as most boring, hated teachers. These teachers were universally disliked and disrespected. The kids often made fun of their physical appearance. One was fat and balding and had wide-set teeth and a crocodile-like smile. He smiled in a way that the kids thought was "weird" and "disgusting." The other was extremely thin, had a pasty-white complexion, and chain-smoked. The kids claimed that he had some horrible disease like T.B. and were appalled by his bad breath. Some called him "hog breath." The third reputedly had a serious mental deficiency or disorder. Rumor had it that a sign had fallen on his head and left him with his lisp. He frequently asked students to repeat themselves, so the kids thought he was also slightly deaf, and definitely slow-witted.

All of these teachers dressed in very unstylish, nondescript, "tacky" clothes. To top off their dull, unstylish appearance, they were noted for their complete lack of humor, boring monotone voices, nitpicking rules, and predictable pedagogy. Kids ridiculed their speech mannerisms: "talks funny," "uses too many big words," "talks down to you," and "talks dry." They also thought their attempts at jokes were hopelessly "corny," "goofy," and "dumb." More importantly, these teachers had very little idea of how to build reciprocity between themselves and their academic workers. They rarely were successful at mediating work either through humor or through grants of free time. Even when they granted free time concessions, students tended not to acknowledge these acts of reciprocity. In short, these teachers were judged extraordinarily "uncool" and lacking in the personal qualities needed to negotiate and humanize the alienating character of academic work.

Collecting stories about teachers who were considered "nerds" evoked memories of my high school teachers. Mr. Dimmitt, or "Mr. Dimwit" as we called him, reappeared like a bad dream. He was an overweight bookkeeping teacher who had puffy red cheeks. Dimmitt had an irritating mannerism that reminded us farm kids of a barnyard pig: pursing his lips in a pompous manner when he spat out orders. He was universally hated, and we were convinced that he would go through life without realizing how "uncool" and "ugly" he was. The least he could have done was try to be less "corny" and "boring." He was a classic nerdy teacher and stood in sharp contrast to Mr. Wagner, the suave, good-looking English teacher. We tried every thing imaginable to irritate him, and he invariably responded in an insufferably "straight" and "self-righteous" manner.

One day, Dimmitt singled me out as the one who had stuck his grade book together with a wad of gooey bubble gum. He used my capture to give me a lecture on being "serious" and something else besides a class clown for my trashy buddies. I remembered this speech because, like the basketball coach's speech, it surprised and confused me at the time. The following is a reasonably accurate recollection of a speech that still angers me:

> What is it with you anyway, Doug? You are a good athlete. You get good grades. You have the potential to make something out of yourself. You could go to college like Carol and Nancy [daughters of local businessmen from the "hill" by the park]. Why do you clown around with Monk and Eddie [sons of workers from "smoky row" by the railroad track] and act like a hoodlum in class? Why do you try to be the class clown in here? They tell me your grandma is a very nice lady. If you come from a good family, why don't you start acting like it? Someday you could be a coach and a teacher like me. You could make a decent salary and be somebody.

Mr. Dimmit had decided that I was aspiring to be in the wrong social class, so he was trying to save me from myself. His arrogance rivaled his physical appearance.

Observing the vatos' making out games constantly summoned Dimmit back to life. He has become a kind of social archetype for me. Many teachers with such attitudes still exist. Although some are technically competent in subject matter, they are sadly lacking in social and communicative skills. Their classrooms often become war zones of rebellion, and they become targets for anti-teacher gossip the way "Mr. Dimwit" did.

127

Discipline in the classes of North Town's "nerd" teachers was generally authoritarian, and students universally agreed that their classes were sheer torture and had few redeeming qualities. Academic workers in these classes were driven to great extremes to make it through the work day. Even the masters of deceit, the socially prominent kids, sometimes "lost their cool" in dealing with these types of teachers. At times, they became as openly rude and aggressive as the vatos. They organized a number of extreme making out games, from highly organized, aggressive, insulting, disruptive behavior to open sleeping and inattention. The vatos generally took center stage and aggressively rebelled against the unrelenting "straightness" and routiness of these classes.

Hip Teaching Performances: The Streetwise Dude Style

The other major teaching style was what the kids called being a "good dude" or "cool dude." To some extent Mr. Read, the liberal Anglo, fits this category, but a Mexicano teacher, Coach Zapata, was considerably more "streetwise" to the vatos' "onda," or "trip." He grew up on the streets of San Antonio and considered himself knowledgeable about gangs, drugs, and street fighting. Judging from several stories he told the players, he handled himself pretty well in a street fight. In spite of these rough edges, he was quiet, socially adept, and quite respectable. He was neither aggressive nor brash, but he did have a sharp, biting, sarcastic wit. Moreover, he was only twenty-five and dressed in an "unstraight" manner. His youth, clothes, and sarcasm gave him a lively, yet cool, controlled air. He always seemed ready for some "action," always ready for some quick verbal repartee.

Coach Zapata's views on the racial unrest were pro-La Raza, although he avoided saying much or being involved publicly. He did not trust the Mexicano politicos. He thought they would "burn him" with some "dumb gossip to the gringos." On the other hand, he thought the kids "used this La Raza stuff to con the teachers." He saw the kids as taking advantage of the teachers' guilt and fear to "get breaks on grades" and avoid work. He exclaimed, "Hell, I would too if I were in their shoes." In spite of his inactivity, he characterized himself a liberal socially and politically. He disliked the social pressure and conservatism of the town and often returned to San Antonio on weekends for his social life.

His attitude toward the Anglo kids was as missionary as Mr. Roy's was toward the Mexicano kids. Coach felt that many of them were "ignorant little red necks" who needed to learn that Mexicanos deserved equal treatment. To reeducate them, he frequently told homilies about Chicanos battling for their civil rights. The Anglos in his stories always learned that they were ignorant and had to change. His attitude toward the Anglo administration was similar to Mr. Roy's. For him, the school board, vice principal, and principal were "bureaucrats" who were more interested in spouting rules and lecturing people than in helping kids learn.

He was one of the few teachers in school who said the vatos were "good kids." For him they were "just trying to be wise asses and were a little immature." His philosophy of discipline was, "Don't let them pull shit that they know is shit, and they will respect you. You have to treat them like young men, not little kids." He meant that "talking down" to and "harping at" the vatos only made them more rebellious. He also rarely threatened them, but he did give out detentions when they broke his rules. He felt the vatos were "wise ass kids who will joke back and accept your authority, because they aren't hard core gang types. What we have here is nothing compared to what goes on in real ghetto schools. These are basically nice kids, but they like to horse around because school means nothing to 'em."

Nor did he condemn the kids for drinking and smoking dope. Like them, he said "that was all there is to do in this town." In short, he had a very generous, liberal, yet tough attitude toward the vatos. He eloquently summed up his views this way: "I know what their game is. And they know that I know, so I get their respect."

Coach Zapata ran his classes in a fairly relaxed, informal manner. His persona or "line" was as a sarcastic, fast-talking, cool teacher. His formal teaching behavior was always framed as, "I'm hip, so cut the bull and do what I tell you." One day, for example, he taught a lesson on liver diseases and cancer. After marching the class through a list of technical names for types of each disease, he then to a discussion of symptoms. The lesson itself was dull and unimaginative, but Coach kept the class lively with repartee. Ray and Elizondo, two very rebellious vatos, were bent on diverting the lesson. One of them commented: "Hey coachie, we saw you in San Antonio this week end with some good-looking chick. What was you doing up there? I thought you was supposed to be workin'?"

Coach shot back: "Never mind where I was this weekend! What were you vatones doing hanging around in the big city? Where did you guys get the money to buy gas to cruise in my territory?"

Ray took up the challenge, "Nombre, listen to the man, his territory! Hey Coach, it's a free country! We work for a livin'. We got a job."

Coach, wanting to get it back to the lesson, cajoled them: "Ya ya, you got a job all right, right here. What are the five major warning signs of cancer? Come on! Come on! Let's get some work done today. You bimbos will never learn this, unless I turn up the heat a little."

The lesson continued, but Ray had shifted his attention to Nancy. They were joking about her being with his friend. She touched him as she asked him to stop teasing her, and Ray jumped back, feigning anger. He did not want anyone to think he was flirting with his best friend's girl. Coach Zapata intervened when Ray jumped up from his seat: "Look, Ray, I told you to pay attention! What is the fifth symptom, when you are yellow, called?"

Of course Ray had no idea, so he began "jiving" the teacher, making far-fetched guesses, to which Coach replied: "Try a word that starts with a J as in junkie or jaundice." Ray acted hurt and shot back in mock anger: "Hey, man, what do you think I am!"

Coach replied: "I think you are somebody who doesn't know shinola about the five symptoms, and I'd enjoy seeing you flunk out of here, if I didn't care so much. So turn to page 47 and read me symptom five, all right? I'm going to take care of you, Ray, and make sure you get this."

Ray had to respond with a sarcastic "Ya ya, sure, Coach," but Coach had one-upped him with this parody of the "concerned" missionary teachers. In effect, he took on the vatos' posture and attitude, thus conveying to them his knowing, streetwise view of school authority. For a brief moment, he "colluded with" Ray and the rebellious vatos, but he quickly shifted it all back to a work frame, demanding that Ray turn to page 47. His "order" to do something serious was framed very differently, however, from Mr. Cain's orders to go to the board.

Unlike Cain, Coach had avoided a rivalry or character contest through several face-saving moves. First, he already had a general joking relationship with Ray. This is apparent in his response to Ray's queries about seeing him in San Antonio. Coach had allowed the vatos to "get a little personal" without losing his cool or control of the situation. As a result, Ray "owed" Coach the sharp, potentially insulting personal jibe about his drug use. Within the context of their general relationship, Coach did not overreact to Ray's playful attempts at "making out" with a boring lesson. He rapped with Ray without shaming him. He was actually as sarcastic as Mr. Cain was, but his brand of sarcasm usually colluded with rather than put down the vatos. He never counted on being respected and followed simply because he was officially in charge. He knew that one had to win respect in a street-style culture through quick wits and fists.

He was enormously effective at humorously transforming making out games into academic work. One day he took a knife away from one of the

vatos in an extremely matter-of-fact manner. The straighter, more conformist kids were all "ohing and ahing" about how Enrique was "going to
get it now." This puffed Enrique up for that great victory of a few days'
vacation from a terrified, enraged teacher. Coach sauntered up and nonchalantly asked to see the knife that Enrique was "scaring everybody
with." He then wondered out loud if it "had a good edge" and asked
if he planned to "cut up the vice principal with it." That brought the
house down, because most people suspected Enrique helping smash out
the vice principal's car window. Coach glanced at the ubiquitous inter-
com and feigned fear as he confided that he could lose his job, "if I let you
keep that knife." He then added, "I can't do that. I got car payments
to make."

This rap appealed to Enrique's practical logic. Coach had explained
that it was either Enrique or him, so Enrique need not take what Coach
had to do as a personal insult. Moreover, the coach was not attacking
Enrique's personal honor. Enrique had no reason to fight back and save
face about losing the knife. Coach had facetiously appealed to Enrique to
save his threatened life style, implying that both he and Enrique were
victims of convention. Here they were, two cool guys, forced to follow
some dumb school rule. Coach had portrayed himself as someone just
doing a job that was not always such fun for him either.

The vatos generally liked Coach Zapata, because he could distance
himself from the formal role of being a teacher and disciplinarian. He was
able to take liberties with his official role, and the more informal and
unofficial he acted, the more he actually enhanced his official authority
with the vatos. The rebellious vatos knew they were being conned into
working or acquiescing. But Coach often gave them the stage and allowed
them to vent their hostilities toward school lessons and teachers. This
made them feel a little better, and they also gained some status and
recognition without seriously disrupting the class.

It is important to note that Coach Zapata's ability to relate to the vatos
was only partially due to his ethnicity. He literally spoke their language
and was sensitive to the nuances of their speech style. More important,
however, was his understanding of their general life style and world view.
These were alienated working class kids with a good deal of collective
pride and personal insecurity about themselves and their future. Coach
Zapata understood that their sense of honor was based on a very macho
view of girls, schoolwork, teachers, their physical appearance, and their
ability to fight.

Nevertheless, other Anglo teachers with very contrasting styles were also partially successful relating to the vatos. Hip Anglo teachers like Mr. Read and straight ones like Mr. Roy, even though they were less empathic, had few discipline problems with the vatos. Some authoritarian, "straight" teachers also developed their own type of reciprocity and trust with these students. It should be added that Coach Zapata's communicative competence did not necessarily produce higher academic results. Had he been a bit more academically oriented, he would have been very similar to the Los Angeles math teacher Jaime Escalante who was idealized in the movie *Stand and Deliver*.

Moreover, not all the Mexicano teachers in North Town related well to the Mexicano students. Some ethnic teachers such as Raul Cisneros, who sought to be a hip Chicano teacher, were less successful than Zapata. Like Coach Zapata's, Mr. Cisneros's classes were also marked by some verbal repartee and joking relationships with students, but the vatos disliked his style. Unlike Coach Zapata, Mr. Cisneros was essentially a "straight" teacher who, as the kids were fond of saying, "tries to be cool and funny but isn't." Students often said that "Mr. Cisneros thinks he is a big shot and a brain." They disliked his intellectual and social pretensions that he had risen above them. Mr. Cisneros admitted the following in an interview:

> Some of the Chicano kids think I favor the Anglos too much, because I call on the Anglos too much. But heck, I try to kid around with both. In the fifth period, I never have this problem. The Chicano kids there like me, but they don't seem to in fourth period. These kids are stuck up. They think they are superior or something. I'm not trying to put them down. I don't know, maybe they are jealous of me.

Mr. Cisneros did not discern that his fifth period was an all-Mexicano class of practicals. In contrast, his fourth period was a highly competitive, racially mixed, advanced academic class. In the fourth period class, the socially prominent Mexicano kids expected him to favor them and to put down the Anglos. When Mr. Cisneros helped stage the making out games of both prominent Anglos and Mexicanos, he was being a vendido who did not support his people. In addition, Mr. Cisneros occasionally made little speeches about how he had "made it" through his hard work. He chided other Mexicanos to live up to his example. On several occasions, he chided the Mexicano student activists to be more active. They took his comments as "putting them down" for their inactivity. He always seemed to be competing with or competing for the attention of the prominent kids, which both they and the vatos disliked.

Summing Up: Making Out Games as Class Role Performances

Making out games occurred in every classroom in North Town High. Every student participated as a key performer or as a passive observer in these often playful, sometimes disruptive events. Students initiated these games, and teachers collaborated, because the school day was long and boring. Academic work simply had to be humanized. I have tried to present enough different types of making out games to show their complexity and variation. These games were routinely initiated by a relatively small number of students. The status groups for "hanging out" formed teams of performers that monopolized "productive" classroom discussions. These same teams of performers staged the making out games that monopolize "unproductive" classroom disruptions. Some making out games were started by one team and were taken over by another. Individuals without a status group could also initiate and participate in others' making out games. These games were too fluid and variable for us to find any absolute correlation between teams of people and types of games. Generally, however, the same student peer groups and individuals tended to orchestrate these games in fairly routine ways.

Moreover, making out games always involved some degree of teacher collaboration, but this varied with the teacher's performance line and the type of game. Aggressive making out games and resistance to teacher authority could develop into character contests that ruptured the teacher's performance and control. Even leader-conformist students occasionally resisted teachers' authority, but these were only moments when they stepped out of their usual role. This signaled that they were unusually powerful players who could actually play the role of conformist *or* rebel—if they chose. Usually, they avoided character contests with teachers and sustained the teacher's performance and authority. Conversely, the rebellious students did not always openly confront teacher authority with verbal repartee or exaggerated inattention. Occasionally, they too would distance themselves from their usual rebellious role and join the audience of passive social "nobodies."

The extent to which these games were mutually constructed also varied with the type of teacher performance. Teachers, like foremen in factories, were trapped in this contradictory role of managing alienating work. Consequently, they found ways of reducing or modifying work loads to make their classrooms function. Some teachers were very skillful at developing a sense of reciprocity and negotiating over student alienation. Mr. Zapata openly collaborated with students and changed school work routines. Mr. Read frequently played with academic work. Mr. Cain and others simply traded free time for a little work to minimize making out games.

Initially, I collected the students' notions of "good" and "bad" teachers. What emerged were the basic notions of reciprocity that all successful North Town teachers had, regardless of their individual communicative styles. First, teachers have to find a balance between work/seriousness and play/joking. Second, they also had to find a balance between being an expert/big shot and being an ordinary person using ordinary, non-technical language. Third, a teacher had to discipline and maintain order but not harp and nitpick about chewing gum and silly answers to questions. Fourth, a teacher had to vary the approach some, but not enough to disrupt the agreed-upon routines. Finally, a teacher had to assign sufficient work and grade strictly enough to keep classes somewhat challenging.

In short, a good teacher struck a balance with all types of students on a variety of issues. Such a teacher stood neither over students with superior airs nor on their level as a buddy. North Town students expected to be disciplined and entertained. In return, they would do the work assigned and help the teacher enact his or her public persona and professional "line." Very different teaching and communicative styles achieved general order and academic production. Different teachers had different ways of striking the reciprocal balance that won the trust, respect, and cooperation of students.

Finally, this account emphasizes how class privileges and roles were practiced and modeled during these classroom rituals. The school leader types, good students, athletes, and cheerleaders of prominent familes were the star performers. They frequently manipulated and deceived teachers for their gain. Teachers and administrators consciously and unconsciously bowed to the pressures and presumptions of socially prominent students and their parents. Meanwhile, more marginal low income students such as the vatos and a few whites openly confronted teachers to their own detriment.

The majority of conforming students provided the main ritual performers—the devious conformists and the openly rebellious—with a willing audience. All the participants in this ritual event learned who the winners and losers were in American society. They also learned that cleverly manipulating authority gains much more than openly confronting authority. An instrumental style of communication or impression management and conformity was ultimately portrayed as the cultural ideal. Teachers ended up staging and rewarding such communicative styles—just as they did in the football and social dating scenes.

F I V E

Looking Back on the 1970s: An Epilogue

During the three summers from 1985 through 1987 I returned to North Town and re-interviewed my "informants." I also attended a ten-year reunion of the class that I knew best. Having been a part of their gossip network for a year, I was an honorary member of the group. These kids had told me many tales of drinking, dope smoking, angry parents, grumpy teachers, and cheating boyfriends. I was the strange guy who was "writing a book" about them. This time around, we all went drinking at the local nightclub, and no one worried about rattlesnakes in the field or cops on the prowl. Even better, no one lied to parents to get out of the house. We talked about old times and good old North Town High. The reunion evoked the same nostalgia that my own high school reunion had. Once again, I was struck by the similarities between my home town and North Town.

I eventually interviewed forty students who had graduated in the 1970s. Aside from collecting the personal views of these youth, I also tried to reconstruct where everyone had gone. The interviewees actually knew where most of their classmates were. By checking and cross checking, I found out what had happened to the vatos, kickers, guzzlers, jocks, and big wheels that I knew. A fuller description of how this survey was done can be found in the appendix on field methods.

Of the 500 in school at the time, I was able to trace where 454 were. My sample had the following demographic characteristics: Mexicano (72%), Anglo (28%), male (52%), female (48%), married (78%), unmarried (22%). A very large number (53%) returned to live in North Town, and the majority (51%) married another North Towner. A much higher percentage of the Mexicanos than Anglos returned (61% vs 34%). The survey also shows that a minority of all North Town youth finished either two (20%) or four years (20%) of higher education. Only a minority of their families (9%) had upper middle class jobs (prominent business and professional occupations). A much larger percentage had lower middle class jobs (small business, trade, and low level office jobs) (36%) or unskilled labor jobs (46%). In general, North Town is a low income, predominantly Mexican American community; consequently, two-thirds of the youth do not continue on to higher education.

Generally, there were no great surprises about which kids succeeded educationally and economically. Many middle class youth, regardless of race and gender, went to college and got the best jobs. Conversely, few working class youth, regardless of race and gender, went to college or got desirable jobs. Tables 1 and 2 in Appendix C show the complete numbers and percentages. Generally, far more upper middle and middle class youth finished college (47% vs. 5%) and got middle class jobs (44% vs. 5%) than working class youth. Youth from families with stable, lower middle class jobs (small businesses, service trades, contractors, low level white collar workers, health and educational aids) also ranked higher than working class youth. More of these youth finished college (21% vs. 5%) and got middle class jobs (24% vs. 5%) than did working class youth.

These numbers confirm what many other studies have shown. Youth from solid lower middle class families have steady incomes, higher aspirations, and a tenuous foothold in the mainstream. As a result, their youth are much more likely to go on to college that the children of farm laborers or domestics. In North Town, approximately one-third of the Mexicano families have already moved from the marginal working-class into the lower middle class. With the desegregation of schools, these families are poised to send their talented children to college and solidify their place in the mainstream.

Comparing this first post-civil rights generation to their parents shows that a larger segment of the Mexicano community actually had achieved upward social mobility. Table 3 (Appendix C) shows the intergenerational difference between the occupations of these youth and their fathers. This new generation had substantially more families in upper middle class occupations than their parents' generation (16% vs. 6%). School desegregation and ethnic politics opened up some new opportunities for these youth, and they joined the middle class. Moreover, approximately twice as many of these new Mexicano professionals returned to North Town, as did Anglo youth with degrees. This new post-civil rights generation of Mexicanos was slowly assuming the leadership positions in North Town and others in this new middle class had pursued opportunities for minorities in the urban areas. The down side of the social mobility data was, however, that the Mexicano working class left behind (58%) remained as poor and uneducated as before.

The segment of the Mexicano community that was least likely to achieve upward social mobility was working class Mexicanas. The majority of Mexicanas married and took part time unskilled jobs (35%) or full-time working class jobs (20%). Like working class Mexicanos, very small numbers went on to college or made it into middle class jobs. A gender difference does appear, however, when one looks for small increments of social mobility. For example, working class Mexicanas were less likely than working class Mexicanos to move up into lower middle class jobs (21% vs. 41%). This difference undoubtedly reflects the greater number of semi-skilled and small business jobs open to males in a more agricultural, less industrialized economy. Conversely, women raising a family have few job options other than part time domestic or clerical work; consequently, Mexicanas were less likely to make even modest social mobility gains. The more difficult circumstance of Mexicanas is also reflected in some mobility differences between them and Anglo females. Anglo girls who were high academically left North Town in larger percentages than Mexicanas (74% vs. 58%). Conversely, Mexicanas who were low academically returned to North Town in larger percentages than Anglos (69% vs. 43%).

All these numbers suggest a continuing pattern of cultural traditionalism in the Mexicano community. As previously indicated, the Mexicano family placed somewhat greater restrictions on the girls. Mexicanas tended to date less, be more family-oriented, marry locals, eschew careers, and stay in North Town. As a result, academically talented Mexicanas from working class families were the least likely to fulfill their potential. They encountered both class and patriarchal restrictions on their educational and economic mobility. In contrast, Mexicanas from middle class families had educational and job mobility profiles very similar to other middle class youth. This suggests that as Mexicanos become middle class, traditional gender role practices may tend to diminish.

Turning to the role of student status groups in social mobility, the survey corroborated the ethnographic portrayal of the student status scene. As indicated previously, the football, dating, and classroom scenes were stages upon which students enacted the social prominence of their families. Youth learned the self-expectations, values, and communicative competences needed for different future civic, political, and economic roles as leaders and followers. Table 4 (Appendix C) shows how strongly family social class background related to the "high" and "low" student status group labels. Generally, the socially prominent youth got the best grades, participated more in sports, band, and student clubs, and used the school most effectively to maintain their social class position. Many more of these youth (73%) than the "kickers" (25%), "nobodies" (21%), "vatos" (10%), and "white trash" (1%) took at least two years of college. Further, most socially prominent youth ended up in professional, white collar, and small business jobs (78%), and most "white trash" (89%), "vatos" (71%), and quiet "nobodies" (61%) ended up in working class jobs.

As these numbers indicate, such labels do not perfectly reflect the social class background of youth. Not all "nobodies" socially were working class. Not all "jocks" were from socially prominent families. These identity labels also reflect one's social acceptability among peers. "Making it" in the social status scene of youth depended generally on money, clothes, and family background, but not entirely. A youth's personality and individual style sometimes made up for her or his family background. Some individuals achieved a high status in this scene in spite of their working class background. Moreover, "making it" in the student status scene was not absolutely necessary for future occupational success. Some youths went to college and got good jobs in adult society in spite of being excluded from the student status scene. Others were high school heroes and very socially accepted but ended up in undesirable jobs.

In short, these status group identity labels were strongly associated with family class background, but individual differences in personality and motivation made a difference. Some talented working class youth who were particularly intelligent and/or personable joined the youth from socially prominent families in running the school and the student social scene. Conversely, some youth from socially prominent families were academically marginal, socially inept, or rebellious. Some of these "underachieved" academically, or were high achievers but socially marginal "loners" or "nerds." The student status scene generally reproduced the class inequalities of the community, but there were some interesting exceptions.

First, "jocks" appear to have been "overachievers" socially and economically. People tended to expect great things from good athletes, and they held a very privileged position in the community. Most jocks were from lower middle class (54%) or working class families (20%) and were generally average in school achievement (60%). Yet many took some college (57%) and ended up in upper middle class (37%) or lower middle class jobs (54%). Second, a small percentage of quiet "nobodies," despite not being involved in the high school social scene, also did very well. The social nobodies included a small percentage of middle class (9%) and lower middle class youth (30%) who became professionals (10%) or got solid lower middle class jobs (28%), although the majority ended up with working class jobs (61%). Third, the majority of "kicker" kids achieved solid economic futures without going on to higher education. Most (65%) became partners in or took over small family farms and ranches (65%), but a substantial minority (35%) ended up in working class jobs.

Finally, although most "vatos" ended up with working class jobs (75%), a substantial minority of vatos (23%) achieved stable, lower middle class jobs much like those of their fathers. In addition to the survey, I made a special effort to trace where the group of ten vatos from the auto mechanics class were. According to the school authorities, these "punks" and "troublemakers" would "never amount to anything." Indeed, these youth have not "made it" into a mainstream middle class life style, except Dario, one of the leaders of the group, who married the daughter of a prominent businessman and politician and became the manager of a gas delivery business. His reflections back on being a vato were particularly revealing:

We thought we'd never need school. We were living day to day. We didn't worry about the future . . . We didn't have much money for beer and drugs, but we always pooled our money to have a weekend party . . . We were fighters, but there wasn't really a gang. It was just that everyone had to protect each other. If you messed with one of us, you messed with all of us. We really stuck together more than the other groups . . . No, we didn't get too personal with each other. It was mostly having fun together. I don't remember telling anybody about my feelings. There was only two feelings, angry or normal. We were really angry about the way teachers treated us. They looked down on us and never really tried to help us. A lot of us were real smart kids, but we never figured that school was going to do anything for us. The talent was there, but probably the majority of the parents weren't really watching out or being strict enough. They didn't watch our grades and get on our case. We didn't have to please nobody. As long as we stayed out of trouble with the law, it was ok. And the teachers were so negative, even the Mexican American ones, that we weren't about to take any of their bullshit . . . We were the violent macho types, I guess. They'd [the teachers] manipulate the "nerds" [the student leader types] into school and books. There was a real separation between us and the nerds and the jocks. Maybe it was jealousy towards each other. The only time we got involved was the Raza Unida. Everybody got involved when the school board let us wear long hair . . . We really didn't know what it [the politics] all meant. We just kinda wanted to be a part of Raza Unida. We were looking at it as the "real Chicanos" verses the gringos. Anything that gringos would say would end up in fist fights. At the end, they'd ignore us, but we'd gang up on them. They'd beat up on one of us, and the next day we'd kick the hell out of them; then they didn't bother us no more. We just kinda wanted to be a part of the Raza Unida. It's [the racial situation] been going on forever, and we wanted to fight them . . . Really this stuff all started in junior high. We became brothers, started drinking together, chasing girls, you know, all that stuff . . . I guess we were trying to prove that we were big shots . . . If I could go back, I wouldn't do it again. It really didn't benefit nobody. I think it was a mistake picking fights with gringos. None of us made it to college. By the end, I think I started realizing that we were messing up . . . Yeah, I suppose I look at it different now because of being married and my wife and her family. I know I don't want my kids to be "vatos."

Dario went on to recount where his "brothers" ended up. Eloy and A.A. had been killed in an automobile crash. Tomas, Raymundo, Carlos, and Jessie worked part time in construction or as roughnecks in the oil fields. They either had never married or were divorced. They still led the "playboy" or bachelor life style of drugs, girl friends, and partying. They had not become "straight," hard-working adults. In contrast, Ray, Juan, Ricardo, and Paco had gotten married and settled down. They worked for the county, a peanut company, a gas station, and as a beekeeper, respectively. Approximately half the old gang has "gone straight," and approximately half were still "hip" or had killed themselves being cool. Compared to the "nerdy," quiet, conformist working class Mexicano youths, the vatos have probably fared about the same or a little worse. Compared to their white trash buddies, they fared about the same. Of the six Anglo girls that used to hang around with the vatos, four had settled into straight, married life styles, and two were still married. The other two still seemed to live swinging single life styles. Tara, one of the brightest and most outspoken Anglo rebels, had been divorced twice, worked sporadically, and still did drugs and scandalized her relatives. She still claimed that she "didn't give a damn what people think."

The two most interesting "honorary vatos," Brian, the Anglo hippie, and Ratonini (the rat), the fast-talking D.J., had also settled in North Town. Brian, the only Anglo longhair who had "hung with" the vatos, had married the daughter of a prominent Anglo farm family and ran his father's produce shed. The vatos remembered him fondly and said he was still friendly, even though he "had gone straight." Brian laughed about his days as a "white vato" and said he still wanted to see Anglos and Mexicanos live and let live. He mused over getting involved in city or school board politics, but had resisted requests to run and play peacemaker. Ratonini was still spinning Spanish records for the local radio station and did dances and parties privately. He was a swinging bachelor and had a son by his young Anglo girl friend. He still dreamed of going to the big city and bigger music scenes and was "king rat" of the airways in North Town.

On the opposite side of the class spectrum, many of the "jocks" and socially prominent youth were running North Town's businesses, schools, welfare agencies, and farms and ranches. Hector, a star linebacker, was on the city council. Pete, a defensive back, and Mark, a wide receiver, were on the school board. Danny, the quarterback, ran the Ford garage, and Rolando, a defensive back, was his right-hand man. Gregorio, the quiet guard who thought himself dumb, ran his own welding shop. Shannon ran her family's cleaners, Mack ran his father's grocery story, and Jenna was an assistant manager at the local bank. A dozen others were teachers, and several were hoping to become principals. A number owned small businesses such as a welding shop, a flower shop, a hauling service, and a plumbing service.

There were a few surprises, however. One of the "coolest" Mexicano jocks, who had starred in football, got good grades, and dated Anglo girls, ended up semi-employed and alcoholic. Despite coming from a self-employed family of truckers, he was unable to take advantage of his family background and his status in the student social scene. He remained a mystery to his old teammates, who were now working at the bank and running their own businesses. Another popular girl had "come out of the closet" and openly become a lesbian; she was driving a truck for a living. Others had survived disastrous divorces rather badly and had slipped below their expectations and family background. In general, however, this first post-civil rights generation was assuming the civic, business, and social service and professional leadership positions. Those who were socially and academically successful in school made up most of this new generation of local leaders.

Recollections on High School Days and an Official TEA Report

I was also intrigued by the way that most students remembered the school and their teachers. The "good students" remembered the "good teachers," Mr. Roy, Mr. Read, and Mr. Vela, fondly. They still mentioned those qualities that they had mentioned as kids. The students who had gone to college also told horror stories about their poor academic preparation. College was a rude shock, even to the "brains" of North Town High. Most admitted that it had taken about two years to adjust to university work loads. These kids had never been forced to read, write, and think much. Everyone told stories about learning basic study skills and a greater respect for ideas, evidence, and argumentation in college. They described college as a good, challenging experience, and looked back on their high school academic preparation with disdain.

What North Towners remembered fondly about high school was all the social life and extracurricular activity. High school was a fun time filled with football games, cute guys and chicks, boozing it up, outwitting adults, and generally being young and irresponsible. Such memories of youth and high school get sentimentalized very quickly through the help of American popular culture magazines, talk shows, TV sitcoms, and movies. Being young has become a major American cultural myth, which helps us forget what growing up was really like. North Towners did not mention having zits, breaking up, and all the adolescent insecurities about appearance, sexual performance, and career. Nor did they mention all the forms of inequality highlighted in this portrayal of youth and high school days. People will admit and talk about these darker sides of growing up, if pressed, but that was not what they recalled naturally.

One particularly thoughtful person explained why people have "amnesia" or selective memory about youth. This person was already a little life-weary, so she pointed out how relative one's triumphs and tragedies are. Making a living and bringing up a family was a good deal harder than she had ever imagined. At thirty or so, she said, life looks like an uphill battle, especially when you have been divorced, fired, and addicted to some drug. In contrast, high school days seem particularly good to young adults struggling to make ends meet and to control their bulging waists and receding hair lines. This nostalgia about youth strikes me as a cultural mechanism for coping with the present. In other words, "Don't mess with our popular memory about youth." The movie *Peggy Sue Gets Married* is an exceptional cinematic reflection on our cultural tendency to sentimentalize youth. Peggy literally goes back in time to sort out the fiction and fantasy of her mythical youth, and thus get on with living. The American mythology of youth dies hard, because it allows us to live with a great deal of personal pain and public injustice, until, like Peggy, we think about it seriously.

I also asked these young adults to evaluate the current North Town schools. This was a timely topic, because the Texas Education Agency had just completed an evaluation that had lowered the schools' accreditation status The report ended with the following ominous conclusion:

The North Town Independent School District is currently classified as Accredited. Because of the number and seriousness of instructional program deficiencies and the number of violations of Texas statute and State Board of Education rules, and the poor performance of a significant number of the student population, the accreditation status of North Town Independent School District is lowered from Accredited to Accredited, Advised.

The report listed a number of improvements, some to be completed within three months, and others to be worked on, that would be necessary if the district wished to maintain its accreditation. Among the listed administrative changes were: displaying lesson plans and curriculum guides; developing a plan for improving student performance; raising test scores through a retesting policy; using a more laboratory/field oriented method in science; allowing for co-educational physical education classes; and providing proper teacher planning periods and reduced lunch supervision duty. Most people I talked with had not actually read the report, but everyone had an opinion. Many of this 1970s generation had a so-what-else-is-new response to TEA's discovery of their school district's "problem." Those worrying about sending their children to a substandard public school were wondering how much a private San Antonio boarding school would cost. They had given up on "reforming" the school or the town, which they viewed as a "lost cause" of bickering and disunity.

Those who worked for the school district and still hoped to change things blamed the present board and school administrators for "causing" a deterioration in the schools. They, especially a handful of ambitious new Mexicano teachers, were chafing to become administrative leaders and reform the school. They agreed with the report's only serious criticism that homogeneous ability grouping and an ethnic imbalance in the staff (70% Anglo) needed changing. Like other middle class Anglo and Mexicano parents, they wanted to raise the school's academic level. Several were considering sending their kids to private schools. According to the achievement test scores (TEAMS), the district was the lowest in the thirteen-county Winter Garden region and was below the national average.

Everyone agreed that the North Town schools needed to improve, but when pressed for ideas about how to change them, most of the new generation repeated the ideas of their elders. They talked about "tougher grading," but complained about the evils of the recent reforms such as the "no-pass, no-play" rule. They wanted "better teachers," but complained about higher school taxes. They extolled "more homework," but admited that they lacked the time and interest to make their children do more schoolwork. In the end, the new generation were looking for the same quick fix that the older one had. They did not see schools as a complex cultural institution that reproduced rather than changed sharp class differences and low aspiration levels.

This new generation was also as quick as the older generation to make political hay over the "school problem." The main reason people ran for the school board was still to fire unpopular coaches and superintendents. Over the past fifteen years, North Town had experienced a kind of musical chairs of educational leadership. The ebb and flow of school board politics had made it an exceedingly difficult district to administer. The result had been little continuity of educational leadership and a high turnover rate (35% annually) of teachers. "Outsiders" invariably ran afoul of local factions and were fired or resigned. This left a core of native North Town teachers and long-staying outsiders. These people became "insiders" who had accumulated the town's best range land, houses, and teaching sections. They were friends and neighbors and knew the right people. Some were reputedly excellent teachers, and some were not. Those who were incompetent, which was not for me to judge, would be difficult to fire. The North Town educational system tended, therefore, to be both unstable and somewhat inbred. The new generation of North Towners recognized these problems, but they had no idea how to minimize this sort of politicization of education.

Race Relations Among the Youth in the 1980s

One topic that the 1970s generation did see differently was race relations. The North Town youth who had lived through the civil rights era had more open, liberal views about socializing with the other race. They were all very positive about how much better Anglo and Mexicano youth related than they themselves had. Everyone pointed to the way the youths openly hung out at drive-ins and dated each other as the patern for the future. A former football star, who became a teacher and city councilman, marveled at the transformation:

Things were real tense in the seventies when this all started. I used to hang around with all the Anglo football studs, but I took some shit for that. It was uncomfortable. These kids feel more comfortable with each other than we did. They have a good time. They joke around more. You see them hanging out at the Dairy Queen and riding around together in cars like we never did. It is more open now. We used to sneak around and try to make out with each other, but now you see this stuff happening everywhere. Let me give you a good example. At our tenth high school reunion, Karl, an old football buddy, didn't know any of the other Mexicanos except me! I envy these kids today, they're out there dating and doing what they want to, like nobody is controlling them the way parents used to. Things are just more out in the open now.

Everyone seemed to agree that the current youth scene was a far cry from the 1970s. One of the vatos who had hung out with white girls said the following:

> Back then you could hang around with a white girl, but now you can sleep with a white girl. You know, it's never been that we didn't get it, but we had girl friends from 8:30 to 3:30 mostly. Now it's changed drastically. Back then, girls who hung around with Mexicans got a lot of shit. Now there isn't the pressure. But really, if I was a white parent, I wouldn't want my daughter fucking around with some of us either. I'd probably try to ship her off to college, too, if I had the money . . . Prejudice is down now. Back then there was a lot, maybe 80 percent prejudice and 20 percent not. Now it's about 50/50. If you're a good kid, you're welcome. But even if I was an honor student back then, I couldn't get in the front door. These kids party together now. If you come from a good family, you got it made now. You can make it with any of them now.

Both teachers and students at the high school claimed that Mexicano and Anglo kids were now socializing together openly. They urged me to "check out the strip" and observe how many multi-racial cars full of cruising kids there were. It was true. The night was full of kids from both races joking, talking, flirting, and cruising. Hector's Taco Bar and the Dairy Queen had been replaced by the Walmart parking lot. This new hangout sat on the strip across from the new Sonic Drive-in and Pizza Hut. Some kids sat on the hoods or in the pickup beds listening to rock music and checking out the cruisers. Other cruised by, so they could be checked out. Kids and cars shuttled in and out looking for action.

Having seen all this new racial mixing, I interviewed some of the younger brothers and sisters of the students of the seventies. The following is a particularly revealing conversation with one of today's school leaders. He is from a prominent professional and political family and is headed for the University of Texas. He was the most articulate of the youths that I interviewed.

> We don't feel much pressure from parents about dating each other. The girls, if they like you, if you are good looking, a good athlete, the other [race] doesn't matter. The main thing that parents worry about is maybe you will run around with reckless types who like to fight. I guess the white parents would get upset, if they thought their kids were hanging out with the concert, T-shirt crowd [the vatos] who likes to fight . . . Yes, they are the ones in the lower sections"

I described how Anglo and Mexicano kids partied separately in the 1970s. He quickly corrected that view of race relations in the 1980s. He recounted a typical interracial party that he attended:

Let me give you a good example of how it is now. There was this real good party last year at this Anglo kid's house. There were, maybe, thirty-five white kids from all grades and back from college, and about twenty Mexicanos. The majority of kids at the party were guys, maybe two-thirds guys, and the rest girls. There were more Anglo girls than Mexicans, because they are more likely to be the type who like to make out. The Hispanic girls are a little more conservative, or have steady guys . . . Naw, there wasn't any trouble at the party. Well, there was a carload of guys that crashed the party. They were the type who likes to get into fights and slash tires. They were about to get into a fight, but people asked them to stay calm or leave. They hung around for a while and left . . . These kinds of parties happen all year long and are mostly on weekends. We just find each other cruising around, and somebody buys some beer, and we have a party . . . Well, ya, I guess it is mostly the kids who are going to college. It's mainly the sharp kids who party together.

The separation between the middle class kids and vatos and low achieving nobodies also carried over into the dating scene. Everyone agreed that kids in the advanced sections still did not date Mexicanos in the practical sections. This generations' vatos were still excluded because of their fighting, clothes, bad manners, and indifference toward success and school. The middle class kids listed, however, more than twenty open, steady interracial couples and claimed many more dated occasionally. This was, of course, a far cry from the handful of secret relationships I witnessed during the 1970s.

In addition, these kids all had stories about "calling for a date" at the house of a prominent Anglo family. The last of the Alonzo clan, a cheerleader and honor role student, regularly invited her Anglo friends to the home of the Anglos' number one nemesis! One student told a story about how the Browns, a prominent ranching family, became irritated with their daughter for openly dating a "skinny Mexican baseball player." When the girl made this known to the other kids, "everyone thought the parents were in the stone age." Both Mexicano and Anglo kids strongly disapproved of such parental pressures. In short, the dating scene had opened up for the middle class Mexicanos, and they report that other Mexicano kids were "jealous," and "always taking about us." Despite continuing class and gender restrictions, the mood and temper of the times had changed. Interracial dating had definitely come out of the closet in North Town.

Race Relations Among North Town Adults in the 1980s

In contrast to the younger generation, North Town adults expressed a greater variety of feelings, but they too portrayed themselves and the town as having "softer" views of race relations. Many claimed that the racial confrontations of the early 1970s and 1980s were an "educational process." They believed that time and reoccurring conflicts had eroded racist feelings and stereotypes. They felt that a small number of "red necks" and "brown necks" existed, but that extreme racism was gone forever. Anglos, particularly the younger educated ones, now more readily admitted that the town had a racist past. Few of them angrily defended the past and portrayed La Raza as a communist plot or criminal conspiracy. Most North Town Anglos felt it was inevitable that Mexicanos, being the majority, should be in leadership positions. They also realized that most Mexicano politicians aspired to be autonomous, not sponsored leaders.

Demographically, Anglos now represented no more than 15 percent of the total population. They found it increasingly difficult to win local elections. Instead, they aspired to find Mexicanos who would be "reasonable" toward Anglo interests and rights and not "anti-gringo." The fear of retribution and revenge for the past still concerned many North Town Anglos, and their trust of Mexicano leaders was a fragile thing. The following testimony of a liberal or moderate teacher illustrates the cautiously optimistic view often expressed:

> I think we've gotten to the point that we [Anglos] will elect a qualified Mexican, except for one man, Mr. Alonzo. He is still too radical, and there has been so much bitterness over what his sons have done. But the Anglo population is dwindling fast. There is nothing here, no future unless you inherit your father's land or business . . . Those [Mexicanos] that are making an effort to better themselves are being accepted. But there are two classes, and the others not making an effort aren't being accepted, still . . . I hope things are settling down, because we are being engulfed. The only thing I worry about is the attitude Mexicans have about certain things, money situations. They don't deal with money and taxes right. It's a Mexico attitude. I can't describe it. It's kind of a payola thing. But I'm hopeful. There are some old-timers who will never change, but I see a gradual change. Unless they try to do something drastic like take your land or raise taxes real high, nobody objects to Mexicans running things. They have some educated leaders now. Some are more educated than the Anglos around here . . . But yes, I am still suspicious of Mr. Rapido and Ms. Serrano. They are closely associated with Mr. Alonzo, and there is that touch of bitterness in them towards Anglos. You can't help but fear that they will want to get even for what the old-timers did to their people.

Mr. Francisco Rapído and Ms. Beatrice Serrano were ex-radicals trying to win Anglo cross-over votes. This had proved to be an uphill battle, even with the more liberal white voters like this teacher. Her family had two mixed marriages, and she generally liked Mexicanos, but she still did not trust the Mexicano political leaders who were associated with the Raza Unida Party.

One can also find Anglos who had not changed much in their racial views. Some younger Anglos back from college described North Town as a "red neck town." They claimed that their relatives would never change. Outspokenly liberal Anglos expressed deep frustration over "the old-timers." One old-timer told me the following story, which shows an enduring racist strain:

> It is getting hard to keep good coaches and superintendents in this town, Doc. Mr. Carter has a pretty little girl in junior high, and he just had to get her out of here to keep her away from Mexican boys. Coach Craig had the same problem. He got himself a nice job up in the hill country where there aren't so many of them. But you know even in Hedley [a hill country town], they are swarming in there, too! They say that Hedley is already forty-five percent Mexican. There just aren't hardly any Anglos left in our grade school. This place is pretty much going downhill. It isn't a place to bring up kids in anymore.

Nevertheless, I was impressed with what younger Anglos had to say about the racial situation. Some socialized in the Mexicano community, and they had a sense of past inequalities. They expressed a greater willingness to live together peacefully and equally. One young professional, who had taken me on during a drinking party for being pro-Mexicano, described her transformation in the following way:

> I've mellowed. I was definitely prejudiced when I was fourteen. I guess I was a little red neck when you were here . . .No, I don't remember giving you hell at the drinking party. I was probably too drunk to remember that. Anyway, nowadays I vote for Mexican candidates. I think I'm like a lot of people here, I am sick of politics and the fighting. Most people would just like to see progress. These are tough economic times. I think the issue now is economic survival. People have dealt with the racial thing pretty well. They say, "Let's find a candidate to do a good job, whatever the race." I'm pretty optimistic about the racial thing. I have lots of Mexican friends, and we argue and drink beer and watch TV and do all the things that any thirty-year-olds do. I don't see any big differences, really.

Increasingly, Mexicanos also mentioned the greater respect shown to them in public by Anglos. One Mexicano educator put it particularly well:

> It's more comfortable now to be a Mexican. It's all right to eat Mexican food and listen to Mexican music and speak like a Mexican. It's kind of like coming out of a closet, or some dark place. This little red neck place still isn't Laredo or

San Antonio, but it's just more comfortable now. I don't have to give a damn what some bollio [Anglo] thinks anymore.

Many of the emerging middle class professionals also expressed disinterest in making a racial fight out of politics. They talked about improving life in North Town for the "community" not for "La Raza." A prominent Mexicano politician reflected:

> We, as a people and I, have come full circle. I grew up in South Texas accepting racism. I went off to college and joined the movimiento (movement) and rallied against racism. Now I find myself working hard to improve this community for both Anglos and Mexicanos. There isn't any other way. We all have to learn to live together.

Some prominent Ciudadano leaders were now busy running their businesses and sending their children to college. They were still interested in politics but accepted a slower, gradual process of change. They expressed optimism about the future for themselves and their children. Others, working-class Mexicanos, said the gringos did not "pick on people much anymore," but that life was still hard. One of the vatos put it this way:

> If I could go back, I wouldn't be like I was in school. It really didn't benefit nobody. I guess I was hanging around with the wrong kids. I don't know any of us that really made it. Most of us are unemployed or working in odd jobs. None of the vatos made it to college. Really, most Mexicanos are still as bad off as their parents. It's only the rich kids who made it to college. I don't think the gringos treat us no better. They think we are a bunch of dumb, dirty Mexicans. They still act like assholes to me. I couldn't date their daughters. I'm still the same Mexican troublemaker I was back then.

North Towners also portrayed the present racial harmony with metaphors like "an ocean with a strong undercurrent" or a "still day that is brewing a thunderstorm." No one who had lived through the past fifteen years was saying that old personal and racial animosities had magically died. Most people believed that racial attitudes had "softened" and that North Towners cooperated more. The adults cited a number of changes that had improved racial relations. People active in the Protestant churches were proud of the way the Baptists and Methodists had opened up the formerly Anglo churches to Mexicanos "who preferred services in English." The Mexicano mission churches on the Westside still gave services in Spanish. Others active in school booster clubs cited the success of the band and football team. People also pointed to the predominantly

Mexicano city council as another sign of racial progress. Yet most North Towners, if pressed, admitted that they expected more strife and disharmony.

One must acknowledge all the talk about softening and mellowing racial attitudes. North Town had come a long way from the segregated racial order of the pre-World War II era. North Towners were grappling with their "race problem" and clearly evolving. But most people who live a while know that everything is relative. As one old-timer said to me, "North Town still has a fair piece to go." For me, one tragic incident punctuates all the talk about improving race relations, and causes me to wonder how deep the cultural change in North Town really is.

The Tale of a Tragic Feud: From Solidarity to Solitude

After so much community conflict, fate seemed to have delivered a tragic, senseless feud to test North Town's soul. Ironically, a conflict between two Mexicano families, not between Anglos and Mexicanos, best illustrates the extent that North Town race relations remain resistant to change. The sons of two prominent Ciudadanos leaders, Commissioner Alberto Alonzo and Paulo Esposito, a former school board leader, became embroiled in a life-threatening conflict. This split within the Mexicano community turned most Anglos and many Mexicanos into spectators who watched, sometimes enthusiastically, this tragic conflict. Ultimately, political opponents and critics of the Chicano civil rights movement interpreted this fight between adolescent boys as an important symbol of the Chicano movement's moral decay and irrationality. Rather than mediating the conflict, onlookers used the incident to argue rhetorically that Mexicanos with a "La Raza mentality" were not rational, responsible citizens.

The conflict between the sons of the Alonzo and Esposito families actually occurred over the attentions an attractive young Mexicana who was the homecoming queen. The two young men argued and fought over this young woman for two years. A teen-age squabble began escalating when Jaime Alonzo threatened Juan Esposito with a rifle, but Jaime ended up losing the rifle and the fight. That left Jaime humiliated and the matter of the girl unsettled. After the shooting, the Alonzo family admitted that Jaime was wrong and tried to make amends to keep their son out of jail. The wives of both families and the local priest tried to bring the families and the boys together. Jaime's father wanted to settle the affair, but he found it hard to talk to and make peace with his old friend, Paulo Esposito. Juan's father wanted the Alonzo boy punished and put in jail.

The Alonzo boy eventually left town, and things began to settle down. But old wounds fester. And one fateful night, Jaime returned for the girl, and Juan readied for another fight. Juan was shot late that night as he exited from his car. What actually happened the night of the shooting may never be known. What *was* clear was the scar on the handsome face of Juan. Juan's father considered the shooting a cowardly and unfair attack on his son, and he sought legal remedy in the courts. Ultimately, Jaime Alonzo was charged with attempted murder of Juan Esposito and a year later a jury found him guilty. This conflict left two families that once laughed and drank together floundering in a pool of distrust and hatred. It drove the final wedge between the old Ciudadanos leaders, and neighbors and friends were forced to take sides. The Mexicano community of North Town was left badly divided.

Despite the misfortune that this incident has caused, I encountered few people outside the Esposito and Alonzo families who were sympathetic, or who tried to prevent the inevitable spiral of youthful passions. North Towners reminded me of the people in Gabriel García Márquez's brilliant allegorical tale *The Chronicle of a Death Foretold* (1982b). In this story, a young man was senselessly murdered over the honor of a woman. The townspeople did little to stop this inevitable murder. Worse still, few were able to realize their own complicity in this tragedy. They accepted the machismo that fueled the murder as natural. Some benefited personally from the murder; others lived in such isolation and solitude that they could not act. North Towners talked about their tragedy in much the same the way that the characters in this tale did.

In the streets of North Town when I was there you could hear many nasty things about Commissioner Alonzo and his family. People called him the "godfather" and claimed that he and some of his children harbored bitterness toward Anglos—that he wanted revenge on the gringos. Some claimed that he had encouraged several of his sons to be brawling machos. They said he threatened ignorant, elderly voters with cutting off their welfare. People told tales about how he once beat up an elderly Anglo woman who was a poll watcher. They told tales that he took payments under the table from cantina owners to pave their parking lots. He was supposed to be both stingy and lavish, giving credit to his customers to cheat them and courting voters with lavish, expensive beer and barbecue parties. Some said he used his political influence to manipulate the judicial process and keep his son out of jail.

In spite of such criticism, Commissioner Alonzo actually has many loyal followers among the "humildes" (the humble poor) who consider him their champion. He has continued to attack the "Anglo establishment" and Mexicano "vendidos." The Alonzos have remained active politically and emerged as *the* Mexicano family that has statewide political connections. If the family were not a symbol of the past racial and political conflicts, they could easily be a symbol of the all-American family. Like many other middle class Mexicano families, the Alonzos are a happily married couple and a tight-knit family. Like the equally close-knit Esposito family, they have accomplished many things that North Towners admire. Upon being fired for political activities, Mr. Alonzo, a labor contractor, started his own auto parts store with several thousand dollars borrowed from friends, one of whom was Paulo Esposito. He gradually built the business up and expanded to other surrounding towns. The family also opened an auto repair shop, an auto wrecker service, and a liquor store, built a new house, and sent their children to college. Nevertheless, various North Towners, including many Anglos, blamed the Alonzo-Esposito tragedy on the "La Raza" mentality that stained their town. The Alonzo boy was perceived as acting out his father's aggressive, vengeful, arrogant racial attitude toward Anglos. They claimed that such racial animosity led to an arrogant, lawless attitude that was directed towards both Mexicanos and Anglos.

But knowing and respecting both families, I can only make sense out of this tragedy as a part of the painful, confusing, political transformation occurring in North Town, *and* as the way North Towners bring up their males. This kind of macho fighting over a girl is hardly surprising. North Towners brought Jaime and Juan up playing football, "kicking ass," and "chasing chicks," but in this case, things got out of hand. The mothers and the priest were unable to prevent the boys from being like any gridiron warrior, or vato, or shit kicker. Moreover, the fathers did not help their sons resolve the conflict in an honorable way. In the end, perhaps, too many townspeople secretly wanted the fight to end in bloodshed and revenge. It is as if the winds of change had dried up the hearts' of some North Towners, and political rhetoric replaced reason. People retreated into their solitude and saw the evils of political and cultural change in what was nothing more than a senseless fight between two boys over a girl.

Some Final Reflections on Democracy in a Capitalist Culture

Watching North Town's civil rights movement sprout, seed itself, and decay has been a sobering experience. Our more detailed study of North Town politics (Foley et al.1988) summarizes the legacy of the civil rights movement. Compared to the Anglo-run political machines of the 1930s and 1940s, North Town in the 1980s had a much more competitive, robust political process. The majority of the population, the Mexicanos, were now participating in large numbers, and many autonomous Mexicano political leaders had emerged. There is a case to be made that a process of democratization was well underway in North Town. A resilient, pluralistic American political system *was* slowly incorporating yet another ethnic group. The inequities of the old segregated order had crumbled, and the new middle class Mexicano politicos had begun making the patronage system and the welfare state better serve the Mexicano working class. In spite of the new gains of social and political autonomy, however, the great majority of working class Mexicanos remained poor. The basic economic structure of North Town had not changed. There was some "trickle down" of new health, educational, housing, and public works programs to the poor of North Town. Consequently, some would argue that American democracy was alive and well in North Town, despite the absence of a major economic transformation of the region's high levels of poverty and unemployment. We (Foley et al. 1988) acknowledged these gains, but argued that this case was ultimately another example of a market economy's failure to redistribute equitably the wealth produced by working men and women.

From another vantage point, a more cultural perspective, perhaps very little had changed. Perhaps the cultural transformation needed to build a genuine democracy still eludes North Towners and America. In some ways, García Márquez's (1970) portrayal of change in a Colombian town best captures the ebb and flow of how North Town is changing. García Márquez (1982a) sees life as essentially a tragic-comic farce of good intentions, fitful starts, and foolish retreats. For him, history moves in cycles rather than in a straight line. The more things change, the more they seem to stay the same. His books are populated with vainglorious politicians, greedy capitalists, obsessive machos, forlorn wives, ruthless dictators, and naive youths. His characters are swallowed up by their isolation, fear, and mistrust. They turn inward and away from others. Idealistic politicians end up making little gold fishes in empty rooms. Men obsessed with power empty passionate women as they do their coal mines. Innocent girls become prostitutes to pay back their family debts. Family plots against family. Neighbors watch innocent people die. His characters seemed doomed to repeat endlessly a tragic cycle of growth and decay. They forsake human solidarity for barren and unloving solitude.

If I could make anthropological jargon speak with García Márquez's eloquence, the streets of North Town would have to be filled with such tragic-comic characters. For years, I have collected the negative things North Towners say about each other. Justifiably, most North Town leaders end up feeling misunderstood and maligned. Over the years, I have watched them grow disillusioned and quietly retire from the intense glare of public life. The incessant gossip about their personal lives, motivations, and honestly simply grinds them down. Some get divorced. Some move away. Others grow vegetables. And I believe some even go mad.

Most of these leaders blame the people's ignorance and lack of gratitude for their disillusionment. What they overlook is that leaders sow the maelstrom they reap. They feed the fires of gossip through their overblown, ingenuous rhetoric about their political enemies. They make these "political enemies" seem like much worse people than they really are. Commissioner Alonzo exaggerates greatly how unproductive Judge Warren is. Judge Warren exaggerates greatly how corrupt Commissioner Alonzo is. During the school board conflicts of 1974, the Anglo board members saw a hateful "La Raza revolt" in brightly colored toilets. Conversely, Mexicano parents saw a hateful racial conspiracy in an inept teacher who forgot the convertibles for their homecoming queen. During the school board conflict of 1980, the Mexicano superintendent spread rumors and innuendos about the "radical school board." The newspaper ridiculed the "fabulous four" as destroyers of the community. Such tales of misunderstanding, fear, and mistrust go on indefinitely.

As election time nears, the barbs and arrows fly, and "the people" retreat in ignorance and confusion. At least in the public sphere, North Towners have taught themselves to believe the worst about each other's intentions and motivations. They judge each other on the images that someone else has invented. They expect each other to be dishonest. Most remain complacently ignorant on the issues and the character of their candidates. No real tradition exists that demands open, face-to-face conversations between candidates or neighbors, for that matter. No mechanism exists for a genuine public discourse. Election campaigns are marked by political rhetoric and misinformation, not rational discourse.

My own explanation of how North Towners can end up watching young boys try to kill each other is influenced by a long tradition of Western social criticism (see Appendix A). Since the nineteenth century, many occidental philosophers, social scientists, and literary critics have argued that the individualism, competition, and materialism of a capitalist culture has a corrosive effect on human relationships. People tend to treat each other as if they were mere objects rather than free subjects with equal rights to life, liberty, and the pursuit of happiness. In such a society, everyday communication tends to degenerate and become instrumental or manipulative. People become better at managing impressions and their images than at communicating openly and honestly. One has to ask whether a genuine, rational political democracy is ever possible without a popular culture with more open and sincere communication.

This study partially answers that question by illustrating how our popular culture practices such as football, dating, and fiddling around in classrooms socialize North Town youth. These rituals are filled with communication that continues to reproduce class and gender inequality. Each new generation of Americans learns our republican ideals of equality and brotherhood from their textbook lessons, *but* we continue to socialize each new generation to communicate in ways that undermine our egalitarian intents and ideals.

The socially prominent youths who are best at impression management in school go on to be the town's political leaders. The communication skills that served them well in the sports, social, and classroom scenes serve them well in the public arena. They create a political discourse filled with rhetoric that distorts what other people are really like. They turn their political enemies into stereotypes and clichés. North Towners still do not know how disagree with each other without reverting to the corrupting influences of gossip and slander. They tell tales that serve their own petty interests rather the the interest of the community.

Several disillusioned North Towners articulated my cultural critique as they joked about what to call this new book I was writing. Our first book was called *From Peones [peons] to Politicos [politicians]* . At least three people suggested that I call this book *From Politicos [politicians] to Pendejos [dumb asses]*. One vato expressed my "fancy" academic theory of "miscommunication and capitalist culture" in his own language. One might call this gem of common sense the vato "folk theory" of miscommunication and capitalist culture. Many other North Towners also expressed these sentiments, although not in such colorful, forceful prose:

We will never learn in this fucking town. We Mexicans want that little job to make a living. This Mexican will run. Then others will, and we will start a little conflict and say this and that and make a big deal out of it. Now we run two or three Mexicans in one slot and the gringos are laughing their asses off. This little community, it's like all others. Politics is nothin' but a bunch of rumors. Everybody [Mexicanos and Anglos] just wants to talk about something and each other. They are all fucking bored, so somebody starts a story. Then somebody's pissed off. Everything gets real personal. They take it out on each other. We aren't fucking ready to lead nobody. Anyway, the fucking gringos are the same. It's all talk, talk, talk.

The juggernaut of cultural change has left many North Towners as frustrated with the progress of their own community as I am. Some leave in despair, and others stay and keep trying to change things. Lest my tale end too sadly, however, I must add that exceptional people do rise out of this swirl of miscommunication and disunity. Like García Márquez, I too see a little magic in unexpected places and people. Some of his characters find loving pursuits and make a real contribution to their fellow human beings. Fame and fortune elude them, but they live life with nobility and dignity. North Town has its fair share of such people, too. They stay and doggedly try to make North Town a better place. For me, one person symbolizes what kind of people are needed to continue the civil rights movement's original goal—a more egalitarian culture and political democracy.

Beyond Disunity and Miscommunication: The Man with a Band

The unlikely story of Dante Aguila, the high school band director, exemplifies what North Town desperately needs to evolve culturally and politically. Ironically, Mr. Aguila came to North Town the same year our research project began. He stayed and quietly built something that goes far beyond the music he plays for Friday night half-time shows. Some North Towners appreciate Mr. Aguila, but to others he is no more miraculous than an evening rain.

So what has he done that might inspire such praise? It is simple. He has ignored all the petty conflict and politics around him and become the best band director he could be. He inherited a small, average, 80-member band that was predominantly white and well off. When our study ended, he had a 220-member band that was the best in the state. Even more important, the band was a cross-section of North Town—rich, poor, white, brown, male, female—and they worked together to achieve their full potential. Unlike the politicians, Dante Aguila leads by quiet example. He has pursued excellence rather than personal glory and power. The result has been a blossoming and harmonizing of youthful talents.

Upon seeing him again, I asked him for my bi-annual rundown on the tribulations of being North Town's band director. During our last conversation, I finally grasped what this man was all about. I congratulated him for winning the state class III marching band contest. He had come close several times, but in 1987 he had finally won it all. We reminisced that he had come a long way since 1973. Then, he admitted knowing nothing about teaching marching band and hated it. He considered himself a musician, not some "damn half-time show." I asked him to explain his transformation, hence the bands.

Aguila had resolved to create a band that reflected his community and his culture, a band that "could play the shit out of good music and march at the same time!" He decided to settle into North Town and meet the challenge. The only thing he wanted was to be left alone to do things his way. The first year he got caught in the racial conflict and saw his young white liberal assistant leave. But he gradually won the confidence of the band boosters and kids and educated himself about marching bands. He went to statewide workshops, visited university band practice sessions, and studied the styles of drum and bugle corps. Over the years, he developed his own style of band that often plays uptempo International Latino sounds to intricate, snappy drum and bugle corps marching routines.

As we watched the videotapes of his band, he explained how the marching movements complemented the music in an esthetic that pleased him. He had made the horrifying idea of marching band music into something artistically challenging and pleasing. Then, over the years, he had figured out how to teach people to march without the military routine and practice that other band directors use. In the end, the band reflected his own sense of music and style. But, as Dante Aguila explained, this was what prevented them from reaching the excellence he desired. The band was technically superior to other bands and performed well, but somehow they never captured the judges' imagination. After several years of soul searching, he came to the realization that he, and therefore his band, lacked "pizzazz." The band, like Aguila, was rock-solid, dependable, and extremely competent, but not "showy" enough. The band constantly understated how good it really was. So he changed the band until it "sold itself better."

The irony of this story is that Dante Aguila, in his quiet pursuit of excellence, has rarely been able to toot his own horn to the school board. In spite of his success, he finds himself without a long-promised band hall. He must also contend with the threat he creates for coaches trying to build a football team. His band has grown so successful that more and more males are choosing it over football—a remarkable accomplishment considering the culture of machismo. I reminded him of the stories I had heard about "band fags," and asked how it was possible to change that. He admitted that football was, and probably always will be, number one. But he had made music and performing well in faraway places attractive. Even "real males" wanted to join in and make music.

He structures his practices so the footballers, if they can play the music, are allowed to miss practices yet still participate. If players cannot march during fall half-time shows, they can during winter concerts or spring contests. This requires him to hold more section practices at night and on weekends, and he does. As a result, everyone who wants to can participate. He listens to their excuses, trusts them, and tells them what he wants. He admits to running a "loose ship" compared to most band directors, but his flexibility creates loyalty. The kids make sure that those who miss practices must catch up, if they want to be a part of the band. Band practices exude a kind of esprit de corps and unity. Dante's democratic leadership inspires this mutual trust and common purpose. In short, the band has a spirit of community that North Town lacks. The town has lost the sense of community it once may have had because of the painful historical process of change. North Town needs many more citizens like Mr. Aguila to end the cycles of conflict and rebuild the trust and communication needed for a more democratic, egalitarian community.

Of course, some social critics will argue that more "good people" will not transform the root cause of what ails most modern societies. They would argue that American society is founded on a ruthlessly competitive, materialistic economy, and that, therefore, these larger historical forces must be changed. The economy that drives us to such great technological heights also resigns us to the solitary pursuit of our own dehumanization. I would tend to agree with such "structuralist" assessments, but that would not stop me from celebrating the good men and women I know. We must find a way to unleash these people and to build a way of life that does not destroy our humanity. I have no blueprint for such a utopia, but I do know that life is too short, and the lives of Juan and Jaime are too precious, to ignore the music that Dante Aguila plays.

A Performance Theory of Cultural Reproduction and Resistance

As I indicated in the Introduction, I have purposely separated these theoretical reflections from the ethnography to better communicate with two distinct audiences. I felt it was impossible to write an engaging popular ethnography full of real people and events that was also full of dense, technical class theory jargon. A separate theoretical essay also makes possible a fuller, more systematic presentation of the ideas used to explain the ethnographic data in Chapters 1 through 5. This essay, which is divided into two parts, represents the intellectual foundation and value premises on which the empirical study is based.

Part 1 of this essay is a more philosophical discussion of how I have rephrased and synthesized general class and cultural theory. Studying existing reproduction and resistance theories, made it clear that these versions of class theory were not sufficiently cultural. Part 1 provides a detailed account of how diverse class and cultural concepts can be unified into a new kind of cultural critique of everyday communication. This represents my general views on doing cultural critiques of capitalism, and it is the philosophical foundation of my performance theory.

Part 2 outlines the concept of cultural reproduction and distinguishes it from economic reproduction. It then conceptualizes the school as a site for the performance of popular culture practices. The major communicative moments of these popular culture practices are highlighted, and a performance theory of reproduction and resistance is presented as an alternative to the existing studies of cultural hegemony. This performance theory is a new explanation of how schools "culturally reproduce" social class inequalities and provoke resistance from working class students.

The Appendix ends with a response to Paul Willis's comments in the

Foreword and suggests some ways in which the perspective of this account differs from his perspective. These concluding remarks also address briefly the concerns of other educational anthropologists and sociologists as to why some American ethnic minorities fail at higher rates than others.

Part I: Philosophical Foundations

In truth, I initiated this study of North Town High School without a fully developed theoretical or interpretive perspective. Many ethnographers go to the field with a provisional set of ideas that develop during and after the fieldwork. Initially, Erving Goffman's dramaturgical theory of role performances seemed like a useful interpretive perspective (see Goffman 1959, 1961a, 1961b, 1963, 1967, 1974, 1979). Goffman describes the petty politics and ritualized communications so characteristic of modern organizations. Students were a good deal like the inmates in Goffman's "total institutions" (mental hospitals, prisons, concentration camps). They were constantly searched, monitored, punished, and resocialized to be more polite, subservient, and orderly, and less individualistic. Schools were middle class bureaucratic organizations dedicated to stripping kids of their ethnic identity and replacing it with an institutional, mainstream identity.

On the other hand, in the face of authoritarian schools, the student inmates endlessly rebelled and created their own identities and spaces. The working class ethnic kids were particularly subjected to the most relentless stripping and resocialization. Goffman's view of these rituals of degradation and rebellion seemed more realistic than the deterministic correspondence model of socialization in early Marxist studies of schools (Bowles and Gintis 1976). In 1974, I substituted the word "worker" for "inmate" in Goffman's studies and was off and running.

At the time, my formal understanding of class theory was still a mishmash of early Marx and various theories of imperialism, dependency, and underdevelopment. My graduate work at Stanford University in the 1960s was primarily a positivist potpourri of psychological behaviorism, abstract sociological empiricism, and anthropological ethnoscience. The main thing I learned at Stanford was a deep respect for grounding theory in empirical fieldwork. Most graduate students I knew learned class theory in the streets and in sit-ins during anti-war protests. I generally followed the early SDS perspective on American society. The young Progressive Labor types, Maoists, and other doctrinaire Marxist sects were too sober and dogmatic. Conversely, the whole hippie movement, with its strong anti-materialist, anti-productivist, anarchistic orientation appealed to me.

Stanford, although a very challenging intellectual environment, was a place that juxtaposed itself against earlier personal experiences full of class lessons. My first, and possibly most enduring, teacher of class theory was Mr. Niel, the owner of the Tama State Bank and our farm. He would visit us in his black Cadillac when he wanted his barns painted white or his share of the crops. When he left, the men in our family always expressed their hatred for him and all landlords and bankers. I have seen Mr. Niel again in many other parts of the world. As a Peace Corps teacher in the Philippines, I saw his international, imperial side. As an anti-war protester, I saw his paranoid, violent side as well as the timidity of the intelligentsia. As an anthropological fieldworker in rural America, I saw his racist, sexist side. Then I spent ten years reading social theory. Mr. Niel was the one kernel of truth that the philosophical tomes on class theory always explained.

Inter-Marxist Ethnographies of Reproduction

Leaving the field, I began searching through the anthropology and sociology of education literature for new models of class analysis. Many earlier sociological studies of schools and youth (Lynd and Lynd 1937; Hollingshead 1949) demonstrated class bias with demographic-type data. Middle class kids got lots of preferential treatment through placement in the top academic tracks, higher grades, less punishment, and higher teacher expectations and rewards (Rist 1973; Persell 1977; Oakes 1985). Moreover, their literacy advantage showed up in research on testing, reading, and general achievement orientation. There was also literature showing that middle class teachers preferred the language, manners, dress, and deportment of kids from their own class. More recently, others have shown that middle class schools and classrooms actually teach or spend more time on tasks, use more varied instructional materials, and have more permissive, trusting discipline patterns (Anyon 1980,1981; Sieber and Gordon 1981; Wilcox 1982).

By the late 1970s a few new Marxist-oriented researchers had studied how classes were "reproduced" in the everday life of schools (Larkin 1977; Apple 1979, 1982; Willis 1981). In addition, several new Marxist or critical theory analyses of schools and classrooms appeared (Everhart 1983; Giroux 1983; Carnoy and Levin 1985; McNiel 1986; Weis 1986; McLaren 1986; MacLeod 1987). Paul Willis (1981), in particular, describes the class struggle over ideological hegemony on the level of everyday classroom interactions in a British school. His fine ethnography details the daily battles of working class lads against the urban school with its bourgeois mentality and middle class teachers. The lads, following the shop floor culture of their fathers, proudly expressed a working class culture that glories in manual labor, physicality, aggressive, bawdy humor and manners, and machismo sexuality. This counter school culture simultaneously preserved the kids' working class cultural style and honor and relegated them to school failure, hence working class jobs.

Without a doubt, Willis's was the first detailed, ethnographic portrayal of exactly how communicative behavior in school reproduced the class relations of the larger society. Willis, himself of working class extraction, shows a keen sensitivity for what these kids experienced in schools. At the time, I thought his concept of class was "pure" and Marxist, rather than some "eclectic," revised Weberian theory of class. In addition, his idea of class cultures purports to introduce anthropological concepts into class theory. At the time, it seemed like the most important piece written for my study, a kind of missing link between class theory and everyday culture and communication. My first reaction was delight, but also envy, since Willis seemed to have beaten me to the proverbial punch. He had produced a new kind of class theory that took the "cultural" into account.

Class Cultures: The View of Paul Willis

The real innovation in Willis's work seemed to be the notion of class cultures, that is, talking about social classes as distinct everyday ways of life. For Willis, following Raymond Williams (1977) and E. P. Thompson (1966), class cultures are lived, profane experiences rooted in working class communities that struggle against bourgeois ideological dominance. Working class people construct their own distinct, rewarding, honorable ways of life. Other work at the Centre for Contemporary Cultural Studies at the University of Birmingham (Clarke et al. 1979) shows this way of life to be rooted in their pubs, soccer matches, row flats and youth gangs, and, most of all, in the manual labor of the shop floors. This class culture values rough physical labor, bravery, loyalty to mates, fighting, dominating women sexually, confronting managers and owners, and surviving as independently as possible from urban corporate lifestyles.

Subsequently, this line of thought was labeled "cultural Marxism," and tedious debates over "culture vs. political economy" and "voluntarism vs. structural determinism" ensued. Several authors chronicle the interminable wrangles between the two titans of French and English Marxism, Louis Althusser and E. P. Thompson, and how Thompson's English peers line up (Samuel 1981). The Birmingham Centre for Cultural Studies (CCCS) has produced a series of in-house theoretical debates on ideology

(CCCS 1977), culture (Hall et al. 1980), history (CCCS 1982), and several empirical critiques of the English state (Hall et al. 1978), student-subcultures (Hall et al. 1976), school reforms (CCCS 1981) and racism (CCCS 1982). These complex theoretical debates filter over to America through interpreters of these interpreters of class theory. From Willis's writings, it is unclear exactly how his theory emerges from these debates or general intellectual discourse. This is, however, the general context of his thought.

Willis is often celebrated here in America for putting subjectivity and voluntarism, that is, people, the heroic working class, back into class analysis. He purportedly rescues class analysis from the structural determinism and functionalism of "reproduction theorists" such as Bowles and Gintis (1976) and Bourdieu and Passeron (1977). Initially, I found myself applauding "cultural Marxism" and Willis's "cultural production" theory of class reproduction for political reasons. If the lads were putting up a good fight, it at least suggested that schools do not easily grind workers into alienating jobs. Moreover, the broad theoretical project of combining cultural and class theory seemed correct. What follows is somewhat critical of Willis, but this work remains indebted to him and should be read as a variation from and a development of his ideas.

Perhaps some of the limitations in Willis's notion of class cultures can be traced back to E. P. Thompson's perspective on class. Thompson claims to have introduced a more anthropological culture concept into class theory. He emphasizes that working class cultural institutions spring from the development of a proletarian labor movement. The working class, particularly the artisan sector of the class, creates a political movement with a nascent socialist ideology and various educational organs, such as newspapers, workers' meetings, festivals, and social events. Each development of an autonomous working class culture is indexed to the degree that it ideologically breaks with bourgeois ideology, Methodism, liberalism, and the literary high culture, thus consciously creating a counter-ideology based on socialist ideology (Thompson 1966).

In Willis's work, these "breakthroughs" during ideological struggles are called "penetrations," and the inegalitarian residues (such as sexism and racism) in working class ideology are called "limitations." The dominant model of culture in both these works is clearly based on an ideal type dichotomy of bourgeois versus socialist ideology. As the working class culture develops a conscious socialist ideology and political organization, it wages an ideological struggle against the hegemony of bourgeois ideas. This emphasis on a counter-culture as the socialist ideology of class consciousness is, of course, strongly reminiscent of Antonio Gramsci

(1971). In Thompson, and Gramsci as well, a working class community is defined in the restricted sense of a political community able to act "for-itself." The culture of that type of community is what political scientists would call its political culture.

Thompson's and Willis's idea of culture as ideology or class conscious-ness is based on their acceptance of the Marxian premise that the route to human freedom and the development of a social self is through control over one's labor. In this view, humans are what they actively create together. They are free subjects only when they have overcome the alienat-ing "objectification" they experience as isolated wage slaves under a ruthlessly competitive capitalist system. The basis of human freedom and a humanizing culture is, therefore, the collective action of alienated workers to create a new, modern egalitarian socialist culture. They throw off the yoke of being individualistic, commodified objects and create a propertyless production system of united, free workers who do not sell their labor and hence their human subjectivity. The essence of a new, democratic socialist society is a way of life that guarantees cooperation and communal property rather than individualism, competitiveness, and private property. Again, all this implies a democratic culture and politics or "political culture."

Willis's concept of working class culture also contains elements of a more anthropological concept of culture. Willis describes the "profane" character of working class cultural forms and expressiveness that he documents with rich descriptive ethnographies of bikers and school lads (1976, 1981). Conversely, one finds in Thompson rather vague discus-sions of "lived experience," which he has struggled to clarify in later works as "lived experience" and "perceived experience" (Samuel 1981). Willis sometimes uses Thompson's metaphors, but he and others at the Birmingham Centre for Contemporary Cultural Studies have done their own working class community studies. These studies often vividly portray the everyday expression of working class culture in community pubs, playing fields, peer groups, families, and dialect speech (Clarke et al. 1979). The working class has a distinct set of what anthropologists would call expressive cultural practices, for example, talking, eating, joking, playing, storytelling, singing, dancing, dressing. They have a distinct life-style and way of living and expressing themselves that is not bourgeois; but this type of cultural distinctiveness may or may not have anything to do with the formation of a working class political culture with a socialist ideology and workers' organizations.

On a general level, Willis's perspective can be applauded for its dy-namic, materialist conception of culture. His concept of class culture suggests that marginalized groups (ethnics, youth, women) actively struggle against the dominant ideology and invent new, counter-hegemonic cultural forms. Willis's view suggests that whatever distinct cultural practices one finds among groups, they have a material base and are socially constructed in struggle. In other words, everyday group cultural practices are what people invent to find dignity in an oppressive class society.

This idea of invented, emergent cultural practices and forms contrasts with the anthropological notion of a historical cultural tradition that is passively inherited. An ethnic culture's cultural practices and forms are, therefore, whatever the group invent from their present struggle *and* from their past. Such a process is ceaseless, is always reflective of deeper societal contradictions, and is always some unpredictable synthesis of the old and new. If "ethnic cultural forms" are produced or created in a historical class context rather than passively inherited, "cultural distinctiveness" becomes problematic and impossible to study without reference to ongoing class struggles.

In terms of general class theory, Willis also makes an important contribution. Apparently following Williams (1977, 1981), he takes a materialist perspective that avoids relying on a copy theory of consciousness. The expression of human consciousness is never a copy or simple reflection of the society's material base. One's position in the production system does ultimately "determine" the cultural forms one expresses. However, the economic "base" does not determine the "superstructure" (consciousness and ideas) in a direct, unproblematic way. For Willis, working class lads invent their cultural forms in opposition to the school's petty bourgeois cultural forms and in solidarity with the "shop floor" culture of their fathers.

In his formulation there is ideological struggle. One cannot predict what working class cultural forms will arise, or when. There are historical moments when cultural forms are created. This process of creation is always dialectical, always depends on the composition and recomposition of classes struggling at a given moment. Although there is nothing new about saying that classes are dialectical moments of struggle, this rephrasing of original Marxian principles does have a new focus on ideology and cultural practices. The study of ideological struggles or clashes between "class cultures" is, therefore, made a relevant part of general class analysis.

On the other hand, Willis's notion of culture remains somewhat ambiguous and undeveloped. He tends to combine at least the following three concepts of culture: culture-as-ideology, culture-as-core-values, and culture-as-cultural-forms. His influential ethnography *Learning to Labor* best illustrates this uneasy synthesis. The first part of the book is a vivid, ethnographic description of what I would call the distinctive, expressive, everyday culture of the rebellious lads. There is no doubt about their distinctiveness from working class "earholes" who conform to main-stream values and teachers in terms of core values and expressive styles. The second part of the book is a long, difficult-to-decipher discourse on class cultures as an ideology. In this section, he clearly privileges the concept of culture as an ideology. As indicated, working class culture is an unfinished egalitarian consciousness marred by sexism and racism. In the theory section, the lads' cultural practices used to resist the bourgeois domination of teachers are indicators of a nascent political consciousness. These cultural expressions and forms are a reflection of the class division of labor in society.

Ultimately, the real difference between working class lads and the "earholes"—and hence working class culture and the bourgeois/petty bourgeois culture—is that the lads value manual labor over mental labor. Willis goes on to suggest that a number of class differences in core cultural values arise from this division of labor. We find working class lads glori-fying a macho style that emphasizes physical prowess, bravery, fighting, drinking, cursing, making fun of authority, and oppressing women and ethnic minorities. The problem with all this, as feminists would point out, is that Willis has described the values of most males, regardless of class. Most of the cultural value differences that supposedly differentiate be-tween classes tend to be true of bourgeois/petty bourgeois males as well. What remains, then, are certain stylistic or expressive cultural differences between the lads and "earholes," but Willis's conception of working class culture as ideology leaves the question of cultural practices somewhat undeveloped. The culture concept that prevails is one that emphasizes ideological consciousness, not distinct expressive cultural practices.

What Willis's data in *Learning to Labor* actually show is that the lads are not a class culture ideologically. Some of his English critics (e.g, Woods 1983) are quick to point out that the lads hardly seem "conscious" of being a political class acting in some planned, rational sense "for themselves." Willis's data do support talking about the lads as a class culture in the sense of their distinct expressive culture practices. In a later article on cultural forms and "cultural politics" Willis and Corrigan (1983) suggest that such behaviors are class phenomena, even though an explicit ideology or consciousness is lacking. This kind of Marxist sleight-of-hand is, of course, unacceptable to most positivists and empiricists. Does a working class culture have to have class consciousness to be a class culture or not?

Ultimately, Willis at least implicitly uses a classic Marxist "false consciousness" defense to answer empiricist critics' demands for "operational measures" of a working class culture. The lads are a working class even if they do not explicitly understand their progressive class role. They understand that the school authorities are offering them false hopes and are busy humiliating them. More importantly, the lads are objectively a class due to their position in the division of labor. They show elements of ideological progressiveness, but their penetration of the ideological fog is only "limited." They have yet to "penetrate" capitalist ideology and discover the truth that Marxist theory reveals. Unfortunately, this discussion of partial consciousness and ideology in this sense leaves unexplained why various expressive cultural practices such as student joking, bad manners, and assorted pranks signify class interests. Willis's concept of their cultural politics as limited class consciousness relies too heavily on one notion of ideology in Marx that ultimately does not explain why such expressive acts are reflections of deeper class realities. Marxian class theory contains a better explanation, which Willis does not use.

Two Views of Ideology in Marx's Original Class Theory

In Marx's writing, there are at least two views of ideology. First, capitalist rulers and their cadre of intellectuals create explicit, conscious sets of ideas about politics, economics, aesthetics, and all aspects of social life. They portray capitalism as the final or universal solution to humanity's problem of materially surviving and prospering. Ideology is the hegemony of one class's ideas over another's. These ideas exist and are taught in a myriad of public institutions and can be empirically studied as the ideological tradition and practices of a particular capitalist political culture. This is essentially the way Willis seems to define classes and class ideology.

I would agree with all that, but would argue that he tends to lose sight of the more philosophical way of defining ideology. This second perspective is a totally different notion of ideology and class consciousness. In this version of class theory, ideology is any form of social activity that enacts the fundamental logic of class relationships. People unreflectively act out this exploitive logic by tending to treat each other like dead objects rather than living subjects. Consequently, the character of our everyday relationships becomes hidden from us. Ideology is not the conscious ideas that people are taught but the unreflective way we treat each other as commodities. In this sense, there is no ruling class socializing a working class.

There is only a vast unspoken, unrecognized, ideological process that makes the commodity logic of capitalism seem normal and natural. Retaining this dual notion of ideology or class consciousness is important if one wants to do more cultural analysis of class phenomena.

In addition, it is important to retain the two distinct views of social classes in Marx. First and foremost, social classes are historical groups that emerge from the new forces of a capitalist mode of production. Two great contradictory classes—capitalists, who own the means of production, and the proletariat, wage laborers, who produce profit for the capitalists—are locked in a struggle of economic interests. A number of other class sectors,—pettybourgeoisie, intelligentsia, peasantry, and "lumpen" proletariat—are intermediary class positions with minimal or no control over the means of production. They also have varying degrees of political influence, privilege, and autonomy as wage laborers or small capitalists. Depending on historical developments, some members of intermediary class sectors can and do become traitors to the capitalist class to which they serve as functionaries. A series of complex debates over "new classes" and class recomposition exists on the intricacies of recent changes in class sectors (Cleaver 1979; Braverman 1974; Gouldner 1980; Gorz 1981). Generally, Willis seems to subscribe to this classical Marxist definition of social classes as historical groups with varying positions in the production system. Without pursuing the discussions of changing class composition in advanced capitalist societies, I would concur with this classical Marxist view of economic classes as real people making history and defending their class interests.

The original Marxist view of social classes contains, however, an additional, more cultural way of talking about social classes that Max Weber subsequently developed. Weber's notion of status groups shifted the discussion of social classes from groups with different positions in the production system to groups with different lifestyles and status displays of consumption. In effect, this view of social classes emphasizes the question of a public social identity that marks a person's group. The market produces a barrage of commodities that people use to mark the boundaries between themselves. The expression of self through consumption becomes the central cultural practice of a capitalist society. Bourgeois sociology subsequently developed elaborate measures of what people think their social class, that is, status group, is. A. B. Hollingshead (1949) aptly labels these lifestyle or status display groups "class cultures." Since, however, mainline sociology perceived its primary task as refuting the Marxist view of classes, a false dichotomy was constructed between cultural status groups and economic classes. Consequently, the bourgeois concept of class cultures was divorced from any view of classes as part of the production system.

Recent critical sociology (Bourdieu 1984) has, however, reconnected this Weberian notion of cultural status groups to the original class formulation. Pierre Bourdieu reintroduces the ideal of a bourgeois class culture that ideologically dominates through its "superior" cultural practices. Such status groups are part of the cultural reproduction of capital that perpetuates class inequalities. This view of classes emphasizes the way that various groups of people enact the cultural logic of the production system rather than who controls the system. Marx would surely not disagree with Bourdieu's more Weberian view of social classes as cultural status display groups, because this "cultural" or subjective view of classes logically follows from his discussion of alienated labor and the riddle of commodity fetishism. Marx never discussed capitalist culture or class cultures of status display practices, but he expected the commodity logic of materialistic bourgeois society to trap people in such alienating, dehumanizing relations and self expressions. The more philosophical discussions of class and class consciousness can, therefore, easily incorporate both an "economic" (controlling the mode of production) and a "cultural" (displaying the cultural logic) definition of social classes. Cultural studies of class need to use both general definitions of social class. The class culture concept is a way of focusing class analysis on the cultural politics of how economic classes are culturally reproduced and resisted.

Redefining the Concept of Labor: Back to Marx Through Habermas

One important key to linking such disparate views of class conceptually is to retain and rephrase Marx's notions of labor and objectification in an idiom more suited to analyzing everyday cultural practices. The recent work of Habermas (1975, 1979, 1985, 1987), although an attempt radically to revise and overturn class theory, is a useful elaboration and rephrasing of Marx's more philosophical view of social classes. The following section will present a general view of Habermas's perspective as the first step in redefining Willis's class culture concept. This perspective allows one to redefine class cultures as alienated communicative labor and qualitatively different types of speech practices. This conceptual move has the general effect of shifting the study of class cultures from the study of ideological hegemony and consciousness to the study of cultural practices that display different class identities.

Alvin Gouldner's (1980) historiography of Marxism suggests two major ways of reading Marx: a positivist, political economy view and a critical, Hegelian philosophical view. Habermas's project is to restate Marx's Hegelian side in a modern social science language. Habermas explicitly drops the whole Marxist-Hegelian labor theory of objectification as alienated wage labor. This severs the connection between Marx's discussion of arrested subjectivity and the rise of a new, progressive subjectivity, the universal class to end all classes, the proletariat. It also drops the teleological assumption Marx inherits from the Enlightenment, that history has a rational, progressive direction.

Instead of ontologically grounding the rational potential of humanity in a particular historical class, Habermas grounds his theory in the general, inherent rational potential of everyday speech acts themselves. Borrowing from J. R. Searle, Habermas argues that a smoothly functioning language game rests on a background consensus between those interacting on the following grounds: (1) the utterance is understandable, (2) its propositional content is true, (3) its speaker is sincere in uttering it, and (4) it is right or appropriate for the speaker to be performing the speech act. In more recent works (1985,1987) this position is further developed with George Mead's view of communication as mutual understanding through taking on the roles of others. Communicative action, therefore, has an inherent social and naively trusting basis. In free, open, trusting dialogic speech lies the ontological basis for uncoerced intersubjectivity, and hence the potential for a rational, truly democratic political culture and society.

In Habermas's formulation, no progressive proletarian class congealed together through political struggle against exploitation is needed to rescue human intersubjectivity. People need only to recognize how the spread of a "technological rationality" and a vast administrative system in late capitalism is threatening the inherent intersubjective and rational qualities of our everyday communication. For those familiar with the gloomy, deterministic views of the early Frankfurt school this probably sounds familiar, yet is also a new optimistic turn. In contrast, the Frankfurt school ended up seeing cultural domination everywhere, and only found hope in avant-garde artistic expressions.

Habermas shares a number of the Frankfurt school's views of capitalist culture. The cultural life in modern capitalism is generally portrayed as far from his notion of ideal communication. A cultural crisis exists in which people live highly privatized lives. Older comprehensive world views based on religion and the work ethic have given way to the new world view of instrumental rationality. Under such a rationality, public policies are justified on the grounds of efficiency. A rational policy is one that works and perpetuates the society. Within such a logic, questions of legal procedure replace questions of distributive justice. We find policy-makers advocating killing efficiently (clean bombs) or "urban renewal" projects that displace massive numbers of people rather than house them. Generally, politics and political thought become forms of disinformation and miscommunication. Ethical considerations of public policies give way to systems-maintenance questions. Habermas calls this new form of rationality the "technological rationality." Engineers, lawyers, and specialists in procedures and techniques replace philosophers and critical thinkers. The technocrats run and maintain rather than question society. The administrative subsystems of a vast new welfare state threaten the "life-world" or everyday culture of people.

In the public sphere of everyday culture, ordinary people also increasingly communicate with each other in instrumental ways. Everyday communication also comes under the sway of these new cultural values. Communicative norms and intentions give way to widespread forms of instrumentality. People increasingly treat each other like objects to be managed rather than free and equal expressive subjects. As policy-makers, intellectuals, and ordinary people unreflectively communicate in this manner, the whole culture is threatened with the loss of its general capacity for rational, critical thought and for open, sincere communication. In effect, modern capitalist culture is not developing the cultural or communicative practices essential for a genuine political democracy.

Habermas (1985, 1987) carefully explicates how Marx's original insight into the "riddle of commodity fetishisms" has been taken up by the Frankfurt school and other major Western social theorists. He outlines how the Weberian concept of "rationalization" and the Lukacsian concept of "reification" extended Marx's ideas and preceded his theory of communicative action. He claims that his theory overcomes the limits of these earlier critiques of capitalist modernity, because he avoids critical theorists' pessimism about ideological hegemony and Marx's and Lukacs's optimism about the progressive proletariat.

In an optimistic turn, Habermas argues that the spread of a technological rationality does not necessarily lobotomize the citizens of modern capitalist states. The inherent character of communication and speech acts, mutual understanding, trust, truthfulness, and sincerity are resistant to total instrumentalization. Consequently, there are signs everywhere (in various new critical social movements of environmentalists, feminists, gays, and so on) that citizens subjected to increasingly administered public policies and cultural life are developing new levels of public morality and consciousness.

In addition, Habermas finds in the developmental psychology of Piaget and Kohlberg the grounds for an evolutionary theory of society to replace Marx's class theory. His later views (1981) are surprisingly like anthropologist Gregory Bateson's (1972) notion of cultural evolution. Bateson sees great potential in "deutero-learning," the growing potential of people to learn how to learn if they avoid certain logical errors of thought. Without presenting a systematic comparison, both of these communication theorists end up suggesting the need for humanity to evolve cognitively as opposed to making class revolutions. Habermas ultimately suggests that cognitive and moral evolution under capitalism may be producing new forms of critical rationality among some citizens.

The other major basis for Habermas's optimism that capitalism is reaching a crisis point is his view of how the capitalist state works. Modern capitalist economies require the political state generally to play a much greater role in managing the economy. This leads to all sorts of attempts to plan growth and manage it through monetary and fiscal policies and direct investments. In addition, a huge welfare state develops to care for the educational, health, aging, and labor market needs of workers. Such state interventionism makes clear to people that class interests are behind the supposedly neutral state and political process; consequently, the state itself becomes "repoliticized" or subject to the increasing redistributive demands of various groups. The state, therefore, increasingly suffers "legitimation crises" trying to justify its own failings and the failings of capitalist business cycles. Big, inefficient government bureaucracies with greater and greater steering tasks and managerial powers have limited capacities. They are unable to rationalize the chaotic capitalist production system, or to institute an effective, efficient state-run alternative. The end result is a paradoxically stronger, more centralized capitalist state, which has more functions and more employees but less capacity to steer the entire international system of capitalist states.

Further, the huge growth of "unproductive" or non-commodity producing labor has also diminished the progressive role of a classic proletariat of angry, underpaid "productive" laborers. This new horde of educated, unproductive workers grow restless, however, because of economic exploitation and increasing cultural hegemony . Their growing political awareness confronts a ruling class that can barely rule. Ultimately, a legitimation crisis emerges from this faltering social system that can neither solve its production problems nor socialize everyone into obedience.

In effect, Habermas substitutes a kind of left-wing systems theory model for Marx's political economy perspective. Various subsystems—cultural, political, economic—undergo crises and ultimately cannot create a new unifying value consensus, despite their cultural hegemony. Nor can the new forms of state interventionism manage and orchestrate economic crises. Capitalism increasingly becomes a dysfunctional social system that breaks down and fails. Ultimately, a new, more rational, cognitively evolved citizenry emerges to challenge and reform capitalism. Habermas sees more progressive potential in the social movements of the educated new middle class than in the old industrial proletariat.

There is much that is interesting in Habermas's synthesis of modern social science writings with Marxian thought. Habermas is the latest, perhaps most thorough revisionist of the Hegelian elements in Marx's theory of capitalism. In all of Habermas's writings, there is, however, no explicit discussion of why Marx's ideas on money, labor markets, capital accumulation, the circuits of capital reproduction, and imperialism no longer explain how the world capitalist economy works. Nor is there any serious discussion of the new class theory debates on how the proletariat is being historically reconstructed in a world capitalist system. Habermas must show that Marx's nineteenth-century model of the capitalist mode of production no longer explains how twentieth-century capitalism works. His argument that increased system complexity and state interventionism has rendered class antagonisms innocuous suffers from the same abstract, ahistorical quality that all systems theory suffers. In the end, his vast conceptual framework is only vaguely connected to any analysis of the changing capitalist political economy or historical events.

Many mainstream social scientists read Habermas as a total and successful revision of Marx. Another way to read him is as an enrichment of class theory that needs to be appropriated back into empirical class analysis. The key assumption this position rests upon is that Marx's notion of labor anticipates Habermas's theory of communicative action. The fundamental idea in Habermas's new critical theory of communicative action is not new. Marx's discussions on the riddle of commodity fetishism have simply been updated with new concepts of speech and communication.

If one reads Marx's notion of labor the way Shlomo Avineri (1968) and Richard Bernstein (1971) do, and examines how Marx talks about "sensuous labor," one discovers a broader concept of labor in Marx's early and later writings (1947, 1964, 1974). For Marx, people also "objectify" themselves outside work and the production system. He talks at length about what most anthropologists would call shared, expressive, "non-productive" cultural practices such as eating, dancing, singing, joking, and myth-making. Such sensuous human activities are intersubjective or communicative. They "objectify" or humanize through social solidarity and communal social practices, and fulfill or express people's inherently social nature. This more cultural notion of activity or labor has disappeared in the discussion of class and class struggle by production-oriented, traditional political Marxists. This broader notion of sensuous labor, although not presented as a formal theory of capitalist culture in Marx, anticipates Habermas's model of capitalist culture as reified communications practices. What Habermas does, which is not a small intellectual feat, is further to develop Marx's idea of alienated labor activity into a general theory of communicative action.

Labor or human activity in the cultural sense is simply everyday communication. Habermas asks, "What is the quality of our everday communication (communicative labor)?" We live in a society with a vast new culture industry that ceaselessly appropriates and shapes our sense of ourselves and our everyday cultural or communicative practices. Without knowing it, are we all laboring in what the Italian new left (Tronti 1973; Baldi 1972) calls the "social factory"? Are we all reproducing a culture that devalues open, honest communication, hence intersubjectivity? This is the same question that Marx raised originally. Perhaps what Habermas and others in Western Marxism have done is to keep alive this question in the face of Marxist dogmatism and economic reductionism. Reading Habermas in this manner allows one to reappropriate his novel rephrasing of Marx's Hegelian labor theory back into a political economy or class perspective. This reformulation focuses the sweeping alienated labor thesis on the qualitative character of everyday communication.

The question then becomes how to study "labor" defined in the broader sense as communication/miscommunication. Such studies would focus on "communicative labor" in the "social factory" of everyday life and in "non-productive" cultural institutions such as schools, media, and families. Marx would have asked how such institutionalized practices of miscommunication or alienated communicative labor reproduce economic social classes and resistance to class domination. Habermas, having abandoned the notion of class altogether, does not, of course, ask such a question. Nor does he ask whether instrumental speech practices, that is, the logic of capital, are more characteristic of the bourgeois/petty bourgeois class than of the proletariat. Instead, Habermas is concerned with the general reification of communication in the "lifeworld" or culture. For him, the process of reification affects everyone living in a capitalist culture, presumably in more or less similar ways.

Habermas's extensive conceptual framework only hints at how to study empirically the reification of everyday communication. He has no analogue to Marx's *Capital* that empirically shows the circuits of reproduction in the cultural sphere or social factory. Nor has he written

extensive popular articles on contemporary cultural politics and communication. We are left, therefore, with the insight that instrumental interactions and a technological rationality are all around us. But we are not sure
when and how cultural managers and administrators run their cultural
labor markets. It is not clear how they get us to labor communicatively to
reproduce our own alienation from others. Nor is it clear how extensively
we rebel and resist the appropriation of our communicative labor. How
do ethnographers describe this appropriation of our communicative labor
and the people's struggle against it?

Describing Alienated Communicative Labor: Erving Goffman

Fortunately for an empiricist like myself, America has already produced
a brilliant ethnographer of Habermas's instrumental speech practices.
Goffman argues that all human communication has a dramaturgical quality. All people generally manage the flow of information, and hence the
impression or image they wish to convey to others concerning their "social identity" and the "social situation" being enacted. Goffman studies
the performances people put on to create a public social order with well
defined territories. Individuals, or "teams" of individuals, maintain roles
and "lines" in most face-to-face "focused" (work groups) or "unfocused"
(sidewalk passersby) encounters. This mutually constructed definition of
a social situation may often break down or constantly need repair,
however, due to threats to the actor's self-portrayal or to the definition of
what is happening.

Goffman (1961a, 1967) develops an elaborate framework of ideas for
describing how people define and maintain their definitions of self and
situation. Face-to-face communication in these mutually constructed social orders involves a good deal of "remedial work" or "protective,
face-saving practices" to avoid "scenes." Consequently, Goffman makes
much of the demeanor, deference, civil inattention, body glosses, and
etiquette that people use to save the performance of a line or scene. In
highly managed communicative settings such as mental hospitals and
prisons, people are often forced to deviate massively from the role performances being staged. A rebellious "underlife" develops among "stigmatized" patients toward their "normal" staff. The contradictions, fictions, and self-deceptions of Goffman's mutually constructed social
orders become, therefore, even more apparent in such settings.

One reading of Goffman's view of people and social life is as an
ethnographic description of what Sartre calls "bad faith." The world of

everyday communication would be impossible without a good deal of fiction and self-deception. This portrayal of human communication is quite different from Habermas's ideal speech of open, honest discursive dialogues. Goffman rarely portrays people as rationally and consciously searching for the truth of propositions they put to each other about reality. The performances people put on in mutually constructed language games seem constantly to violate the background consensus that Habermas claims is necessary for real communication. Everyday communication is often marked by untrue propositional content "performed" insincerely and inappropriately. People seem frequently to deceive each other and themselves, then simply "repair" their false definitions of self and situation so that the show goes on.

Goffman's work is also filled with a curious ambivalence about attributing social structural effects to the social "scenes," "encounters," and "gatherings" he studies. He carefully defines his small studies of face-to-face interactions as a new field of sociological study, somewhere between psychological studies of the self and sociological studies of social organization. Goffman's realm is the shadowy world of fleeting, temporary social orders. He studies the ritualized interactional conventions that make communication possible. He conceptually isolates this type of human behavior the way anthropologists once studied "primitive tribal societies" as cultures living beyond world history.

Goffman ultimately becomes engrossed in studying this paradoxically real yet make-believe social life. His studies plunge deeper and deeper into the intricacies and mechanics of this dramaturgical world until he ends up studying "frames" or communication about communication (1974). His reflection on the extraordinary communicative practice of framing leaves the following sober reference to his political critics in the introduction:

> He who would combat false consciousness and awaken people to their true interests has much to do because the sleep is very deep. And I do not intend here to provide a lullaby but merely to sneak in and watch the people snore.

One must take seriously Goffman's perspective that everyday communication is unthinkable without dramaturgical fictions. One only has to imagine telling boring colleagues what you really think, or literally explaining how you're feeling to the neighbor's morning greeting, to realize quickly the importance of "performances." They are the lifeblood of our privacy, peace of mind, and functioning social order, as Goffman claims. We must, however, also read Goffman as an ethnographer of communication in late capitalist society, despite his claims of universality. We must scrutinize the pervasive cultural tendency he finds to dramatize and construct social reality for forms of inequality. Not all mutually constructed dramaturgical performances may be mutually beneficial to all the performers. Dramaturgical performances in public institutions are not as free of historical context as Goffman's own "framing" of his studies tends to imply.

Goffman generally expresses no interest in doing cultural critique, but he has nevertheless written excellent, critical portrayals of modern mental institutions (1961a) and mass media advertising (1979). He shows how these cultural institutions deceive the public and themselves as they dehumanize patients and women. His general work on communication remains, however, a search for the universals of conversations and dramaturgical performances. He exhibits little interest in exploring whether the mutually constructed fictions and performances he sees everywhere create or "reproduce" forms of inequality.

The closest he comes to such a project is his account of the "stigmatized social identities" of social groups, from the physically disfigured to the ethnically/racially different (1963). The effect of historical, social structural factors is clearest in this portrayal of how "normals" and "stigmatized" individuals accommodate each other. Curiously, however, Goffman completely leaves out the stigma of class, one of our most well-documented "identity stigmas" (Sennett and Cobb 1972). Why class identity fails to qualify as a powerful form of stigmatization is never explained. Goffman clearly has his blind spots, but he is hardly as apolitical or uncritical as some critics have suggested (Meltzer, Petras, and Reynolds 1975).

To utilize Goffman's insights, one needs to interject critical ideas such as ideal speech and class interest into the study of everyday communication. We need to explore what else is being constructed besides a smooth-flowing conversation. We need to ask when this type of communication becomes miscommunication that arrests intersubjectivity and reproduces class divisions. Habermas provides us, therefore, with such critical questions, and Goffman provides us with a set of categories for empirically describing actual everyday speech performances that may be reproducing class inequalities.

Class Cultures as a Situational Speech Performance of Status Groups

In terms of class theory, Goffman's concept of identity has much in common with the Marxian notion of alienated labor. In this regard,

Goffman, a symbolic interactionist, gives interactionism a very different twist. In Goffman, George Mead's well-known theory of the self becoming social never gets enacted. For Mead (1934), the development of a social self depends on the mutual recognition of others and the ability to put oneself in their role, to achieve an empathic relationship. Such interactions occur through social acts in which meaningful symbols and gestures are shared. In the Meadian world of open, rational discourse, people intentionally share social identities and roles. A workable society is built through speech interactions. Human consciousness or the mind takes on, therefore, a distinctly social, environmental character. This view of intersubjectivity or objectification of the self through sympathetic others has real affinities with Marx's notion of sensuous labor and Habermas's notion of communicative action.

In contrast, Goffman's concept of identity emphasizes displays of the self that lead to misrecognition and to an avoidance of intersubjectivity. Some such interactions construct workable social fictions and interactional performances, but others are turned into an audience or parallel parts in a script. The self is usually not revealed or shared. Actors play their roles with little emotion or empathy, or they compete intensely with each other in relative anonymity. Consequently, intersubjectivity is arrested and blocked through deception and mistrust. The objectification of the self through sensuous labor or role taking becomes instead role playing that distances the self from others. Without ever using the term, Goffman's empirical descriptions of communication look very like what Habermas calls instrumental action, or what a class theorist would call alienated communicative labor.

Ultimately, Goffman provides what could be called a "situational speech performance" concept of class cultures. He suggests that public face-to-face interactions become highly routinized aspects of a social order. They are reoccurring rituals in which people act out their proper roles. Although Goffman does not look for performances that stage class roles and identities, nothing in his general approach restricts such an interpretive posture. Dramaturgically, class groups are socialized to use distinct styles of speech. They select a speech style that fits the general social identity that "normal" society bestows upon them and marks the performers' social status.

In a situational speech performance, the two classes who are mutually constructing and performing their social identities are not necessarily a speech community in the traditional sense. Goffman uses a much vaguer notion of community or society. The roles and identities people perform daily, and hence the style of their speech, flow from their general understanding of "normal." Class stigmatization is learned very early in many forms of communicative labor in the social factory of capitalist culture. Each class performs its speech style during ritualized class interactions in various institutional settings. In this view, "speech communities" only exist in a relational sense during moments of class performances. The origin of speech practices is in the logic and general character of class society and not in some fixed territorial speech group with a tradition. This definition follows the call for a less idealized, homogeneous, and unitary concept of speech communities in the field of ethnography of speaking (Bauman and Sherzer 1975).

Two generalized class roles are routinely enacted in reoccurring everyday situational speech performances. Bourgeois/petty bourgeois actors typically assume they are leaders with "normal" identities and superior speech, who have the right to speak often and in an official manner. Standard, official speech is authoritative and proper. Proper, polite speech and etiquette can become a strategic weapon in their everyday communication. Such instrumental, manipulative speech practices help preserve the image of bourgeois class privilege as cultural models and as political leaders. Conversely, working class actors assume they are outsiders and subordinates with "stigmatized" identities and inferior speech, who only have the right to speak when allowed by others or when rudely demanded by themselves. Unofficial speech is often non-standard, informal, and lacking in politeness forms. Impolite speech becomes an unstrategic form of expressiveness that either meekly enacts the subordinate, stigmatized role of outsider or openly, hostilely rejects it. These more open, dialogic speech practices help preserve the dual role and identity of an uncultured, inferior outsider and rebel.

The major difference between Goffman's view of identity and the more anthropological view found in Willis is that an expressive culture perspective contains a diverse variety of traditional expressive practices or communicative channels. An anthropological view of culture as a shared, learned set of expressive cultural practices emphasizes the group's folklore, music, dance, humor, and general speech style. Each group has a specific historical tradition and a place or territory. These expressive traditions are self-generated, "authentic" symbolic practices that express group social identity. Such cultural practices are the basis of a group's sense of primordiality or origin. These practices are symbolic boundary-maintaining devices that both the group and "normal," mainstream society mutually recognize (Barth 1969; Royce 1982).

In the complicated process of intergroup relations, disputes may arise over the identities of cultural groups. Mainstream or "normal" society may seek to impose a stigmatic, inauthentic image upon a "stigmatized" group. Stigmatized groups may either maintain their stigmatized social identities or seek to symbolically reverse them. Such battles over the definitions of social identities may lead to cultural resistance and to the creation of entirely new, self-generated cultural forms and group identity definitions. Such struggles over symbols and identities can be described as distinct cultural traditions that are both "primordial" and invented.

Goffman tends to banish history and cultural traditions from his model; consequently his idea of a "social identity" is largely situational and psychological. He emphasizes practices such as face-saving, character, and correctness of social form and etiquette. What links these two disparate perspectives are, however, the ideas of performance and intersubjectivity. More recent theoretical formulations in folklore emphasize the performance dimension of all expressive culture practices (Bauman 1986). The expression of one's personal identity is ultimately a product of mutual social construction and/or struggle. Social identity only has an objective reality when expressed or performed on a cultural stage with others. The self is completed through intersubjectivity. Without others, there is no personal self. This fact suggests that thinking about social classes as some sort of historical speech community may be a useful, complementary extension of Goffman's more phenomenological perspective.

Class Cultures as the Historical Speech Traditions of Status Groups

A more sociolinguistic notion of class cultures broadens a phenomenological perspective in several ways. First, a historical view of "speech communities" conceptually ties situational class role performances to a larger, ongoing process of cultural assimilation and resistance. Class cultures, as historical speech communities, cannot be studied as if they are beyond the forces of capitalist development or "modernization." Second, as indicated, the notion of language and culture in a more historical view of speech communities implies a strong concept of a complex cultural tradition. Class-based speech communities would be more expressively complex, therefore, than the speech practices portrayed in Habermas's and Goffman's models of communication and language. The speech styles of classes would be expressed through many channels, and would be a very dynamic mix of traditional and invented forms.

On the other hand, empirically demonstrating that class-based historical speech groups in the anthropological sense exist is still very problematic. Anthropological studies of speech communities are rarely located in a larger class context. They are usually not conceptualized as studies of cultural assimilation and resistance to world capitalist development or "modernity." Anthropological linguistics, although rich in empirical studies of distinct cultural speech groups, has not generally studied speech communities as emerging class cultures. To my knowledge, there are no studies of whether social classes tend to use a distinct expressive tradition or qualitatively different speech styles in everyday communication. There are, however, a few classic studies of classes as historical speech groups. Basil Bernstein's work (1976) on the middle class "elaborated code" and the working class "restricted code" is a well-known example. His work and that of Jenny Cook-Gumperz (1973) provide some empirical evidence for these codes, but his notion of speech code differences is a very narrow, cognitive view of language and communication. Various studies also document that speech "registers" and standard/non-standard or dialect differences between classes exist.

What follows is a brief review of modernization studies that provide suggestive, indirect evidence that class-based speech groups in the folkloristic and sociolinguistic sense may be emerging. Scattered studies of peasant and proletarian communities' response to capitalist domination do suggest the importance of expressive class cultures in class struggles. First, local level anthropological studies of third world peasants and proletarians show considerable cultural resistance to modernity. Various groups use traditional cultural rituals and practices in active political struggles against capitalist economic development (Taussig 1980; Scott 1985; Delgado 1987; Mota 1987). In these cases the proletarians are resisting both economic domination and cultural assimilation.

In addition, anthropological studies of non-white American ethnic groups also suggest that cultural assimilation into world capitalist culture creates many new oppositional cultural forms and practices. Distinct expressive cultural practices in music and language survive among working class Mexicanos and blacks (Peña 1985; Keil 1966, 1985; Límon 1983, 1984, 1989). Dan Rose's (1987) study of black American street life is particularly suggestive. He describes the traditional concept of reciprocity that underlines public verbal performances such as the "hustle." Other work on black speech, music, and folklore suggest a distinct black proletarian cultural style (Levine 1977; Baugh 1983; Abrahams 1964).

These studies describe both powerful forces of traditionalism and invention in these emergent proletarian cultural communities. These communities are invariably in a state of cultural transition and change. Some recent work on ethnic communities show that many working class Mexican Americans and Afro-Americans are quite "mainstream" in terms of values (Williams 1981; Anchor 1978). Other studies on ethnic identity indicate that Blacks and Mexicanos increasingly use poverty and socio-economic status indicators as cultural identity markers (Lawrence 1982; Fukumoto 1983). For these people, being ethnic means being poor and displaying their stigmatized ethnic social identities with the symbols of a low income lifestyle. These working class ethnics are being culturally assimilated into modern capitalist consumer culture and are bicultural and bilingual in the expressive culture sense.

Various general studies on modernity suggest that fine-grained studies of speech communities need to be included. In the classic portrayal of "becoming modern" (Inkeles and Smith 1974), a modern person becomes an individualistic, aggressive entrepreneurial types who is unencumbered by traditional values and social organization. This portrayal leaves out the linguistic description of the modern bourgeois person implied in the work of Habermas, Bourdieu, and Goffman. Conversely, a "proletarian person," whether in urban ghettos or in traditional third world agrarian societies, typically scores low on Alex Inkeles's modernity scale, and retains more traditional cultural practices and forms of social organization. This group are more marginalized as consumers and display less modern entrepreneurial and individualistic behavior.

Other studies of modernity suggest specific social organizational factors that may affect the development of distinct class cultures as speech communities. Recent historical studies of American working class communities suggest less cultural assimilation or embourgeoisment than mainline sociology often portrays (Dawley 1976; Rubin 1976; Gutman 1977). Studies of working class families also suggest that they retain more traditional, extended kinship-oriented practices (Stack 1974; Poster 1981; Foley et al. 1988). Studies of cognitive style differences (Ramírez and Casteñeda 1974) and literacy (Heath 1983) show that working class families and communities have less bourgeois or "mainstream" cognitive styles and literacy practices.

A Plausible Argument for Class-based Historical Speech Communities

These various studies of modernization suggest a plausible explanation for why proletarians may be less culturally assimilated in a communicative action sense. In general, low income proletarian communities seem to retain a more traditionalistic organizational character. The practices of an extended family system and fictive kin are more intact in such communities. The neighborhood provides a relatively strong web of social relationships. This greater social complexity and communality leads to a stronger normative emphasis on various forms of social reciprocity or social obligation. Life in these peasant villages, low income ghettos, and small rural working class towns is less anonymous and individualistic and has more traditional patterns of resource sharing and social interaction.

A more collective organizational context may create speech communities that are generally more context-bound or indexical in character. The grounds for mutual recognition and role taking are greater in such traditionalistic communities, because people share a greater stock of background knowledge about each other. Lies and deceits are more transparent in a communicative context where everyone has a long "career" as communicator and role-taker. Consequently, a higher degree of normative consensus exists about members' proper communicative roles and styles. Creating new, variant impressions of the self through instrumental verbal performances is contextually constrained. As a result, the management of reality through words or discourse may be practiced less successfully, and thus less frequently. As a result, people develop less communicative competence in deceit and impression management. In the end, actors in more traditionalistic, context-bound speech communities judge themselves more by their deeds than by their public situational speech performances.

In contrast, more anonymous communicative contexts such as modern suburban communities and corporate work groups are marked by intense individualism, competition, restricted information, and considerable impression management. In such market-like modern speech contexts, the split between public and private self is much greater than in more traditionalistic communities. Such relatively unindexical, ahistorical, anonymous communicative contexts give rise to the greater use of strategic, instrumental speech and impression management. As a result, people in such speech contexts develop greater communicative competencies in instrumental speech and impression management.

Living and practicing the constant construction of factitious realities ultimately socializes one to believe that discourse or words, not deeds, are reality. Discourse and "displaying" an image of reality gradually become what Roland Barthes (1972) calls a second-order language or "mythology." A second-order language is one in which the signifiers of meaning, the gestures of a managed line or image, become detached from the meaning or signification. In this case, the signifiers, the gestures of a managed line or image, are "detached" (have the opposite meaning) from the impression of self and situation that the impression manager wants to convey. Ultimately, these deceits or "mythologies" about the self and one's social situations, like Barthes's mythologies in popular culture advertising, become "naturalized." The interactional mythologies or self-advertisements that people use seem natural and true to those constantly using them.

Put in Marxian terminology, a person's everyday discourse practices become reified. Increasingly, people who are men and women of words and are skillful at deceit come to believe that their discursive practice of impression management *is* reality. They become less reflective about the gap between their words and deeds. Consequently, traditional normative ideals about doing what one says and being sincere and truthful become less of a constraint on communicative action. A pecuniary, instrumental logic, "what sells is true," becomes the normative ground of their communicative style. The more one is in, or wants to be in, the "mainstream," the more one uses instrumental communicative practices rhetorically to define and manage social reality.

The other aspect of modernization that may also be creating distinct class-based speech communities is the reaction that cultural homogenization and administration creates. Worldwide capitalist modernization also evokes strong counter-cultural movements and expressions of cultural politics. As modern life becomes highly administered and culturally homogenized, traditional ethnic cultural forms and practices become freely circulating commodity forms. Class and ethnic signifiers meld together in economically marginal groups, and ethnicity can become a class stigma in the status sense. This often provokes cultural revitalization movements. Such conflicts over social identities represent a new dynamic in late or advanced capitalist societies. The youth in marginalized working class ethnic communities create new counter-cultural practices that appropriate and invert mainstream, bourgeois expressive practices. These new counter-cultural practices may be additional temporary barriers that slow the spread of the cultural logic of instrumentalism, and hence the complete assimilation of everyday proletarian culture and communication.

Habermas's critique of capitalist culture suggests that the appropriation of people's communicative labor in the cultural sphere is a new level of dehumanization. When society thoroughly commodifies all human expressiveness, the ontological basis for a human culture ("a lifeworld of uncoerced communicative action") is threatened. A new reason for revolt emerges, therefore, with the growing theft of communicative labor. This creates a great deal of oppositional expressive behavior that valorizes stylistic markers of social identity and deepens the gap between "normal mainstream" and stigmatized, non-mainstream social identities.

The general class struggle takes on, therefore, many new forms in advanced capitalist societies. The great ideological struggle in advanced capitalist societies is not only over explicit political ideologies but also over one's mode of identity expression in an overly administered world of manufactured symbols and identities. The signs of such struggles are everywhere in the "unproductive labor" or expressive cultural practices of various segments of the proletariat such as break dancing, low-rider cars, the racism of "white ethnics," spiked haircuts, and reggae music. Such expressions of cultural resistance may also become commercialized, however, and expressiveness itself does not necessarily culminate in a progressive class acting "for" itself politically. It does, however, often represent an anti-bourgeois, anti-mainstream reaction to capitalist culture, even when expressing reactionary, racist, and sexist values.

Summing Up: Studying Class More Anthropologically

This synthesis of Marxist class theory with ideas of communication from critical theory, symbolic interactionism, and sociolinguistics rephrases Marx's original perspective in a more anthropological way. Anthropologically, this translates into the empirical study of the cultural practices of expressive speech that people perform to establish class identities. These practices occur in situational speech performances, and they may also represent emerging class-based historical speech communities being assimilated into a world capitalist culture.

This particular field study ends up using the more restricted notion of class cultures as situational speech performances. No attempt was made to document the existence or importance of class-based historical speech communities. More studies of the ethnography of speaking and folklore are needed to shed light on whether class-based speech communities are emerging in capitalist cultures. Although plausible, this notion of social classes as emerging speech communities still has little empirical support. This field study does, however, present extensive evidence that ritualized, daily situational speech performances stage or enact different class role identities and communicative styles in schools.

Theoretically, this study suggests that original class theory can incorporate the conceptual distinction between economic classes and class cultures as emerging cultural status groups with expressive cultures and speech styles. Studies of such communicative labor are the logical extension of Marx's more philosophical notions of class and ideology or class consciousness. The key idea that links these reputedly disparate views is

Marx's concept of human labor and objectification. Although Marx did no cultural critiques of everyday communication, his notion of commodity fetishism anticipates such studies. One need not jettison the concept of political economy to do such cultural critiques of capitalism. Contemporary "cultural Marxism" both originates in and articulates class theory in some new directions.

Indeed, as the following discussion of "cultural reproduction" will show, a more cultural view of social classes opens up new ways of studying how class inequalities are perpetuated. Having presented my notions of class and culture, I have laid the philosophical foundation for a new theory of cultural reproduction and resistance in schools. Part 2 will clarify the concept of "cultural reproduction" and then elaborate a performance theory of cultural reproduction and resistance. This theory was used to describe how North Town High School reproduces class inequalities culturally.

Part 2: A Performance View of Class Culture Reproduction in Schools

The previous discussion redefines class cultures as situational speech performances that enact class identities. Given this concept of culture, what then does it mean to say that the social class structure is "culturally reproduced"? The first concept that needs clarifying is "reproduction," and the second is "cultural reproduction." In classical Marxist theory the reproduction of a capitalist mode of production is clearly spelled out in *Capital*. A debate exists over the continuing utility of the theory of value (Steedman et al. 1981), but a paradigm for talking about "reproduction" and "crises" in the cycle and circuits of reproduction exists (Bell and Cleaver 1982). When Marxist economists study "reproduction," they study capital accumulation, the flows of capital and commodities, the ebb and flow of rates of profit, and the ensuing struggles over wages.

These are the cycles that reproduce or sustain the structuring of vast groups of people into a systemic historical pattern of production and consumption. Reproduction refers to the perpetuation and expansion of a particular kind of society and production system over time. One can measure the rate of exploitation of labor and the rate of profit that sustains this particular mode of production's growth or reproduction. This historical ebb and flow is reflected in labor strikes, falling wage rates, repressive state labor policies, immigration policies and flows, ideological campaigns against rival capitalist states, leaps in applied production techniques, and a multitude of measures of income distribution, homelessness, pre-natal deaths, crime, youth rebellion, and so on.

In sharp contrast, the Marxist paradigm is less explicit about how society is "reproduced" culturally. Numerous intellectual histories detail the complex debates within Marxism that have produced scholars who claim to be rescuing and developing the cultural or less economistic, positivistic side of Marxist thought (Gouldner 1979; Kolakowski 1978). The more clearly articulated perspectives in the new "cultural Marxism" do not necessarily focus, however, on everyday cultural practices that somehow "reproduce" class society. Nor do they always spell out the relationship between "economic" and "cultural" reproduction processes.

One key difference in economic and cultural reproduction is that the "cultural reproduction" of classes is not a direct, primary mechanism for maintaining capital accumulation. The human capital perspective in mainstream economics factors in the education and training of a work force to increase productivity. Capitalist companies undoubtedly profit from taxpayers' subsidizing the training and welfare maintenance of their workers. The same can be said of the general socialization of workers to be loyal, patriotic citizens. This also enhances the stability of the political economy and creates the general grounds for productivity, but "socialization" is not a major macro-economic mechanism that arrests falling rates of profit during an accumulation cycle. Marx does not state any specific mechanism of cultural reproduction that is analogous to the reserve labor army or the replacement of living labor (people) with "dead" labor (technology). Besides the general notion of socialization, what does it really mean to say that cultural institutions like schools "culturally reproduce" social class inequality?

On the cultural side, Marx presents a complex philosophical discussion of alienated labor, the loss of species-being, and the objectification and loss of self through commodity fetishism. Philosophically, a Marxist discussion of the "cultural reproduction" of class society must be founded on an analysis of alienated labor. Marx contends that human activity in a capitalist society comes under the materialist logic of commodity form, and we literally become what we do and consume. This type of Marxist critique develops from his Hegelian notions of the subjectivity and identity formation. Ultimately, this kind of analysis has been labeled "cultural Marxism," and European "culturalists" and "structuralists" have been hashing out these differences (Samuel 1981).

To date, the major outcome of those debates has been a analytical orientation centered on "ideology" and "ideological struggles." Tortuous metalanguage debates developed around the meaning of ideology (CCCS 1977). The most influential perspective that emerged from these debates was Gramsci's notion of hegemony and counter-hegemony. This formulation stresses the creation of an ideological realm in which people are socialized to have different levels of class awareness or consciousness. Recent discussions of this cultural struggle center on the production and consumption of popular culture forms (S. Hall 1981; Bennett et al. 1986; Chambers 1986; Fiske 1989a, 1989b).

Most cultural critics using this perspective assume that certain everyday cultural practices in the "cultural sphere" produce a contested "hegemonic consensus." The efforts of the "ideological apparatus" (Althusser 1971) or the "culture industry" (Horkheimer and Adorno 1982) are never passively accepted, thus no general cultural consensus or stable state of political legitimacy ever exists. The ceaseless attempts to "administer" the cultural sphere and produce some homogeneous set of cultural forms or cultural norms engender a creative rebellion in both the popular culture and the "avant-garde" arts.

In short, the cultural sphere never quite secures a hegemonic consent for the ruling bourgeois ideology. Cultural practices on the everyday material plane alter people's sense of personal and group identity and their understanding of their traditions. People with different types and levels of cultural consciousness sometimes band together to change society through direct political action. Or people can consciously or unconsciously acquiese to the dominant ideas and ideologies about their historical reality. As Hall (1981) put it, the cultural realm or sphere is best thought of as contested and always in the process of change, without fixed forms and practices.

This version of class theory does not postulate a strong or absolute notion of causality between these "cultural struggles" and "economic" class structures. It postulates a conditional and dialectic relationship between the "cultural" and the "economic." Consequently, most cultural critiques of "hegemonic" or "counter-hegemonic" ideology describe either the levels and types of political consciousness in a dominating or a dominated group, or the various ideological practices and mechanisms of a given societal institution such as the media, family, factory, state, or school. Such studies portray the "cultural politics" of social control in institutions between the managers and their clients, workers, consumers, subordinates, or citizens.

Studies of Cultural Hegemony and Ideological Struggle in Schools

As previously indicated, studies of "cultural resistance" in schools have shown how marginalized working class and ethnic youth resist "mainstream" teachers and their "straight," patriotic, work-oriented ideals. The Birmingham Centre for Contemporary Cultural Studies (CCCS) has influenced several recent critical ethnograpic studies. One alternative way of conceptualizing "cultural reproduction" has been as a distribution of "symbolic capital" (Bourdieu and Passeron 1977) or school credentials (Collins 1979). Neo-Marxists with a Gramscian orientation have generally written this perspective off as too functionalist and lacking a notion of struggle and resistance.

In subsequent works, Pierre Bourdieu (1984) redefines class and class differences as differences in consumption and taste. This formulation of "taste cultures" does indeed jettison the classic Marxian concept of classes as competing economic groups. In this perspective, the cultural reproduction of the economic structure becomes the reproduction of status groups with distinct, relatively privileged lifestyles. He now seeks to demonstrate empirically the connections between everyday cultural practices and social classes through surveys of people's different life styles and consumption practices.

His school reproduction studies did not demonstrate how schools reproduced different taste cultures, or how students with different cultural capital fare in classrooms or after earning credentials. They generally describe the bourgeois bias found in the teachers' language, social comportment, and curriculum preferences of French lycées and universities (Bourdieu and Passeron 1977). Despite these conceptual and empirical limitations, Bourdieu's "cultural" and "linguistic capital" concepts have intrigued a few non-Marxist "micro-ethnographers." Hugh Mehan and his associates (1986) propose that "constitutive ethnography" must begin studying how students with different "linguistic" and "cultural capital" construct "student careers" and enhance their status. Sociolinguists Jenny Cook-Gumperz and John Gumperz (1982) also advocate more studies of class differences in linguistic and cultural capital. One American sociolinguist, Shirley Brice Heath (1983), has produced an excellent ethnographic study of how differences in linguistic and cultural capital affect language use in schools. In contrast to Bourdieu, Heath studies the process of acquiring and using linguistic capital, rather than its general distribution.

A Performance View of Class Reproduction and Resistance in Schools

My "performance theory" has affinities with the work of Heath and the proposals of Mehan and associates that give Bourdeiu an interactional turn. What seems promising and problematic about their synthesis of class and cultural theory is spelled out elsewhere (Foley 1990a). No coherent "school of thought" has emerged from these various "micro" studies of cultural capital, but they do suggest a nascent synthesis of "macro" class theory and non-Marxist "micro" ethnographic approaches. They also suggest a way out of the problematic dichotomy of "structuralists" and "culturalists" that reproduction and resistance theorists have erected between themselves.

As Part 1 indicated, this performance theory is built on Marx's discussion of self-objectification through alienated labor. Using Habermas's theory of communicative action, Marx's notion of alienated labor was rephrased as "alienated communicative labor." To do empirical studies of "alienated communicative labor," I articulated Habermas's notions of communication with Goffman's dramaturgical concept of self and social interaction. Reading Goffman this way historicizes his theory and makes his perspective the empiricist analogue of Habermas's philosophical critique.

Goffman provides a body of mid-range descriptive concepts for empirically describing the art of impression management, or what Habermas would call "instrumental speech acts." This description of communication in one youth scene and high school uses Goffman's concepts of impression management, territories, performance teams, performance lines and loyalty, rituals of degradation, character contests, face work, underlife, collusion, role distancing, and frames. I have avoided elaborate discussions of these concepts in this text, but the portrayal of this youth scene is very Goffmanesque.

Unlike Goffman, however, I paid much more attention to class factors. This study describes how youth from different classes use communicative competencies in impression management. In this case, middle class youth from both races have more of this "cultural" or "linguistic capital" than working class youth in either race. These differing interactional skills of youth are described in various classrooms and extra-curricular activities.

In the anthropological sense, these various interactional moments can be thought of as a general ritual process. These ritualized communicative events are a vital part of how youth are generally socialized into "mainstream" American "capitalist culture." Such situational speech acts are performances in Goffman's sense, which dramatically and symbolically present the societies' ideal class roles and communicative styles. During these communicative moments, some youth become socially prominent and leaders, some passive and conformist and others rebellious and marginal. Economic classes and inequality are "culturally reproduced," therefore, through this ritual process that schools constantly stage.

The Major Situational Speech Performances of Cultural Reproduction

In North Town, the situational speech performances that all students and teachers routinely enacted typically occurred during community sports contests, student status group displays, and classroom making out games. Youths practice, learn, and anticipate their different class identities and roles through the way they play football, display peer status, and horse around in classrooms. The concept of "making out games" discussed in

Chapter 4 best illustrates how micro studies of everyday communication "link" with macro class analysis of inequality.

In one way or another, most of the situational speech performances described are connected to American popular or leisure culture practices. Schools are a site for the enactment of American popular culture. They are very diffuse community institutions pervaded by these local traditions and practices. These community-level popular culture practices such as football, dating, and classroom making out games are at least partly the product of a national leisure culture. Institutions of entertainment and artistic expression produce a kind of national popular culture that is distinctly American. The spectacles of professional football, rock concerts, hit movies, and television sit-coms, talk shows, tabloids, romance novels, and popular magazines transmit cultural models for our youth. Their ideas of gender roles, friendship, romance, and expressive cultural styles reflect the values and styles of our national popular culture.

As Willis and others (Fiske 1989a, 1989b; Chambers 1986) have suggested, however, different local status groups appropriate and create their own versions of these mass-mediated cultural forms. This fact suggests a complex process of transmission, mediation, and production of cultural forms and styles. Cultural traditions are constantly being homogenized *and* invented in modern capitalist cultures. This culture concept makes problematic the anthropological notion of an "authentic" stable cultural tradition that produces stable social identities. The idea of shifting "lifestyles" tends to replace the idea of distinct, unchanging social identities.

A whole new field of interdisciplinary critical cultural studies is emerging to address these questions (Aronowitz 1981; Bennett et al. 1986; Chambers 1986; Grossman and Nelson 1988; Fiske 1989a, 1989b). The field still lacks definitive models of how invented local popular culture practices articulate with older high and folk cultural practices and forms. The use of a popular culture perspective generally signals a reformulation of the anthropological culture concept used to describe less technological, traditional societies. A more dynamic, historical, and political concept of culture is needed to describe the culture of a complex capitalist society.

The concept of "capitalist culture" guiding the field study remains provisional and partial. Following Habermas, I argued that our everyday national popular culture is generally inculcating people with an instrumental style of speech. Americans "culturally reproduce" their individualistic, competitive, and materialistic society through using this alienating, manipulative communicative styles. Those class segments most deeply integrated into the popular culture practices of leisure and consumption are the most thoroughly socialized and consequently they become the most competent in impression management techniques. As indicated, cultural institutions like schools showcase and valorize these moments of instrumental communication.

The Habermasian critique implies that a new kind of "deep" linguistic socialization is occurring in advanced capitalist cultures. This socialization into a new communication style is not simply imposed through a cultural hegemony of ideas. The enactment of this logic of commodity fetishim has become a "natural" way of living and communicating. People do not reflect on their impression management competencies as being instrumental, manipulative, and dehumanizing. Moreover, enacting one's class identity and position in these social dramas does not directly "cause" one to end up in a particular class. Participants who play different roles in these moments of symbolic reproduction do, in fact, often end up in different social classes.

Concluding Remarks and a Response to the Foreword by Paul Willis

Paul Willis and several other reviewers have raised a variety of questions that merit a response. Willis worries that my study downplays working class "resistance" and makes too strong a case for dominance and "reproduction." He suggests that the critical theory perspective I advocate might slip into simply classifying expressive practices and merely reflect dominance rather than illuminating the creative and "rational" potential of youthful resistance. He fears that I tend to overlook what he studies so well—namely the lads' understanding of and creative resistance to ideological domination. This leads him to characterize my political position as not unlike that of the early Frankfurt school critical theorists—a kind of elitist high culture lament on the irrationality all around them. He urges me to explore the dialectical, contradictory relationship among expressive practices, the critical elements of their thought, and the whole leisure culture apparatus of cultural reproduction.

He also suggests that the ethnographic text is rich enough to present the "content" of the vatos' and white trash kids' worldviews. Like Willis's study, my study shows how conscious the Pacos and Taras were of the school and youth scene, therefore of adult society as rigged against them. But he is right when he says that I did not place the same emphasis on their awareness and "resistance" that he did. In my tale, the vatos and white trash kids end up with a vague populist or cultural nationalist discontent rather than with a clear counter-hegemonic class consciousness. In Willis's language, their "penetrations" of the ideological hegemony, like those of his lads, were only partial. Racist and sexist thinking remained in substantial doses. Moreover, as the follow-up study in Chapter 5 documents, most North Town working class kids, like Willis's lads, also ended up in working class jobs.

In addition, I presented more of what Sennett and Cobb (1972) call the "hidden injuries of class" that Willis does. The vatos' fathers, mostly an unorganized rural proletariat of migrant and day laborers, did not extoll their jobs the way an older unionized urban proletariat might. Their tendency to glorify physical labor, bravery, and pain, as the patriarchal football scene suggests, was a very male thing, not simply a working class cultural phenomenon. Such considerations led me to downplay, somewhat more than Willis did, the importance of a strong, positive working class culture that loves manual labor. I was not entirely comfortable with

Willis's idea that one's view of labor, mental versus manual, was the fundamental difference between a "working class culture" and a "bourgeois class culture." Bourdieu's recent attempts to spell out class cultures as taste cultures, although lacking a notion of struggle and agency, adds some important dimensions to Willis's perspective. My discussion in Part 1 on communicative competencies tried to add some other dimensions to the general discussion of class cultures.

Willis developed his model of a working class culture from a diachronic ethnography of one neighborhood in an old English industrial city. Since Willis did not do a historical study of class recomposition and struggle, the extent of class differentiation within the working class community he studied is unclear. Moreover, since he studied only a white working class group, he did not address the whole issue of race or ethnicity. Perhaps wisely, Willis limited his study to the rebelliousness of a few lads at one historical moment in time. This made it possible for him to construct a model of working class culture that makes a fairly persuasive case for the intergenerational continuity between fathers and sons. The real achievement in this is to counter psychologistic culture-of-poverty views of the working class with a portrait of a strong, robust, positive, enduring working class culture.

In constrast, talking about "a working class culture" in North Town was considerably more complicated because I tried to analyze one multi-ethnic community historically. Chapter 1 summmarized our study (Foley et al. 1988) of how the political economy of North Town's capitalist racial order has changed since 1900. To recapitulate, this region and working class community went through a major class recomposition that undermined its segregated racial order. This eighty-year process of economic development spawned a new Mexicano middle class that rode the civil rights movement to individual upward mobility. By the mid-1970s the Mexicano community had become increasingly proud of being "ethnic" at the very moment it was becoming increasingly differentiated by social classes. This led to intergroup divisions over the use of "ethnic" and "mainstream" cultural symbols to express self-valorizing ethnic and class cultural identities.

As a result of these larger historical forces, a growing numbers of Mexicano youth from middle and stable working class backgrounds wanted to participate in the "mainstream." They *also* wanted to transform their stigmatized ethnic identity that equates being poor with being Mexican. Consequently, this account of adolescent rebellion or "resistance" portrayed ethnically conscious Mexicanos with very small differences in class background fighting back in rather different ways. Some of this "ethnic resistance" actually led away from the valorization of a Mexicano working class or "barrio" and "street" culture. Nevertheless, such "resistance" had roots in class and racial oppression and also had creative and progressive elements.

Unlike Willis's study, this study ultimately had to grapple with the conceptual problem of how to study "cultural assimilation" in a class society. In this particular case, many middle class and a few working class Mexicano youth, were culturally assimilating into mainstream "capitalist culture" in some sense. My notion of "cultural assimilation" makes a critical distinction than most theories of assimilation do not make. Most theories of cultural assimilation do not suggest particularly well how to handle the race-class dialectic conceptually. Consequently, I developed two complementary notions of culture, and differentiated between an acquired "qualitative speech style" and an inherited "expressive cultural style."

This allowed me to "see" that middle class Mexicanos who were "making it" did not necessarily abandon their historical ethnic expressive cultural practices. Instead, they simply added competencies in deceptive communication to the general expressive repertory that they learned growing up in a vibrant regional and ethnic speech community. They learned how to work the system, to be "clean cut jocks" publicly, to get the pretty girls with "straight arrow" raps, and to con teachers while entertaining their peers. These middle class Mexicano youth ended up having it both ways. They became mainstream conformists, yet still maintained a cool ethnic image among the silent majority of working class Mexicano "nobodies." They creatively blended mainstream Anglo communicative behaviors with emerging "Chicano" ethnic political symbols.

Only the more politicized, rebellious working class vatos, a variation of Willis's lads, criticized these youth as "vendidos" (sell outs) and "cocos" (coconuts that are brown on the outside and white on the inside). These youth, taking their lead from the cultural nationalists, tended to glorify working class "barrio" or "street" culture as being the "real" or "authentic" ethnic culture. In addition, the vatos adopted a cultural identity that creatively blended marginalized "hippie" counter-cultural symbols with emerging "Chicano" political and traditional Mexicano "ethnic" symbols. This strong regional and ethnic orientation led them to define their economic oppression in racial terms. Despite a strong sense of ethnic unity, however, the vatos also set themselves apart from the "rich" and "straight" middle class Mexicans by emphasizing the social class difference they felt. This suggests a growing working class consciousness, but not the same sense of class unity and sense of autonomy that Willis's lads had. In this case, it was the Jacintos of the new Mexicano middle class who actually felt empowered and went on to fight for the rights of working class ethnics, not the vatos like Paco.

In short, I simply did not find it as easy as Willis did to portray a tight connection between my lads' (the vatos) expressive style, their rebellious attitude and ideological "penetrations," and their fathers' shop floor culture. In this South Texas context, it would seem that the American political system has absorbed another progressive, reformist impulse, in this case the Chicano civil rights movement. American society and its schools incorporated and rewarded the Jacintos and "pushed out" the Pacos. This political incorporation of "ethnic resistance" was greatly aided by the capitalist popular culture practices of sports and dating that these youths learned growing up. That touches upon another closely related theoretical problematic in my work that concerned Willis.

Willis also entreats me to explore more fully how everyday popular cultures are more progressive than mass culture theorists claimed. He wants me to show how popular culture practices such as sports and dating "resist" commodification, how these youth turn this capitalist culture around for their own purposes. Willis's earlier work, and apparently his latest work on *Common Culture* (1990), has consistently and somewhat more exclusively focused on the creative potential of human agency. If I understand Willis's new theoretical directions, he is searching for additional ways of talking about how popular or leisure culture practices undermine the productivist capitalist work ethic. When he urges me to look for more ways in which people creatively turn the commodification of everyday life to their advantage, he make an excellent point.

His general perspective has a strong affinity with John Fiske's (1989a, b) important new statement on popular culture. Fiske emphasizes that people appropriate and use all sorts of commercialized "mass culture" forms and commodities in quite unexpected, creative, and empowering ways. In his formulation, they get pleasure out of playing with these contradictory cultural forms and producing their own meanings. These forms of "resistance" to generalized commodification are neither revolutionary nor hedonist, but they are life and self affirming. They do not always lead to "progressive" political agendas and movements, but the potential is always there. In short, human agency that produces meaning, beauty, intersubjectivity, and sheer pleasure is always possible within the flux of capitalist commodification, or for that matter under the yoke of Stalinist socialism. This perspective restates Marx's idea that capitalist development is progressively abolishing archaic cultural traditions. Indeed, as Willis and Fiske seem to be suggesting, advanced capitalism may be creating a kind of circulation of the symbolic that melts down traditional cultural forms and practices in very liberating ways. These processes of cultural change were not apparent during the early stages of capitalist development.

As I indicated earlier, this general notion of culture and cultural forms provides anthropologists like me with an exciting alternative culture concept for studying advanced capitalist societies. Cultural traditions and cultural identities—be they ethnic, gender, or class identities—are always in flux, and they are always a product of "the folk." Many anthropologists are still guided by a "high-mass-folk-culture" distinction. A popular culture perspective forces us to let go of invidious dichotomies in traditional cultural theory such as authentic folk versus inauthentic mainstream culture or authentic cultures of substance versus invented cultures of style. It forces us to talk about the cultural politics surrounding shifting cultural forms and identities in a highly fluid cultural tradition. Once our absolutist assumptions about venerable cultural traditions has been undermined, we can see more clearly that the ethnic, class, or gendered "other" we construct is often a static, ahistorical, and bloodless ideal typology.

Because I generally see "culture" in capitalist societies as a "popular culture" of power relations filled with contradiction and struggle, this ethnographic text also shows some of the creative, rebellious, pleasurable side of "cultural reproduction." But Willis is right: I do tend to emphasize what he considers the negative side of popular cultures. Apparently my anthropological training leads me not to celebrate the progressiveness of popular and leisure culture practices *too* quickly. To be sure, the football players found their aesthetic moments of pleasure and joy in "hitting" and in humiliating "band fags" and pleasing those who controlled the summer jobs. Males also generally pleased themselves in courtship rituals because young women generally believed in romance and practiced "bonded sexuality." Moreover, the classroom "making out games" were definitely fun and somewhat empowering for some youth, especially the middle class youth who were more communicatively competent at deceit. All of these youthful popular culture practices were celebrated and enjoyed by adults in sports, drinking, womanizing, and twerking-the-teacher tales. But all of these "natural" and good cultural practices had their price, and not everyone enjoyed them in the same ways.

My holistic anthropological orientation prompted me to contextualize this analysis of classroom "resistance" or "making out games" in quite different ways than Willis did. I used much broader conceptual frames such as "capitalist culture" and "community ritual," and that forced me to record much more of the traditional character of sports and dating. Like Willis, I interpreted the "resistance" in school classrooms as an expression of class culture struggle between working class and middle class youth. But, unlike Willis, I also saw this adolescent "resistance" as an extension of the whole youth scene and the community's way of socializing each new generation through sports and courtship rituals. I acknowlege the potential of popular culture practices to be progressive, but sports, dating, and making out games also had very negative structural consequences for many North Town youth. These youth were still being socialized in very traditional ways, even though the Chicano civil rights movement had challenged and circumscribed, to some extent, traditional racial forms of dominance. It was hard for me to extoll these forms of popular culture as resistance to the cultural hegemony of classist, sexist, and racist ideologies. To do that would have been to leave out what everyday life is really like in North Town.

Popular culture theorists generally seem to minimize how "unprogressive" sports and dating practices are. Part of this tendency may be a function of their desire conceptually to revise orthodox and pessimistic class and mass culture theories. Part may also be a function of their methodological orientation. When popular culture theorists actually conduct detailed empirical studies, they often focus on isolated texts, cultural forms, or small groups of performers creatively resisting hegemony rather than on historical communities. This study generally suggests the need for students of popular culture to take a more classical community studies approach to interpreting everyday popular culture practices. This view is spelled out in more detail in a paper on sports as a form of community popular culture (Foley 1990c). That article reviews recent theoretical work in the sociology of sports (Gruneau 1983; A. Hall 1984; Critcher 1986; Hargreaves 1986; Messner 1988; Deem 1988) and develops more explicitly the discussion in Chapter 2 of sports as a community ritual. I think of this as a sober view of capitalist leisure's and popular culture's contradictory character. Anyone hoping to transform capitalist popular culture must be realistic about the durability of the politically unprogressive cultural traditions that "the people" find pleasurable and self-serving.

Finally, in fairness to Willis, I must grant him the point that he is far too sophisticated a thinker and unorthodox Marxist simply to reduce the culture concept to political ideology. I never meant to say that a false consciousness view of culture was at the very heart of his perspective, but I did say that his perspective seemed like an uneasy synthesis of several culture concepts—one of which was an orthodox Marxist notion of ideology and consciousness. My point was that he seemed to lean a little too much on an that view of ideology and consciousness in the theory section of *Learning to Labor*. On the other hand, his earlier notion of profane culture, as he says, is a very rich, full-bodied culture concept. This is precisely why I took his writings so seriously and tried to develop what he was doing with anthropological notions of expressive culture and with critical theory notions of communication. As much as I admire the creative outpouring from the Centre for Contemporary Cultural Studies at Birmingham, I wanted to take their studies of "ideology" in some new, hopefully, equally productive directions.

The other reason I did not probe too deeply into the content and form of North Town youths' popular culture expressions was undoubtedly my preoccupation with other theoretical issues. This book was also shaped by the academic debates of fellow anthropologists and sociologists who study schooling in more ways than this theory essay may have suggested. Part 2 of this essay was my attempt to get beyond the conceptual barriers that "macro" and "micro" ethnographers and "reproduction" and "resistance" theorist had erected between themselves. I wanted to suggest some new ways of integrating macro and micro ethnographic approaches through my performance theory. In retrospect, I was as preoccupied with those conceptual problems as I was with the broader issue of class culture theory outlined in part 1.

On the Policy Question of Ethnic Failure in Schools

Despite my preoccupation with the education-as-cultural-reproduction question, some educational anthropologists who reviewed the manuscript took me to task for making few statements on the policy question of ethnic school failure. They asked how my performance theory better explains why some American ethnic minorities fail. My initial response (to myself) was that I never designed this study to explain why Mexicano kids fail and drop out of school. Had that question guided this study, I would have focused much more on individual kids' "educational careers" or life histories and on their school achievement scores. This question of school failure is a much narrower question than the problem of showing how American popular culture practices reproduce various forms of social inequality. In spite of this limitation, my study *does* provide some food for thought on the question of school success and failure.

Chapters 1 through 5 show that a historically oppressed ethnic group in South Texas have begun to succeed in their newly desegregated public schools. The longitudinal data on social mobility in Chapter 5 suggest that

10 percent more Mexicanos (than their fathers) were finishing at least two years of higher education. I would add that my quantitative intergenerational mobility measure of "school success" understates this new trend. My impression was that perhaps twice that number of Mexicanos were aspiring to obtain advanced educational credentials. Explanations of ethnic school failure (Ogbu 1987) that emphasize the negative psychological orientations of racially oppressed native-born ethnics such as blacks, Mexicanos, and native Americans tend to underestimate these new trends among politicized, middle class ethnics. Unfortunately, I cannot say how generalizable these empirical findings are to Mexicano communities outside South Texas that lack a civil rights movement and/or a demographic majority. I do think this study generally captures the dynamics of change occurring in many rural Southwestern communities, however, and I would expect to find similar trends elsewhere.

In my explanation of school success and failure, the key variable that predicts individual success and social mobility is how these ethnic youths use social class styles of speech. The American system of class, race, and gender dominance is powerful, but by paying careful attention to the "micro-politics" of ethnic resistance this case shows how one American ethnic group is gradually overcoming historical patterns of economic exploitation and ethnic stigmatization. This generally follows the suggestions of various "micro-ethnographers" to study why some ethnic youths from historically oppressed groups succeed rather than why they fail (McDermott 1987; Erickson 1987; Trueba 1988). The study describes, therefore, two different styles of "ethnic resistance" rather than just "working class resistance." I argue that class differences in communicative competence to use instrumental speech help "explain" general differences in school success and failure.

Generally, I found that the more middle class Mexicano kids, the "earholes" in Willis's study, tended to use the mainstream communicative code skillfully to succeed in school and "Anglo society." Even in a historically red neck town, enterprising Mexicano youth were learning behaviors that the society and schools admired, constantly staged, and graciously rewarded. They saw their success as ethnic resistance and "beating the gringos at their own game," and most of these youth maintained their ethnic expressive culture practices. This new assertiveness of middle class Mexicano youth cannot be called working class cultural resistance, but if one accepts the notion of multiple forms of oppression and struggle, these middle class Mexicano youths were "resisting" the ideological hegemony of their historical capitalist racial order. Rather than form an anti-school counter-culture, they developed and used the cultural capital of the mainstream to break with local traditions.

On the other side of the class divide, vatos tended to valorize both their class and ethnic status and "resisted" through open and dialogic verbal confrontations with school authorities. They saw their failure as ethnic and class resistance, and class theorists will recognize this as a variant of "working class resistance." The results of this resistance were the same as in Willis's study. In this case, the vast majority of Mexicano youth were not getting ahead, escaping the sting of class and racial prejudice, or developing a well-articulated class consciousness. They were tracked into practical sections of semi-literates and passed on through social promotion policies until more than 50 percent dropped out. The vatos ended up being a thorn in the administration's side and amusing entertainers that enlivened the deadening routine of academic work—and school failures.

All forms of social inequality die hard, and this study emphasizes multiple forms of dominance. Chapters 2 and 3 show how deeply entwined class inequality is with the patriarchal cultural practices of sports and dating. Working class Mexicanas were clearly the most at-risk students. They had to overcome a youth scene that put them down for class, race, and gender. I try to describe the patriarchal character of this youth scene in great detail, but as I indicate in Appendix B, female ethnographers need to tell the untold story of the "vatas" and female "nobodies" better than I have. Nevertheless, middle class females generally did far better than their working class counterparts from either race. But not all middle class Mexicanos got ahead, and not all social "nobodies" and working class Mexicano kids failed. These were the general tendencies, and, of course, there were exceptions to this general explanation or model.

Generally, this explanation complements Willis's and other anthropologists' attempts to explain school failure. Anthropologists and sociologists have debated the question of ethnic school failure quite vigorously (Ogbu 1987; Erickson 1987; McDermott 1987; Trueba 1988). John Ogbu (1987) and associates (Obgu and Matute-Bianchi 1986; Gibson 1988) have done the most extensive work on ethnic school failure in the field. Ogbu's explanation of how oppressed racial minorities defeat themselves through low expectations, which the self-fulfilling prophecy and expectations literatures replicate, obviously has merit. Nevertheless, his caste theory is built upon some notions of stratification, culture, and ethnicity that limit the way he studies the failure and success of native-born American ethnics in schools. My portrayal of the growing class differences among North Town Mexicanos does not fit easily into his sweeping notions of an oppressed "involuntary immigrant groups" or of a negative ethnic "oppositional culture." Elsewhere, I have tried to spell out in detail what I find problematic and useful about his and other anthropological explanations of ethnic school failure (Foley 1990a).

As previously indicated, I found the work of micro-ethnographers Shirley Heath (1983) and Hugh Mehan and associates (1986) particularly useful. They suggest focusing on cultural capital as linguistic competence and socially constructed reality. I outline my reasons for reframing their suggestive studies with different own notions of class, culture, and communication. Ultimately, Ogbu and other anthropologists, myself included, offer only partial explanations for why some ethnic kids fail, and until recently, little explanation for why some ethnic kids in oppressed ethnic groups succeed. Perhaps my main contribution to the debate over explaining ethnic school failure is more conceptual and methodological than empirical.

Having now made some claims for contributing to this debate, I hope, however, that educational anthropologists and sociologists will read this as a study of the riddle of commodity fetishism. This is a broad cultural critique of the ideological side of learning American culture, *not* a carefully designed empirical study of one ethnic group's school achievement. I have tried to raise the same question that Jules Henry (1965) raised about post-World War II America, but I revised his rather dated Freudian perspective with ideas from critical and class theory. Like Henry's *Culture Against Man,* this study asks Americans to reflect on the materialistic and dehumanizing side of our everyday cultural practices. I "read" this youth scene of sports, dating, and making out games as a metaphor of American culture in general. Ultimately, this study tries to challenge our notions of "winners" and "losers" and asks whether anyone actually wins in a capitalist culture so at odds with its ideals.

As a contribution to American studies, my goal for both this and the previous volume was to record accurately the complex process of political and cultural change that the social movements of the 1960s and 1970s spawned in one South Texas town. This meant highlighting the struggles of groups and individuals who transforming the patterns of American society and culture found in North Town. Despite my tendency to present a negative view of "capitalist culture," I also see the resilient, life-affirming quality in many people who "live" American capitalist culture. Consequently, I ended this volume with the story of Dante Aguila. For me, Mr. Aguila, the band director, is a lovely paradoxical symbol. He is one among a number of people who I found "resisting" and preserving their humanity. In popular culture jargon, he is an example of how to transform a potentially deadening, dominating mass cultural practice—halftime band music—into something much more liberating and pleasurable for the kids and himself. He is one of those people who tries to soar above our materialistic way of living and communicating and just enjoy life, music, and human solidarity. In spite of my critical perspective, I have no alternative blueprint for a new society and am peddling no particular political ideology. In an epoch when our ideal models of society and culture are blurring, I am left celebrating people and profane culture—until we invent something better.

Appendix B

Field Methods, Narrative Style, and Hermeneutic Interpretation

In this essay, I would like to convey in a more personal and philosophical way how I worked in the field and interpreted my experience. This essay describes in detail my style of communication with North Towners. It characterizes the extent that my fieldwork techniques were "dialogic" or deceptive. Various technical problems such as interpreting "making out games" and conducting the follow-up survey are also detailed. I also characterize the narrative writing style used and show how it flows from my philosophy of interpretation and science. The essay ends with a more philosophical discussion of hermeneutic and critical theory interpretive approaches. That discussion ends with my notions of a non-positivistic science and rationality grounded in personal experience. This provides the basis for my knowledge claims and invites the reader to argue about them.

Arriving in North Town

When we arrived in North Town, the Chicano movement had burst onto the local scene, and local Mexicano politicians had just won the school board and city council elections. Soon after the election, Anglos began suspecting that North Town Mexicanos had organized a "takeover" of the town. Anglos were convinced that Partido Raza Unida, a radical Chicano third party, had spread to North Town. As a result, we arrived at a very tense moment in the history of North Town ethnic relations. I and a research team of three settled into a large old house near the center of town and two smaller houses in the Mexicano barrio. We were generally greeted with a cordial if somwhat suspicious and curious politeness.

Gaining entrée into the North Town schools proved somewhat difficult. Don Post, a doctoral student of mine, had spent six months developing a relationship with the political leaders in both ethnic groups. He initially introduced me to the key leaders and set up a presentation to the local school board. Prior to the meeting, I met with most of the board members. Anglo board members expressed concern about the low achievement rates of many Mexican American students. They urged me to study the "poor home environment," which they characterized as overly permissive and unsupervised. Mexicano board members expressed concern about racial prejudice and discrimination in the schools toward their children. They urged me to study the "poor quality of white teachers and administrators," which they characterized as racist and indifferent to their needs. I responded by promising each warring side that I would look into their concerns.

The board meeting proved to be a very strange exchange between the townspeople and outside academics. I was introduced and asked to describe what I intended to do. As briefly and as untechnically as possible, I tried to explain what an ethnographic study of a school was. In retrospect, this was no small task for someone fresh from the "discourse wars" of graduate seminars. I translated ethnographic study as a kind of "descriptive local history." The idea of writing a history of the town and school seemed to make some sense to the board. At one point a local rancher asked: "What good will one of these, what did you say, 'ethnographic studies,' whatever that is, do? What will we get out of it?" Swallowing rather deeply, I countered with a longish speech that I, being relatively young and without authority over the youth, would be able to talk to "the troublemakers" and figure out why they were uncooperative. I argued that teachers and principals lacked the time to do this sort of thing. That response received several approving but skeptical grunts. In addition, I also promised to visit the homes of these students and see what parents were doing about their childrens' problems. Implying that the problem may lie in the home got a good response, and several board members offered suggestions how to approach the parents. Considerable discussion ensued over possible disruptions of the classroom and whether teachers would be required to participate. I stressed that no classes would be disrupted, and that participation would be purely voluntary. With those final assurances, the board unanimously agreed to let me spend the school year observing in the North Town public schools. A closing comment by one of the ranchers wryly expressed the ambiguity of the moment: "Well, I guess we will find out what an ethnography is."

In actuality, the board meeting requesting access to the schools was largely a ceremonial event. Each ethnic group had already decided to give us access to observe in the schools. We, particularly Don, had lobbied hard to convince board members that we could help them understand their educational problems. Years later, we found out the real reasons for the unanimous vote we received the night of the presentation, however. Anglo Better Government League (BGL) leaders determined through their state political contacts that cooperating with a Department of Health, Education and Welfare (HEW) sponsored researcher might avoid political trouble. They investigated us through the offices of U.S. Senator Loyd Bentsen. They determined that we were "bleeding heart liberal academics" but not agents of HEW or the U.S. Justice Department.

On the other hand, Mexicano political leaders hoped to win over an outside Anglo liberal to their demands for greater equality. They investigated what we had been doing in Crystal City, home of the movement. They perceived us as potential advocates for their civil rights cause. Both sides hoped to persuade us to write a report advocating their respective point of view. In the end, perhaps we appeared to be only a minor threat, and possibly an ally. This was particularly true for the Mexicanos, who had less power and less to lose. The Anglo BGL leaders in power, like the Crystal City Raza Unida leaders, never trusted us. Some of the basis of this mistrust is chronicled in greater detail in the community study (Foley et al. 1988) as well as in the next sections.

My Public Persona and Gaining Acceptance

Becoming accepted and established in a community is always a long, sometimes difficult process. North Town was a racially divided community, and many of the leaders were involved in intense political competition. I came into this environment as a researcher with a team of graduate assistants. Being from the University of Texas, I was afforded a great deal of courtesy. On the other hand, my entire purpose for being there was clearly suspect. The way I related to the kids and teachers has already been portrayed episodically in the ethnography, but the following discussion is a more detailed, explicit account of my field methods and of various methodological issues.

At school, my persona was a curious mixture of serious researcher and down-home jock. Being an ex-college basketball and tennis player, I worked out regularly with both teams. Not infrequently, I was running around the high school campus in shorts and a t-shirt. I went to all the extra-curricular sports events, even the out-of-town games. I also hung around the field house and rode on the player bus to games. I became identified as an "ex-college player," and kids used to ask me questions about college sports. I also helped the "father of North Town tennis," a retired coach, give his protégés a few pointers as we played.

My acceptance by the kids was an interesting progression. Initially the rumor went around school that I was a narcotics agent. The year before, a number of high school kids had been busted for drugs in an undercover operation. When I went to my first football game, the entire student section chanted "narc, narc, narc" when I walked by. Needless to say, this amused the adults and turned me a pale shade of red. It was a good-natured taunt, but there was some suspicion. Many students came up to me in school and asked directly if I was a narc. For a month or so, that was a source of endless joking.

Gradually, however, I began being invited to Anglo student drinking-dope smoking parties after football games. Some of the dope smoking kids also made it a practice of letting me know when they were stoned. They would come up in the halls and show me their joints, and ask if I had noticed how "ripped" they were in class. During the first two months, all the kids put me through a series of tests, the usual wisecracks and public putdowns. One day a student passed the following note to me from another student:

> Do you believe someone should come around and write a book about our school? I think it is a good idea, if both good and bad points are put in. It should also be showed to both teachers and students to show what should be corrected and what shouldn't be. Most people are friendly to the guy, but I heard a friend of mine [in this class now] wearing dark glasses call him a missing link. Do you think it is a good or bad idea?

One of the teachers had introduced me to the class as "an anthropologist searching for the missing link in North Town." One of the kids replied that maybe *I* was the missing link. This led to an amusing discussion about what a bunch of animals they were, and what archaeologists in old horror movies really do besides search for lost treasures.

On another occasion, I was riding on the pep squad bus home from the game. Three of the girls wanted me to sit between them to "keep them warm." We shared some popcorn and a couple of sandwiches as they joked about cute guys. A couple of the band guys came up and gave me the Chicano handshake and asked: "Hey man, what are you doing with these chicks?" What they meant to say was "What's an old guy like you doing hustling our chicks?" After they left, this was an invitation for the girls to get personal. One kidded me about my age (gasp! Over thirty!). Another joked about going home with me, and she asked which one of them I was

209

going to pick. I retorted, why not all three, which was definitely the correct response. They laughed and dropped that line of sexual joking. They then wrote my name on a team-spirit balloon and told me to let it float up to heaven when I got home. The poetry of that gesture swallowed up any cute comeback I was harboring.

Initially, the kids accepted me with a good deal of curiosity and kidding. They were constantly trying to guess exactly what I was going to write. Many wanted to know how I lived and who paid me. One came up and asked me when I was going to turn my report in to HEW. Another asked if I was going to write a book like *Up the Down Staircase*, a novel about a teacher in a ghetto school. Upon hearing that I had been in the Philippines, one student asked, "How do you say I don't trust you in Filipino?" Another asked if I was "putting them under a microscope."

Having responded to their tests in various cool, ironic ways, I became "Doc." I took that diminutive as a sign of respect and familiarity for this strange guy who was "writing a book about us." They knew I was some kind of doctor or professor, but as Tara said:

> You are smart. Everybody likes you. You don't act like a big shit. Why do they call you "Doc"? Are you really some kind of professor from UT? You walk around, but you know. You're real quiet and slow and friendly, but man, can you play tennis and basketball. The teachers think you're a genius or something. Cain and Jones and Cisneros all told us to be good and be quiet when you were around. They didn't want us to act like animals in front of you. They probably want you to think they're hot shit teachers.

Eventually, some kids also asked me for very personal advice about dating, drinking, and parental problems. Others borrowed books from me and asked about the university and what college life was like. I was closer to the male athletes, because I was always around and obviously was one of them in spirit. This group had a fairly good racial, class, and student achievement level mix of males. Generally, I had a smaller sample of female informants, but I did talk frequently with six or seven females of varying ages, class, and racial background. I also "rapped" a good deal with the Mexicano kids in auto mechanics who were considered the "troublemakers." At the time, I had a Ford van with ex-hippie trappings, a carpeted sleeping area, and a tape deck. In what turned out to be a bit of good fortune, my van engine blew a piston. The vatos and I rebuilt my engine in the school shop. That proved to be a good entrée, and we spent many hours talking about sex, drugs, and cars while fiddling with my van.

The other major part of my "style" that fit nicely into rural North Town was being "down-home." I grew up on an Iowa farm, so wearing blue jeans and talking about animals and crops and land comes quite naturally. North Towners reminded me of former friends and relatives. They were unpretentious, practical, straightforward people. I often felt like I was in some kind of time warp in North Town. On the other hand, living in small-town America also felt strange to me. Having lived abroad and in several cities, I am now culturally both an "insider" and an "outsider." I do not like the cultural conservatism and social pressures of small town life anymore. Nevertheless, coming home to rural America was easy, even though I am no longer a farm boy.

Some Limits to My Acceptance and Credibility

One of the most difficult aspects of the research was maintaining good relations with the badly divided, politicized school board. During the first weeks in town, I successfully presented my research to the school board, who then publicly invited us to spend the year observing in North Town schools. As I indicated, each ethnic group believed that I was writing something partisan supporting its viewpoint. The Mexicano board members wanted us to record the racial discrimination by whites. The Anglos wanted us to document the cultural deficiencies of Mexican American family life. Being accommodating and somewhat deceptive, we told each side what they wanted to hear. Judging from repeated questions, few people actually believed our studiously vague descriptions of the research. Various parents and students said they "knew" I was "really studying the race problem."

Later on in the research, the school board summoned me to give a mid-year progress report on my research. This summons came shortly after I received a mysterious call from a Mexicano friend who was playing "deep throat." He called to warn me that my research into the city and county records had upset the county judge and mayor. Of course, these are public records open to anyone, but I was apparently not supposed to be looking at them. The school had restricted me from looking at any personnel files, so when I began reading old city minutes and county tax and debtor records, they had second thoughts about my observing in the schools. My protector told me to "cool it," and I did. Nevertheless, within a week, I was asked to present a "progress report."

I was the first item on the agenda, and their businesslike manner signaled that they intended to grill me. The purpose of the meeting was apparently to expose publicly my "real reason" for coming to North Town. They wanted me to acknowledge publicly that I was more interested in race relations and politics than in education and children's learning.

The local doctor and staunch BGL leader initiated the inquisition: "I thought you were going to study motivational problems of the children?"

I responded that much of my work had been to talk with students about their teachers and classes. I assured them that I now knew many of the vocational education students who were considered "troublemakers." The president of the board, a very forceful woman, followed up this response by asking: "I thought you were going to study family background factors? Didn't you tell us that you were going to look into the breakdown in a lot of these kids' families? Was that all just a lot of talk?" I began to say that we had interviewed as many as a hundred parents, but the good doctor was getting his second wind. He interrupted and asked what I expected to find in the county and city records. He wanted to know if I was looking for materials on race relations and discrimination. I retorted that the records had little on what I would call race relations. I emphasized how the record could be used to learn about past issues, leaders, and economic development.

The board president escalated the questioning and asked what the title of my proposal was. I said rather meekly, "Anglo and Chicano Models of Educational and Social Change." At that moment, I deeply regretted writing the proposal in a language that endeared me to liberal federal bureaucrats but was a red flag to North Town Anglos. The board president sensed that I was in a corner and asked: "Which is the Chicano model? Isn't it Crystal City? Aren't you comparing us to Crystal City? Didn't you do research there last year? Didn't you pick North Town as an Anglo-controlled school?"

To all these pointed questions I responded in what my fieldnotes describe as an "evasive, weasel-like manner." "Yes, Crystal City seemed like a 'Chicano model' at the time." The words burned in my mouth on that occasion. "Yes, I had been there briefly, but a graduate student of mine was actually doing the research." Five months was hardly a brief visit to Crystal. I hedged that North Town was not exactly an Anglo-controlled school, but that Anglos were still active and influential. I wanted to express approval that Anglos had *not* left North Town as they had in Crystal, but Mexicano board members might have thought I was being disingenuous.

Eventually, the questions trailed off to a few comments about watching me carefully and keeping the school files private. I felt like I had stood before my inquisitors with no clothes, and I was relieved to get off the hook. They never actually took any further actions to restrict my research in the schools. Apparently, the main purpose of the meeting was to make public my pro-Mexicano bias, thus showing what a hypocrite I was. The tone of the meeting was who-are-you-trying-to-kid-Foley. They wanted to see what color a bleeding-heart liberal bled, and my unjudiciously written proposal was my undoing.

Several years later, during the community review of the *Peones* manuscript, I was told how the Better Government League had investigated me. They obtained a copy of the original research proposal to the National Institute of Education through Senator Bentsen's office. They could see from the original proposal that we were sympathetic to the new Raza Unida movement. We portrayed it as a progressive new break in South Texas race relations. They also had a somewhat laundered version of the proposal that Don Post and I had furiously edited and reprinted for that first board meeting. That version was essentially the same, except that it was somewhat more even-handed and downplayed the virtues of the Chicano civil rights movement. I was told later that this deception had led the Better Government League leaders to close their meetings to us.

On Our Openness and Sense of Ethics

In retrospect, I am not proud of laundering the research proposal. I do not portray this incident to my students as a "good field technique." On the other hand, I am not sure how negatively it affected the data collection. Throughout fieldwork, many Anglo leaders still talked to me freely, especially after some reviewed the manuscript. At that point, the reviewers tried to correct my biased, pro-Mexican views. During this era, everyday communication was filled with deception. Many North Towners seemed to expect that you were conning them the way they were conning you. The norms of everday open, honest, sincere communication were under attack, and public trust was quite low.

This does not absolve us for being deceptive, but North Towners probably agonized less about our deceptions than I did. The low expectations they had for us probably help explain why we got away with the deceptive proposal. In addition, some North Towners still felt that the federal government must have sent us, therefore, they felt obligated to cooperate. The idea that such research was simply part of a professor's job was unbelievable to most people. I explained about inventing research projects, applying for competitive grants, and the publish-or-perish syndrome to absolutely no avail. I doubt if most people understood or believed that no one "sent me."

In spite of this serious deception, we tried to be fairly open about what we were doing. Our major way of being open and ethical was to have North Towners criticize our manuscript. At the time, I felt that social scientists wrote accounts about people, but people were never asked to critique these accounts. After leaving the community, I spent several years writing *From Peones to Politicos*. I wrote the manuscript with a minimum of obscure technical language so North Towners could read and criticize it, then returned to the community with a draft of the manuscript and gave it to twenty-five people from the various groups and viewpoints. Approximately half the reviewers had been informants and about half were people we knew less well.

After a month had passed, I returned again and tape recorded sixty-five hours of discussions on the manuscript. This proved to be an enormously rewarding yet difficult experience. Some people wondered why I had "dug up all this racial stuff" and how it was possible to learn so many secrets in such a short time. One school board member, who threatened to sue me for libel, made me go over the manuscript page by page for six hours. Even more menacing, the school counselor challenged me to a fist fight. Finally, the local priest accused me of being a propagandist for the Raza Unida party. Conversely, some Mexicanos claimed that I was the savior of the community who would bring the "feds" in to clean up the town. Several people showed me the book with the pseudonyms scratched out and the real names written in. They were proud of their accomplishments and wanted their children to know that they had made history.

I promised people who read the manuscript that I would publish their comments in "the book." I did, and that endures as one of the best features of the community study. One unintended consequence of the review process was to generate a great deal of new data. I did not anticipate the extent that some people would open up because of the review process. Anglo political leaders treated us much the way the Crystal City Raza Unida leaders had during our research there. They were very suspicious and closed their political meetings to us. Returning with the manuscript made several Anglo leaders become more talkative, however. If I really was going to publish a book, they wanted to set the record straight and tell their side of the story. Moreover, they also respected me for coming back and taking their criticisms, as one rancher put it, "like a man." During the fieldwork, the Mexicanos were unusually open with us. We actually attended several private political strategy meetings of Mexicano leaders. They had very little new to say about the manuscript and were generally pleased with the presentation of their views. A full account of what was said can be found in *From Peones to Politicos* (Foley et al. 1988).

Being open about the manuscript and getting community reviews ultimately made our account much more balanced and better informed. It also made me feel more ethical about how we had done the fieldwork. This helped spread word about the manuscript and assured that some North Towners would read it. Ultimately, most city employees and some teachers looked at the published version of the book. The local radio station sold and promoted the book, and I went on a talk show to discuss it with other people. Whatever its effect, which has been difficult to judge, returning with the manuscript was an important part of trying to be "dialogic" in a literal, communicative sense.

In general, I believe that we did the day-to-day data collection in a relatively open manner as well. At times, I colluded with students in the games they played with teachers. At times, I was caught in the middle of warring ethnic groups. I was courted. I was snubbed. We generally followed the usual practice of strict confidentiality. We listened to a great deal of gossip and hearsay, but tried not to repeat it or other things that people told us.

The manner in which we talked with people was informal, open, and occasionally even confrontational. The more we became a part of the community and people's personal histories, the more we talked to people like friends and colleagues rather than interviewees. The more we talked to people without tape recorders and notepads, the more they talked back in an outspoken way. We started out being rather passive participant-observers, asking few questions, and we ended up actively involved in community events, people's lives, and animated conversations. This progression was particularly true of my relations with the youth. I certainly did not become a teenager again, but North Town youth were surprisingly open and frank about themselves and about their town and school.

On the other hand, being open as a field researcher is also a performance of sorts. A researcher can probably never be a friend or be open in the same sense that a real member of a family or community can. I was always an outsider playing the role of researcher. This creates a degree of ambiguity, and you cannot escape being deceptive. You are often hiding what you are actually studying and what you are most critical about in regard to the community. I never told obviously racist Anglos that they were red necks. I never told Mexicanos when they misjudged an Anglo friend. I never told blatantly incompetent teachers that they should look for another line of work. Much of what I privately felt went into fieldnotes and laments to colleagues, rather than into frank conversations with North Towners.

The worst thing about being a field anthropologist is the nagging feeling that you are like Willie Loman in *Death of a Salesman*. Consequently, you invariably find ways of distancing yourself from this contradictory role of "friendly spy" or "intimate stranger." You create a private life that is "authentic," and you bend the conventions of your public performance as an anthropologist.

The idea that we practiced an open, dialogic style of fieldwork is, therefore, very relative. Compared to standard field techniques extolled in how-to-do-it manuals, we did do some unconventional, experimental things. Yet we were also deceptive in many small and some not-so-small ways. We never understood the extent to which North Towners saw through our "fronts" until we learned much later about their investigation into the research proposal.

We generally justified our big deceptions on the grounds that we would write a good critical piece about how Americans were solving the American dilemma of race. I fell back on the it-is-good-for-society rationale, which, of course, can and has led to many abuses of power by various leaders and intellectuals (Bok 1978). Where do you draw the line on such a utilitarian argument? Douglas (1976) has a more cynical justification for deception. He argues that a well-intentioned intellectual has the right to be deceptive in order to get the goods on corrupt leaders or to expose socially damaging cultural practices. I still have mixed feelings about the white lies of omission that we told during the fieldwork, but I would probably do it again. I think of our books as a cultural critique that creates dialogue. We have taken our lumps over what we claim to know about North Town and American ethnic/race relations. As time passes, others will judge if our small lies led to some greater good.

Observing in North Town High

My initial observations in the North Town schools were more like ethology or bird-watching. I was a passive observer who never asked any questions. I was like a giant Rorschach inkblot. Kids would come up to me and start trying to guess why I was there. They would begin telling me all sorts of information without being asked questions. My silent vigil on their frantic activities produced talk. They filled my space, invariably with talk of politics and race. Those topics were the great unspoken secret. They hovered over the school and were on everybody's mind. This was so true that teachers were loath to mention such matters. Their job was to ignore it all, so the nasty issue of race might go away. If asked directly, the teachers were willing to talk about racial issues, but it was the kids who wanted to hear another adult's opinion besides that of their parents.

One section of my fieldnotes seems particularly appropriate to illustrate how I felt after three months in the schools. It gives some sense of the patience and attention to communication needed to get your "story":

> *On Being a Hunter:* Waiting is extremely frustrating. I could be going so much faster, if only everyone would trust me and cooperate, or if I wasn't so inhibited, perhaps? There is an invisible line which some are beginning to cross. Kids are beginning to bump into me in the halls. They tap me on the shoulder, shake hands, "Que paso-me" [ask me what's happening?], give me friendly taunts, come up and give their opinion of teachers and school without me asking. Some now call me Doc. Others say, "Hello compadre" [godparent, friend]. They are beginning to ask me personal questions, too. Where did I grow up? Did I really play ball there? Was I all-state? Am I really a professor at UT? One joked that Kara was just being nice to me so she could be in the book, be the star. Yesterday, Bubba pulled the oldest joke of all on me. He put a quarter up to his eye and held it in like a monocle. He then challenged me to do it. I did, but in the meantime he had put lead around the edges, which left me with a "black eye" and everyone else roaring with delight. They are playing with me more, and I am less like a hunter sitting up-wind. My waiting is a state of moving softly without pounding expectations. I am just trying to be in the same life/work/play space. I just want to be quietly visible and reach out with my presence. They come to me, because I don't move too quickly or say too much. Unlike a real hunter, I have no gun. I do not kill them with bullets or words. But like a hunter, I do try to stay up-wind, and these kids come to feed in my field. I'm this adult from the outside world that knows things that they don't. They wonder about all this growing up, all the stuff happening in their town. They are beginning to share things about themselves with me, tell me how they feel about their "race problem." Some want me to come to their drinking parties, to smoke dope with them, to let them ride around in my van. Things are moving, even though I seem to be doing nothing more than living here and hanging out at school. Am I the hunter or the hunted?

During those first three months, I mostly hung around the school and visited classes, played ping-pong in the gym at lunch time, and participated in the sports programs. I avoided getting too identified with any particular group of kids or teachers. I wanted to convey to everyone that I was open to talk to as many people as possible. I often watched students during the lunch hours and after school. During these observations and casual conversations I never took notes. Upon returning to my house, I wrote up my recollections of what happened. I quickly learned who the key student status groups were, and how the two ethnic groups organized their territories. As I came to know many of the principal civic and

217

political and business families, I began crudely locating kids on a community class continuum as well.

As indicated briefly in Chapter 2, I used no formal questionnaires or sociometric instruments to verify the various status identity groups. When I had long, private conversations with students whom I knew well, I took extensive notes while they talked. Most of my conversations with youth were informal, however, and took place in the hallways, school buses, sports fields, and "hangouts" of North Town. I never recorded these conversations until I returned home. Formal opinion surveys would have been far too obtrusive in this racially tense situation. Moreover, It would have felt awkward and obtrusive to be constantly framing my conversations as "interviews."

Earlier studies of "the adolescent society" used peer rating questionnaires and sociometric surveys to meticulously classify students. It seemed unnecessary to measure these groups quantitatively for several reasons. First, the large status display groups were not really groups in the classic corporate sense. To force kids to label and locate themselves under these labels and "groups" would have reified these labels and groups into something they were not. Second, taking a performance view of this scene required me to avoid getting bogged down in classifying people into status groups or in counting dyadic pairs. My goal was to capture how popular culture rituals among the youth reproduced various forms of inequality. I ultimately constructed a general cultural model of the North Town youth scene.

In sharp contrast to quantitative studies of adolescents, I used a much more ethnographic method of studying adolescent status groups. Initially, I asked a number of students to identify the groups and to classify specific students in their correct groups. We usually discussed groups of students I had observed "hanging out" together at school or at sports events. I started out with specific observations and asked students to verify or correct my impressions. Since the school had only five hundred students, it was easy to locate the main high and low status groups quickly. We also came to know what kinds of families they were from without doing an obtrusive, time-consuming formal survey.

Several students who became key informants taught me how to see the student groups the way they did. The characterization of group labels and social organizational patterns was originally based, therefore, on many observations, casual conversations, and intensive informant work over a year, not a set of quantifiable survey questionnaires. This generalized account was created from hundreds of hours of listening to these youth and observing how they interacted with each other. In the end, my characterization is rooted in the views of Paco, Tara, Jack, Reggie, Chuckie, and many others. I can, therefore, describe the pattern of their feelings and practices, but I cannot cite precise numbers for group membership or a particular type of behavior.

One additional, important way that I have cross-checked the original participant-observation and informant work was through the follow-up study reported in Chapter 5. During several weeks of intensive interviewing, I was able to contact and talk to as many as forty former North Town students who were students during the original fieldwork. I selected at least four members from each high school class, and using the high school annuals, we traced where their classmates had gone. Those former students who had organized the ten-year reunion were particularly knowledgeable. It was necessary to use both Mexicano and Anglo informants to learn what everyone was doing as adults. Astonishingly, perhaps 90 percent of the information from informants was reliable. There are undoubtedly still errors, but the cross-checking process produced reasonably accurate information in a short time. North Town is still a relatively small, traditional community where people tend to know everyone and their families.

During these interviews, which often lasted two or three hours, I also engaged the respondents in more general discussions on the various status groups of selected youth. This proved to be a very useful cross-check on my original interviews and observations and made me very certain about my original classifications of kids as "vatos," "kickers," "nerds," and "school leaders." Ten years later, people's memories were still quite vivid on who hung out or went steady with whom. Moreover, as we talked about what hanging out, friendship, and dating meant, it was clear that I had gotten the story right during the original fieldwork. In effect, the follow-up survey gives the original fieldwork a somewhat more quantitative character without being obtrusive. Being able to return to the original research site some years later strikes me as a very good way of blending quantitative and qualitative techniques.

For the analysis of classroom rituals, I initially observed a wide range of classes and subjects. During the first three months of observations, I took no notes whatsoever, and I wrote up my observations from memory each day. During later observations, I made sketchy notes of the sequence of events, key characters, and choice dialogue. In the evenings, I elaborated those notes. Initially, I wanted to get a feel or flavor of the school and to meet most of the teachers in a less obtrusive manner. Later, I began focusing on specific classrooms that had interesting mixes of student groups and ethnicity. My log of teacher observations indicates that I observed 125 hours of formal classes over a six-month period. I observed twenty teachers at least twice, but concentrated on eight. They were all observed from eight to ten hours.

After generally classifying these teachers according to their communicative style, I selected what I considered interesting differences. The idea was to cover a variety of teachers that the kids judged "good" and "bad" who were "cool" and "nerdy." I also wanted both Mexicano and Anglo and male and female teachers. Finally, I selected different types of sections, practical and advanced, to get a sense of which type of class the teachers preferred. Ultimately, I did several observations of the sections or classes that had an interesting racial mix of students and/or an interesting pattern of making out games. In short, sampling of teachers and sections to observe was done purposefully for variety and contrast in performance styles. Although I did not randomly sample, I ended up with a very extensive, and, I believe, representative sample of classroom behavior.

In addition, I supplemented these observations with extensive conversations with many of these teachers. They generously gave me time during their off periods, and we talked in their rooms about their views of teaching, the students, and their families. I took extensive notes during these somewhat formal interview sessions. I kept no precise records of the total time spent talking with teachers, which includes an occasional dinner party, cafeteria lunches, in-service workshops, faculty meetings, and "hanging out" in the teacher lounge. I am quite certain I spent more time talking with them than I did observing their teaching. Although this ethnography is written more from the students' point of view, I also collected the teachers' views on many topics. The sections on school board politics, classroom making out games, and sports use a great deal of information collected from teachers and coaches.

In general, teachers were so cooperative and helpful that I usually visited them on a day's notice. At other times, I visited them spontaneously when invited. Several of the teachers, who were long-time residents of North Town, were also valuable informants for the community study. Initially, teachers feared that I was evaluating their teaching. Gradually, several expressed relief that I never tried to tell them how to teach. I apparently "asked a lot of questions" but was a "good listener." Several of the younger, more liberal teachers invited me to socialize with them in their homes.

School administrators were, however, another matter. The principal and vice principal were always on their guard in interviews, and they were very protective of the school records. School administrators always seemed to fear saying something that might jeopardize their positions or future careers. Several openly admitted that it would not serve their interest to be too "chummy" with me. They knew the school board was skeptical of me, and they had apparently been warned to cooperate—but with caution. The Mexicano administrators were more open about school policies, but they were still more circumspect than either Mexicano or Anglo teachers. Except for the principal, I never had any particularly revealing conversations with administrators.

The observation of making out games initially proved somewhat difficult, because I had no precise definition of what I was looking for. I knew I wanted to focus on student-teacher negotiations and the humorous breaks in classroom lessons. I also wanted to record patterns of racial and class inequality. I started with a Goffmanesque notion of performance and dramaturgical events, and a class theory notion of alienated labor. Initially, I tried to track student status groups' behavior as soon as I could. I was looking for how ethnic and class factors affected student status group performances in the classroom.

Initially, it was not always easy to define when a making out game began and ended. At times, these events were not clearly marked. At other times, groups of kids clearly staged well orchestrated, though usually spontaneous, "scams" or teacher "cons." After observing many of these games, it became easier to see them as rather well marked "speech events" or "speech acts" with beginnings, sequences, and ends. I have not described these events in as great a linguistic detail as a sociolinguist would, however, because my focus was more on the dramaturgical roles than the speech itself.

At first, it appeared that all kids played all the roles in these little dramas to slow down work. Since, however, I still did not know the youths well enough to classify them, I frequently returned to my fieldnotes to add information. The classroom vignettes of student-teacher interactions were recorded with as many names of the students as I knew. Later, I went back and filled in other names and any status background information I had on the family or the kid's standing with other kids. After a number of months, most of the making out games that I had recorded in detail included the names and status ranking of the given performers. Since the various roles were played by a small number of students, this became predictable and relatively easy. Ultimately, I focused on selected sections with certain teachers, which allowed me to see a small number of kids initiating similar making out games week after week.

Eventually, I could see that these games had an ethnic and class pattern with distinct normative roles for different youth. When students failed to enact their parts, teachers demanded greater loyalty to these roles. They rewarded, punished, or disattended to such breaks. Such disjunctions or ruptures in these dramas signaled, therefore, the overall normative structure and meaning of the games. Moreover, students signaled their intentions to be deceptive or dialogic through body language, through verbal repartee, or by simply telling me a con was on. At times, I was unable to be a detached "scientific observer" and ended up an active participant in these playful exchanges. It became apparent that students used different communicative competences and speech styles for different purposes.

The ethnographic description of class reproduction was based, therefore, on actual observed performances rather than on self-reports. Ultimately, my fieldnotes distinguished the specific class backgrounds of performers during each classroom performance. This was possible because we were also doing a historical study of class recomposition in the community itself. I knew the family backgrounds of most of the participants in these making out games. Moreover, I participated directly in these language games and observed them first-hand.

In ethnomethodological jargon, my interpretations of school events became highly indexical or contextualized. I finally "saw" children performing class roles when I knew many of the youths' families and understood the class structure of the community. Much later, I labeled or explained these recorded patterns as illustrations of "instrumental speech" and "alienated communicative labor." In a positivist approach to fieldwork, I would have started out with these concepts operationalized into discrete behaviors. Certain ways of acting would have meant "instrumental" behavior, and others would have meant "non-instrumental" behavior. Having done this study and generated a conceptual framework, it could now be replicated in a more quantifiable, positivistic manner.

While attempting to record how making out games staged class culture performances, I also noticed many sex role performances. The students were more preoccupied with sex and sexual play than with any other topic. Daily classroom life and humor was filled with sexual jokes and teasing. My notes actually reflect my consciously avoiding such topics due to my conceptual programming to "see" ethnicity and class. But my "conceptual shields" broke down, and a fair amount of the sexual play and sex role performances intruded into the fieldnotes. Female performance roles such as "the dumb blond" and "helpless female" were obviously reproducing both class and patriarchal norms. The descriptions of powder-puff football games, the pep squad, going steady, and interracial dating illustrate these patriarchal practices. Several female students became key informants, and the ethnography does give some sense of what growing up female in North Town was like. I ultimately included a great deal on gender performance roles and the reproduction of patriarchy.

Nevertheless, my ethnographic account tends to be a male account of a very male-dominated world of sports, bonded sexuality, and male-led making out games. As I indicated previously, being a male and ex-jock, I tended to have better access to the males. I found it particularly difficult to talk with young females about intimate topics like sex and sexuality. No matter what my views might be on feminist topics, I could probably never talk to a young girl about her feelings as another woman could. I could have presented more detailed data on the female view of sports, friendship, dating, and marriage, but I ended up writing about what I knew best.

Ideally, the research team should have included a female ethnographer in the high school. The research team did include female ethnographers to do work on elementary school teachers and on the Mexicano family. Jean Meadowcroft spent four months in the elementary schools and has written on the racial attitudes of teachers (Meadowcroft and Foley 1977). Clarice Mota worked primarily with older women and families, and this material was included in the community study (Foley et al. 1988). Her work also provided some insights into the changing values of her informants' daughters. Some of that material helped corroborate what my female informants were telling me. Unfortunately, Clarice had no access to the schools and could not serve as a counterpart female ethnographer in the youth scene.

On Narrative Style

Having described the way I related to North Towners and recorded my experience, I would like to shift to a more philosophical discussion of field methods. First, I would like to characterize the narrative account that I have written. Second, I would like to show how this narrative flows from my assumptions about ethnography as a critical interpretive enterprise.

This ethnographic account of the youth scene and growing up in North Town remains within a narrative tradition that Marcus and Cushman (1984) label "ethnographic realism." I use several distinct narrative conventions, however, to establish the text's authority and truth claims on different grounds. For example, the language used is often much closer to ordinary speech than to technical social science discourse. My manner of expression is obviously personal and conveys a distinct authorial voice. One friend called it "full of Foleyisms," meaning my manner of conversing, sense of humor, and general way of being and communicating. Others praised it as "natural," "open," and "accessible." My language style also provoked other reviewers to call it "breezy," "informal," "self-serving," and "casual." At many points, however, the narrative does "code-switch" into an analytic, more formal language that uses social science ideas. A particular anthropological and political perspective intrudes into the text and is explicitly stated in the appendices.

Nevertheless, the text contains many real people expressing their views and actual social scenes. There are also recognizable, although not highly developed, characters in a literary sense. These experiential moments and characters keep the formal, interpretive moments from dominating the narrative. I selected these real events and people because I judged them to capture best what I saw over and over again. One might call these incidents and characters a series of "ethnographic metaphors." In other words, these carefully chosen moments act like metaphors because they are unusually fecund and suggestive. They evoke memories of adolescence and growing up and draw the reader into the scene. They come to mean, therefore, more than the literal scene that they represent.

Unlike the usual ethnographic constructions of "a typical day," or "a typical conversation," these "ethnographic metaphors" do not have a detached, distilled, generic quality. In a generic ethnography, the narrator stands apart from what he or she is describing and reconstructs the scene in an analytic language. This language becomes a tool rather than the ground of experience. The language of such portrayals often lacks the playfulness, a sense of time, place, and voice that suggests a real experience. These timeless ethnographic portraits are above history, hence more monologic and less likely to engage the reader.

In searching for a general narrative style that at least implicitly had a more dialogic character, I was drawn to "new journalism" (Wolfe 1974). "New" journalists use a variety of literary narrative techniques such as scene-by-scene story telling, realistic dialogue, third person point of view, and "relentless symbolic detail" of people's expressive style. Wolfe claims, at times grandiosely, that new journalists capture a whole side of American life abandoned by psychologically oriented novelists. Modern day new journalists like Wolfe, Truman Capote, Norman Mailer, Joan Didion, Jimmy Breslin, Hunter Thompson, and George Plimpton are writing first-hand accounts or "non-fiction" novels about life in America. Wolfe claims that they are recording the manners and morals of society the way great historical novelists such as Balzac and Dickens did. This involves living in these settings for a period of time and/or extensive library research and supplementary interviews.

These accounts are often autobiographical, and the language used is highly personal. These first-person narratives are filled with the writers' judgments about everything from the tea cups to their characters' voices and motivations. The narratives are so personal and authorial that little formal, technical language stands between the observer and the observed. Their aim is generally to take the reader deep into a social scene, which is revealed through the eyes of all the participants. In this regard, they engage the scene and its characters in such an open, subjective manner that their dramatic portrayals of others become, in some ways, more "objective." One has the sense of witnessing an honest confrontation between the investigator and the investigated. Moreover, in some of these accounts, a genuine blending of world views between observer and observed seems to occur. New journalism texts have an experiential quality that many generic ethnographies lack. In the name of science and objectivity, ethnographers usually excuse themselves from their texts. In addition, they tend to portray their analytical model rather than their actual field experience. New Journalists never lose their "subjects" in a pool of technical jargon.

Anthropologists can learn a great deal from new journalists about openness to a scene and to language. What seems like philosophical naiveté allows their intuitions and imagination to guide the field experience. They simply want to be in the flow of history and to write interesting, provocative accounts. Consequently, they convey their experience in more open, commonly shared language. The "methodological naiveté" of this open posture fulfills Hans-Georg Gadamer's (1975) most fundamental conditions for hermeneutic interpretation. They have no positivist pretenses about finding truth through formal methods or expressing it in an artificial, objective language. They have not been trained to look for truth and objectivity outside of experience and the historical tradition they are trying to understand.

It should be added, however, that the great strength of the new journalism is also its weakness. These accounts of new journalists contain many forms of personal excess that ethnographers usually avoid. Too often, the accounts stage the egos of these free-wheeling investigators. The commercial lure to produce timely, trendy, entertaining accounts is enormous, and some of these writers become celebrities and entertainers. At times, they only stay in a scene for a few weeks, or write pieces based on a few interviews and little cross-checking. It is hard to imagine building trust and getting "inside" a social scene that quickly, much less understanding it. They apparently to have no tradition of fieldwork practices or concepts of society and culture that serve as a standard for interpretation and argumentation. The "fieldwork" of new journalists seems more akin to the chronicles of travelers. If the travelers were interesting, perceptive people, like some of the new journalists, they wrote interesting travelogues. Or their travels forced them to be self-reflexive, and they said interesting things about themselves. If not, they simply wrote chauvinistic moral tirades about the strange savages they endured.

The new journalists do not make explicit their interpretive world views. They seem to have no explicit philosophy of how to interpret social scenes. If they are aware of the general debates on epistemology and ontology, they do not feel obligated to discuss them. Consequently, they offer little defense of their claims to be representing reality beyond simply "being there." Gaye Tuchman's (1978) incisive ethnography illustrates how various institutional practices constrain journalists. Apparently, the conventions of journalistic fieldwork and reporting do not demand that they be self-reflexive about their interpretive practices. New journalists could learn much from the social science tradition that would improve their general practices.

Another source of ideas about new ethnographic narrative styles comes from within anthropology itself. A small but growing number of anthropologists advocate more "dialogic" and "polyvocal" texts (Tedlock 1983; Clifford and Marcus 1986; Clifford 1988; Rosaldo 1989). No one agrees what exactly that means, but a very serious search is on for new narrative forms that reflect new notions of interpretation. My text is "dialogic" in both a narrative and a methodological sense. This narrative is dialogic, because it presents multiple points of view and conversations with "informants" that capture the give and take of my field experience. The characters' uncensored views of football, dating, school work, politics, and race relations are presented. Generally, I reconstructed these views from memory or copied them during interviews or observations. I present the particular views of Tara, Paco, Jacinto, and Coach Zapata as widely shared "folk theories" of social change or race relations.

At times, the literal dialogue with the community breaks down, and the BGL perceives my deceptions or the school board seeks to discredit me. There is trust and distrust, and the dialogue ebbs and flows, but it is, nevertheless, a dialogue. My conversation with this community is neither completely open nor simply monologic. North Towners talk back, and sometimes they front and con me. The qualitative and quantitative character of this dialogue is portrayed in the text and explicitly assessed in the previous sections. I have not tried not to stage the account to look more open and dialogical than it was, but I can offer no independent proof of that.

On Interpretive "Methods"

One thoughtful reviewer questioned how "dialogic" and open a text could be that had such an explicit interpretive perspective. He wondered if North Town youth played football, dated, and outwitted teachers to "prove" my theory of alienated communication. Unlike novels or new journalist accounts, the plot or structure to this tale is my interpretive worldview. One reviewer of the manuscript, a friend who has written in innovate "ethnographic novel" (O'Brennan and Smith 1981), viewed this narrative as a contrived, dogmatic, monologic morality tale that had "duped him." It was "a great story with great data," which ended up being "the mouthpiece for some goddamn Marxist ideology!" What this reading of the text misses is the extent that the narrative is dialogic in a philosophical sense. The main narrative device that makes this account more "objective" and "scientific" is the "sub-plot" of this text—my search for ways to put my class experiences in academic words and do a "scientific" ethnography.

Like Smith and many new journalists, I also use an autobiographical narrative style. In this case, however, this narrative convention is used for methodological reasons rather than to tell my personal story and recount my inner feelings. The autobiographical narrative literally situates me within the American cultural tradition. This immediately shatters the fiction that I stand above my cultural tradition and explain it through my all-powerful rational theory. In deconstructionist language, this move "decenters" the authorial privilege to claim an ultimate, objective interpretive position. Being in the account helps convey, therefore, how hermeneutic this interpretation really is. In addition, it also conveys the general continuity of the American cultural tradition.

In hermeneutic jargon, this critical reflection on my culture and my life contains a triple hermeneutic circle of interpretation. The experience among North Town youth forces me to confront my experience as a youth. The interplay of these two experiences creates a dialogue both with North Towners and with my past. In addition, I am also busy reading social theories that purport to grasp the meaning of American culture and class. This represents a third dialogue with other interpreters of the American experience. Ultimately, the ground of my understanding about North Town rests in experiences with Mr. Niel, American colonialism in the Philippines, academic patricians, and South Texas racists. The dialogue with social theorists simply puts into words what I knew already at the age of ten. I can explain better how I was brought up, because I understand my historical time and space. This enables me to live in and judge how North Town is a variation of that same historical tradition.

I have made sense of my life, and life in North Town, therefore, from a particular "prejudice" or worldview. In Gadamer's terms, this is the "horizon" that I used as I encounter the commonsense "horizon" of North Towners. Over the years, I have developed a set of ideas about "capitalist culture" from my own cultural tradition. These ideas are no more inherently rational and "objective" than other ideas, but they do represent a more expanded "horizon" than my youthful, commonsensical understanding. When I live in North Town, I project this "old" *and* "new" worldview onto my new experience. That forces me to sort out further what I believe. I end up going back and forth between my general model of capitalist culture and society and my specific experiences of lived capitalist culture. I go from Paco's threats and Jack's deceits back to the whole of a class perspective, then back to my past and "Mr. Dimwit," then return, yet another time, to the whole and the notion of instrumental speech.

In more positivist language, this process of abduction includes deduction of behavioral laws and speech acts based on the assumptions of my model of capitalist culture. This interpretive process also includes induction from behavior in North Town and from my remembrances. These experiences act back upon my world view, in positivist language, like a feedback loop. I am an "open system," or more accurately, am simply open to experience. I "ground" my ideas in "data" or, more accurately, am simply in history or being. In the end, a revised "model" of capitalist culture in action, lived out by Paco and Jack, speaks to my experience and makes sense to me.

In engaging North Towners' commonsense understandings of their culture, many new elements of patriarchy and racial inequality became apparent as part of the whole. My understanding of capitalist culture became infinitely more complex from this direct experience, which is to say that historical reality is far more complex than our "models" of it. My final text looks nothing like I imagined before arriving in North Town. It includes a vast array of topics and experiences I never dreamed would best capture and portray the meaning of the experience.

And what does all this imply for someone using ideas from class theory? Does that somehow automatically banish one to the realm of subjectivity and mere propaganda? Smith and many others assume that class theory and anyone using it are inherently more ideological and biased. Unfortunately, many class theorists *have* presented class analysis as a science that has discovered the universal laws of society. This leads them to believe that they can predict a future, for which they have the blueprint. Many Marxist dogmatists have turned the original critical insights of Marx into a kind of pseudo science that prophesies a secular utopia. When analyzing historical reality, they often stand arrogantly above history and stuff people's experiences into their analytical categories. But as Sartre (1963) points out so well, Marx himself did not analyze history in such an undialectical or undialogic manner. His descriptions of the French revolution show an undogmatic mind at work engaging reality with his world view.

Another way of reading Marx is, therefore, as a brilliant hermeneutic interpreter of his historical tradition. He situates himself within the rise of capitalism and sees it for what it is, a paradoxically progressive yet destructive human cultural invention. His discussion of commodity fetishism lays out historical reasons why a capitalist culture also has this progressive, yet dehumanizing quality. He argues that this type of society will force us to create a better one—if we are to evolve still further. Subsequent cultural critics like Habermas have extended and refocused these original insights on our flawed modern tradition of public communication. In different ways, Marx and Habermas *have* tried to create a rational scientific foundation for their practical philosophy and moral-ethical world view. Predictably, neither of them found an archimedean point, or a method that frees them from history and the hermeneutic circle. Their perspectives, like everyone else's, are partial and embedded in their historical times.

Nevertheless, they do avoid the tendencies of positivistic social scientists who uncritically extoll the ideology of a superior rational Western science and its idealized society. The historical, hermeneutic character of these theories helps one avoid the enlightenment legacy of a positivistic epistemology for the human sciences. Mainstream social scientists often make ontological claims for their political and economic theories because they believe in the magic of science to make their ideas more inherently rational, unideological, and universal. Or they simply embrace the rise of capitalism and parliamentary democracy as some final, true social order—rather than just another historical phase in cultural evolution. From this perspective, it is "mainstream" social scientists who are more likely to become idealogues, because they uncritically accept the assumptions of western rationalism and capitalism.

A critical posture toward enlightenment ideals of scientific methods and modern society puts "intellectual distance" between the interpreter and his or her tradition. This intellectual distance makes interpreters somewhat like "strangers" in their own historical time and space. The critical stance of being "inside" *and* "against" the tradition creates a hermeneutic circle or dialogic posture necessary to question our cultural tradition. It is in this deep-rooted skepticism that one is more likely to find some basis for a more "objective" interpretive posture.

In this particular case, I used Habermas's distinction between instrumental speech and communication or ideal speech as a criterion for judging when everyday speech acts were violating rational discourse. The earlier discussions of recording "making out games" and verifying student status groups illustrate how systematically these judgments were based on the field experience. The political reality of North Town youths' language games was not simply deduced from my general model of capitalist culture. The basis for my interpretive claims goes beyond simply "grounding" Habermas's notions of distorted communication empirically. Unfortunately, a complex process of hermeneutic reflection cannot be easily described as a tidy set of repeatable technical procedures. In lieu of that, I have displayed the dialogic character of my interpretation in ways that even non-technical readers can critique.

This manner of interpreting historical situation is the only way we have to produce quasi-objective accounts of our lived reality. Once we abandon the conceit of standing above experience and divining its meaning through our technological prowess, we are left with creating serious dialogues within ourselves and between others. In Habermas's ideal world, we are left to redeem discursively our truth claims about reality through uncoercive argument. The truth of our historical reality is never absolute and is always a momentary understanding, a consensus worked out among ourselves. It is simply the best we can do, given our finite understanding of an infinite temporality.

As I indicated in the introduction, I still believe in a "rationally motivated" social science. But the idea of a social scientist discovering universal laws and predicting the future, either deductively or inductively, seems touchingly naive and colossally conceited. One has only to honestly try and figure out what is going on in a real, historical setting to experience the Faustian paradox of knowing that the more you know, the less you seem to know. Interpretive studies like this one are at least provisionally objective and will generate serious discussion over their meaning. Such an intellectual labor has little to do, however, with the positivistic enterprise of academic specialists' studying people and history as an object outside themselves.

In the end, this text about South Texas is also about me putting my class experiences in an academic language. While growing up, I was praised for being an all-American jock and put down for being a rude rural, working class type. Upon reaching adulthood, I took an odd turn into the strange, patrician world of academia. Contrary to its high-minded pretensions, the university is the ideal place to refine futher the communicative logic being learned in North Town High School. Academia is full of gifted impression managers who are busy honing the "communicative competences" they learned as preppies, guzzlers, jocks, and brains. Most vatos and white trash kickers never make it to the academy, except perhaps as janitors or gardeners. Ultimately, even they must learn how to "front" authority and bite their tongues—as graduate students and assistant professors do—if they are to survive. With this study of South Texas, I have finally discovered why communication in academia has always felt more alien and alienating than communication in rural Iowa.

I have also discovered a way to be a social "scientist" that makes sense to me. Finding a version of "science" and "rationality" that expresses my intuitive understanding of class consciousness has been difficult. The "rationalism" that one learns in the university is usually what the French feminists call the phallocentric, rationalist conceit of Western high culture (Marks and de Courtivron 1981). The latest version of this self-serving ideological posture is Allan Bloom's popular book about the closing of everyone else's mind but his (1987). As self-appointed head philosopher-king, Bloom pronounces judgment on my generation's alleged moral deficiency and irrationality. Bloom notwithstanding, a critical rationality is hardly dependent on being steeped in Western high culture. Only the privileged class would peddle that line, since they monopolize the "cultural capital," guard their ivory towers with meaningless I.Q. and GRE tests, and decide which "great ideas" are true.

In contrast, I grounded my critique in Jurgen Habermas's notion of the rational, dialogic potential of communication. His idea of rationality forces us to be critical about our commonsensical, ideological understanding of our culture. I tried to temper whatever "rationalist conceit" class theory still has with Gadamer's wise admonition about "standing above" tradition. This style of cultural criticism is meant to show what a detached, patrician notion of culture, tradition, and rationality some of the intelligentsia have. If the paradox of life is to smile upon us, "rationality" and "science" must plunge a little deeper into the heart of darkness than some intellectuals do.

Appendix C

Data Tables

Table 1. Educational Mobility: Percentage of North Town Students Completing, Attending, or Not Attending College (by Family Social Class Background)

	College graduate	Two years higher ed.	No college
Upper middle class	49%	19%	33%
	(21)	(8)	(14)
High white collar	50%	25%	25%
	(18)	(9)	(9)
Low white collar	21%	27%	52%
	(35)	(44)	(45)
Blue collar	5%	11%	85%
	(10)	(22)	(178)

chi square = .00001, N = 413 of 454

Table 2. Educational Mobility: Percentage of North Town Youth Holding White and Blue Collar Jobs (by Family Social Class Background)

	Upper middle class	High white collar	Low white collar	Blue collar	Domestic
Upper middle	26%	40%	16%	7%	11%
	(11)	(17)	(7)	(3)	(5)
High white	0%	64%	17%	3%	17%
	(0)	(23)	(6)	(1)	(6)
Low white	1%	24%	48%	12%	15%
	(1)	(40)	(78)	(20)	(25)
Blue collar	0%	5%	25%	46%	23%
	(0)	(11)	(53)	(97)	(49)

chi square = .00001, N = 453 of 454

Table 3. Intergenerational Mobility: Percentage of Mexican Americans Belonging to Four Economic Classes (by Generation)

	Pre-civil rights generation	Post-civil rights generation
Upper middle class	2%	1%
	(9)	(3)
High white collar	3%	14%
	(11)	(45)
Low white collar	36%	31%
	(115)	(110)
Blue collar	58	54%
	(158)	(166)

no chi square

Table 4. Class Background of Student Status Groups

	Upper middle class	High white collar	Low white collar	Blue collar
Big wheels/stars	18%	18%	42%	21%
	(20)	(20)	(46)	(23)
Jocks	12%	15%	54%	20%
	(7)	(9)	(33)	(12)
Kickers	15%	0%	65%	20%
	(3)	(0)	(13)	(4)
White trash	0%	0%	11%	89%
	(0)	(0)	(2)	(17)
Vatos	4%	2%	22%	71%
	(2)	(1)	(11)	(35)
Nobodies/inactive	6%	3%	30%	61%
	(11)	(6)	(59)	(119)

chi square = .00001

REFERENCES

Abrahams, Roger (1970/1964). *Deep Down in the Jungle: Negro Narratives from the Streets of Philadelpia*. Chicago: Aldine.

Althusser, Louis (1971). *Lenin and Philosophy and Other Essays*. London: New Left Books.

Anchor, Shirley (1978). *Mexican Americans in a Dallas Barrio*. Tucson: University of Arizona Press.

Anyon, Jean (1980). "Social Class and the Hidden Curriculum of Work." *Journal of Education* 162 (1): 67–72.

——— (1981). "Social Class and School Knowledge." *Curriculum Inquiry* 11 (1) (spring):3–42.

Apple, Michael W. (1979). *Ideology and Curriculum*. Boston: Routledge & Kegan Paul.

——— (1982). "Curricular Form and the Logic of Technical Control: Building the Possessive Individual." In Michael Apple (ed.) *Cultural and Economic Reproduction in Education: Essays on Class, Ideology and the State*. London: Routledge & Kegan Paul, pp. 247–76.

Aronowitz, Stanley (1981). *The Crisis in Historical Materialism: Class, Politics and Culture in Marxist Theory*. New York: J. F. Bergin Publishers.

Avineri, Shlomo (1968). *The Social and Political Thought of Karl Marx*. Cambridge: Cambridge University Press.

Babcock, Barbara (ed.) (1978). *The Reversible World: Symbolic Inversion in Art and Society*. Ithaca, N.Y.: Cornell University Press.

Baldi, Guido (1972). "Thesis on the Mass Worker and Social Capital." *Radical America* 6(3):3–20

Barth, Frederick (ed.) (1969). *Ethnic Groups and Boundaries*. Boston: Little & Brown.

Barthes, Roland (1972). *Mythologies*. Trans. Annette Lavers. New York: Hill and Wang.

Bateson, Gregory (1972). *Steps to an Ecology of Mind*. New York: Ballantine.

Baugh, John (1983). *Black Street Speech: Its History, Structure, and Survival*. Austin: University of Texas Press.

Bauman, Richard (1986). *Story, Performance and Event: Contextual Studies of Oral Narrative*. Cambridge: Cambridge University Press.

Bauman, Richard and Joel Sherzer (1975). "The Ethnography of Speaking." *Annual Review of Anthropology* 4:95–119

Bell, Peter and Harry Cleaver (1982) "Marx's Crisis Theory as a Theory of Class Struggle." *Research in Political Economy* 5:189–261.

References

Bennett, Tony, Colin Mercer, and Jane Wollacott (1986). *Popular Culture and Social Relations*. London: Open University Press.

Berger, Peter and Thomas Luckmann. (1967). *The Social Construction of Reality: A Treatise in the Sociology of Knowledge*. New York: Anchor.

Bernstein, Basil B. (1975). *Class, Codes and Control*. London: Routledge & Kegan Paul.

Bernstein, Richard (1971). *Praxis and Action*. Philadelphia: University of Pennsylvania Press.

——— (1983). *Beyond Objectivism and Relativism*. Philadelphia: University of Pennsylvania Press.

Bloom, Allan (1987). *The Closing of the American Mind*. New York: Touchstone.

Bok, Sissela. *Lying: Moral Choices in Public and Private Life*. New York: Pantheon, 1978.

Borman, Kathryn M. and Jane Reisman (eds.) (1984). *Becoming a Worker*. Norwood, N.J.: Ablex.

Bourdieu, Pierre (1984). *Distinctions: The Social Critique of the Judgement of Taste*. Cambridge, Mass: Harvard University Press.

Bourdieu, Pierre and Jean-Claude Passeron (1977). *Reproduction in Education, Society and Culture*. Beverly Hills, Calif.: Sage.

Bowles, Samuel and Herbert Gintis (1976). *Schooling in Capitalist America: Educational Reform and the Contradictions of Economic Life*. New York: Basic Books.

Brake, Mike (1980). *The Sociology of Youth Culture and Youth Subcultures: Sex and Drugs and Rock 'n' Roll*. London: Routledge & Kegan Paul.

Braverman, Harry (1974). *The Degradation of Work in Twentieth Century Capitalism*. New York: Monthly Review.

Burawoy, Michael (1979). *Manufacturing Consent: Changes in the Labor Process Under Monopoly Capitalism*. Chicago: University of Chicago Press.

Canaan, Joyce (1987). "A Comparative Analysis of American Suburban Middle Class, Middle School, and High School Teenage Cliques." In George and Louise Spindler (eds.) *Interpretive Ethnography of Education: At Home and Abroad*. Hillsdale, N. J.: Lawrence Erlbaum, pp.385–406.

Carew, Jean V. and Sara Lawrence Lightfoot (1979). *Beyond Bias: Perspectives On Classrooms*. Cambridge, Mass.: Harvard University Press.

Carnoy, Martin (1974). *Education as Cultural Imperialism*. New York: McKay Publishers.

Carnoy, Martin and Henry Levin (1985). *Schooling and Work in the Democratic State*. Stanford, Calif.: Stanford University Press.

Centre for Contemporary Cultural Studies (CCCS). (1977). *On Ideology*. London: Hutchinson.

——— (1981). *Unpopular Education: Schooling and Social Democracy in England Since 1944*. London: Hutchinson.

——— (1982). *The Empire Strikes Back: Race & Racism in 70's Britain*. London: Hutchinson.

References

Chambers, Ian (1986). *Popular Culture: The Metropolitan Experience*. London: Methuen.

Clarke, John and Charles Critcher (1985). *The Devil Makes Work*. London: Macmillan.

Clarke, John, Charles Critcher, and Richard Johnson (1979). *Working Class Culture*. London: Hutchinson.

Cleaver, Harry (1979). *Reading Capital Politically*. Austin: University of Texas Press.

Clifford, James and George Marcus (eds.) (1986). *Writing Culture: The Politics and Poetics of Ethnography*. Berkeley: University of California Press.

Clifford, James (1988). *The Predicament of Culture: Twentieth-Century Ethnography, Literature, and Art*. Cambridge, Mass.: Harvard University Press.

Coleman, James (1961). *The Adolescent Society: the Social Life of the Teeager and Its Impact on Education*. New York: Free Press.

Collins, Randall (1979). *The Credentialed Society: A Historical Sociology of Education and Stratification*. New York: Academic Press.

Cook-Gumperz, Jenny (1973). *Social Control and Socialization: A Study of Class Differences in the Language of Maternal Control*. London: Routledge & Kegan Paul.

Cook-Gumperz, Jenny and John J. Gumperz (1982). "Communicative Competence in Educational Perspective." In C. L. Wilkinson (ed.) *Communicating in the Classroom*. New York: Academic Press, pp. 13–24.

Counts, George (1969/1922). *Social Composition of Boards of Education*. New York: Ayers.

Critcher, Charles (1986). "Radical Theorists of Sport: The State of Play." *Sociology of Sport Journal* 3: 333–43.

Cusick, Philip (1974). *Inside High School: A Student's View*. New York: Holt, Rinehart and Winston.

Dawley, Alan (1976). *Class and Community: The Industrial Revolution in Lynn*. Cambridge, Mass.: Harvard University Press.

Deem, Rosemary (1988). "Together We Stand, Divided We Fall: Social Criticism and the Sociology of Sport and Leisure." *Sociology of Sport Journal* 5:341–54.

Delgado, Guillero (1987). "Articulations of Group Identity and Class Formation Among Bolivian Tin Mines." Unpublished dissertation. Austin: University of Texas.

Douglas, Jack (1976). *Investigative Social Research: Individual and Team Field Research*. Beverly Hills, Calif.: Sage, 1976.

Dundes, Alan (1978). "Into the Endzone for a Touchdown: A Psychoanalytic Consideration of American Football." *Western Folklore* 37:75–88.

Dwyer, Kevin (1982). *Moroccan Dialogues: Anthropology in Question*. Baltimore: Johns Hopkins University Press.

Eckert, Penelope (1989). *Jocks and Burnouts: Social Categories and Identity in the High School*. New York: Teachers College Press.

References

Eddy, Elizabeth M. (1967). *Walk the White Line: A Profile of Urban Education.* New York: Anchor.

Erickson, Frederick (1987). "Transformation and School Success: The Politics and Politics of Educational Achievement." *Anthropology and Education Quarterly* 18(4): 336–55.

Everhart, Robert (1983). *Reading, Writing and Resistance: Adolescence and Labor in a Junior High School.* London: Routledge & Kegan Paul.

Fabian, Johannes (l983). *Time and the Other: How Anthropology Makes Its Object.* New York: Columbia University Press.

Fiske, John (1989a). *Understanding Popular Culture.* Boston: Unwin Hyman.

(1989b). *Reading the Popular.* Boston: Unwin Hyman.

Foley, Douglas. (1990a) "Reconsidering Anthropological Explanations of School Failure." Submitted to *Anthropology and Education Quarterly.*

(1990b). "Rethinking School Ethnographies of Colonial Settings: A Performance Theory of Reproduction and Resistance." Submitted to *Comparative Education Review.*

(1990c). "The Great American Football Ritual: Reproducing Class, Gender and Racial Inequality." Submitted to *Sociology of Sport Journal.*

Foley, Douglas with Clarice Mota, Donald Post, and Ignacio Lozano (1988). *From Peones to Politicos: Class and Ethnicity in a Texas Town, 1900 to 1987.* Austin: University of Texas Press.

Fukumoto, Mary (1983). "Perception of Ethnic Distinctiveness by a Group of Mexican Americans: Case Study in a Housing Project in East Austin." Unpublished dissertation. Austin: University of Texas.

Gadamer, Hans-Georg (1988/1975). Trans. and ed. Garrett Barden and John Cumming. *Truth and Method.* New York: Crossroads

García Márquez, Gabriel (l970). *One Hundred Years of Solitude.* New York: Harper & Row.

(1982a). *The Fragrance of Guava.* London: Verso.

(1982b). *Chronicle of a Death Foretold.* New York: Ballantine.

Garza-Lubeck, María (1987). "A Case Study of Academic Work and Student Productivity in an Inner-City Urban School." Unpublished dissertation. Austin: University of Texas.

Gibson, Margaret (1988). *Accommodation Without Assimilation: Punjabi Sikh Immigrants in an American High School and Community.* Ithaca, N.Y.: Cornell University Press.

Giroux, Henry A. (1983). *Theory and Resistance in Education: A Pedagogy for the Opposition.* London: Heinemann Books.

Giroux, Henry A. and Roger I. Simon (eds.). (1989). *Popular Culture, Schooling, and Everyday Life.* Cambridge, Mass: Bergin and Garvey.

Goffman, Erving (1959). *The Presentation of Self in Everyday Life.* Garden City, N.Y.: Anchor Doubleday.

(1961a). *Asylums: Essays on the Social Situation of Mental Patients and Other Inmates.* New York: Anchor.

References

(1961b). *Encounters*. Indianapolis, Ind.: Bobbs-Merrill.

(1963). *Stigma: Notes on the Management of Spoiled Identity* Englewood Cliffs, N.J.: Prentice Hall.

(1967). *Interaction Rituals: Essays on Face-to-Face Interaction*. New York: Anchor.

(1974). *Frame Analysis: An Essay on the Organization of Experience*. New York: Harper & Row.

(1979). *Gender Advertisements*. Cambridge, Mass.: Harvard University Press.

Gorz, Andre (1981). *Farewell to the Working Class: An Essay on Post-Industrial Socialism*. Boston: South End Press.

Gouldner, Alvin (1970). *The Coming Crisis in Western Sociology*. New York: Basic Books.

(1979). *The Future of Intellectuals and The Rise of the New Class*. New York: Oxford University Press.

(1980). *The Two Marxisms: Contradictions and Anomalies in the Development of Theory*. New York: Oxford University Press.

Gramsci, Antonio (1971). *Selections from the Prison Notebooks*. New York: International Publishing.

Grossberg, Lawrence and Cary Nelson (1988). *Marxism and the Interpretation of Culture*. Urbana: University of Illinois Press.

Gruneau, Richard (1983). *Class, Sports, and Social Development*. Amherst: University of Massachusetts Press.

Gutman, Herbert (1977). *Work, Culture and Society in Industrializing America: Essays in American Working-Class and Social History*. New York: Vintage.

Habermas, Jürgen (1975). *Legitimation Crisis*. Trans. Thomas McCarthy. Boston: Beacon Press.

(1979). *Communication and The Evolution of Society*. Trans. Thomas McCarthy. Boston: Beacon Press.

(1985). *The Theory of Communicative Action*. Vol. 1. *Reason and the Rationalization of Society*. Boston: Beacon Press.

(1987). *The Theory of Communicative Action*. Vol. 2. *Life World and System: A Critique of Functionalist Reason*. Boston: Beacon Press.

Hall, Anne M. (1984). "Toward a Feminist Analysis of Gender Inequality in Sport." In Nancy Therberge and Peter Donnelly (eds.) *Sport and the Sociological Imagination*. Forth Worth, Tex: Texas Christian University Press, pp. 82–103.

Hall, Stuart (1981). "Notes on Deconstructing the Popular." In Ralph Samuel (ed.) *People's History and Socialist Theory*. London: Routledge & Kegan Paul, pp. 227–40.

Hall, Stuart, Charles Critcher, Tony Jefferson, John Clarke, and Brian Roberts (eds.) (1978). *Policing the Crises: Mugging the State, and Law and Order*. London: Macmillan.

Hall, Stuart, Dorothy Hobson, Alan Lowe, and Paul Willis (eds.) (1980). *Culture, Media, Language*. London: Hutchinson.

References

Hall, Stuart and Tony Jefferson (eds.) (1976). *Resistance Through Rituals: Youth Sub-Cultures in Post-War Britain.* London: Hutchinson.

Hanna, Judith (1982). "Public Social Policy and the Children's World: Implications of Ethnographic Research for Desegregated Schooling." In George Spindler (ed.) *Doing the Ethnography of Schooling: Educational Anthropology in Action.* New York: Holt, Rinehart and Winston, pp. 316–55.

Hargreaves, John (1986). *Sport, Power and Culture.* Cambridge: Polity Press.

Heath, Shirley Brice (1983). *Ways with Words: Language, Life and Work in Communities and Classrooms.* New York: Cambridge University Press.

Henry, Jules (1965). *Culture Against Man.* New York: Vintage.

Hobsbawm, Eric and Terance Ranger (eds.) (1983). *The Invention of Tradition.* London: Cambridge University Press.

Hollingshead, A. B. (1949). *Elmtown's Youth.* New York: Wiley & Sons.

Horkheimer, Max and Theodor W. Adorno (1972). *Dialectic of Enlightenment.* Trans. John Cumming. New York: Herder and Herder.

Horowitz, Ruth (1983). *Honor and the American Dream: Culture.and Identity in a Chicano Community.* New Brunswick, N. J.: Rutgers University Press.

Hymes, Dell (1974). *Foundations in Sociolinguistics: An Ethnographic Approach.* Philadelphia: University of Pennsylvania Press.

Inkeles, Alex and David H. Smith (1974). *Becoming Modern: Individual Change in Six Developing Countries.* Cambridge, Mass.: Harvard University Press.

Johnson, N. Brock (1985). *West Haven Classroom Culture and Society in a Rural Elementary School.* Chapel Hill: University of North Carolina Press.

Johnson, Richard, Gregor McLennan, Bill Schwartz, and David Sutton (eds.)(1982). *Making History: Studies in History Writing and Politics.* London: Hutchinson, for the Centre for Contemporary Cultural Studies.

Katz, Michael B. (1971). *Class, Bureaucracy, and Schools: The Illusion of Educational Change in America.* New York: Praeger.

Keil, Charles (1966). *Urban Blues.* Chicago: University of Chicago Press.

——— (1985). "People's Music Comparatively: Style and Stereotype, Class and Hegemony." *Dialectical Anthropology* 10:110–30.

Kirst, Michael W. (1985). *Who Controls Our Schools? American Values in Conflict.* New York: W.H. Freeman.

Kolakowski, Leszek (1978). *Main Currents of Marxism: Its Rise, Growth and Dissolution: The Breakdown.* Vol 3. New York: Oxford University Press.

Labov, William (1972). *Language in the Inner City: Studies in the Black English Vernacular.* Philadelphia: University of Pennsylvania Press.

Larkin, Ralph (1977). *Suburban Youth in Cultural Crisis.* New York: Oxford University Press.

Lawrence, Robert. (1982). "Cultural Codes in Social Discourse: A Phenomenological Perspective on Ethnic Drinking and Urban Indentity." Unpublished dissertation. Austin: University of Texas

Leacock, Eleanor Burke (1969). *Teaching and Learning in City Schools: A Comparative Study.* New York: Basic Books.

References

Levine, Lawrence W. (1977). *Black Culture and Black Consciousness: Afro-American Folk Thought from Slavery to Freedom*. New York: Vintage.

Límon, José E. (1983). "Western Marxism and Folklore: A Critical Introduction." *Journal of American Folklore* 96: 34–52.

(1984). "Agringado Joking in Texas Mexican Society: Folklore and Differential Identity." In Ricardo Romo and Raymond Paredes (eds.) *New Directions in Chicano Scholarship*. Santa Barbara: University of California Press, pp. 33–50.

(1989). "Carne, Carnales, and the Carnivalesque: Bakhtinian Batos, Disorder and Narrative Discourses." Forthcoming in *American Ethnologist*.

Lynd, Robert. S. and Helen M. Lynd (1937) *Middletown in Transition: A Study in Cultural Conflict*. New York: Harcourt Brace and Company.

MacLeod, Jay (1987). *Ain't No Makin' It: Leveled Aspirations in a Low-Income Neighborhood*. Boulder, Col.: Westview Press.

Marcus, George E. Richard and Cushman. (1984). "Ethnographies as Texts." *Annual Review of Anthropology* 11:25–69.

Marcus, George E. and Michael J. Fischer (1986). *Anthropology as Cultural Critique: An Experimental Moment in the Human Sciences*. Chicago: University of Chicago Press.

Marks, Elaine and Isabelle de Courtivron (1981). *New French Feminism: An Anthology*. New York: Shocken.

Marx, Karl (1947). *The German Ideology*. New York: International Publishing.

(1964). *Early Writings*. New York: McGraw-Hill.

(1974). *Capital: A Critique of Politial Economy*. Vol. 1., *The Process of Capital Production*. Trans. Samuel Moore and Edward Aveling. New York: International Publishing.

McDermott, Ray (1987). "The Explanation of Minority School Failure, Again." *Anthropology and Education Quarterly* 18 (4):361–67.

McLaren, Peter (1986). *Schooling as a Ritual Performance: Towards a Political Economy of Educational Symbols and Gestures*. London: Routledge & Kegan Paul.

McNeil, Linda (1986). *Contradictions of Control: School Structure and School Knowledge*. London: Routledge & Kegan Paul.

Mead, George H. (1962/1934). *Mind, Self and Society from the Standpoint of a Social Behaviorist*. Vol.1. Chicago: University of Chicago Press.

Meadowcroft, Jean and Douglas Foley (1977). "Life in a Changing Multi-Ethnic School: Anglo Teachers and Their Views of Mexicano Children." In Hernan Lafontaine, Barry Persky, and Leonard H. Golubchick (eds.) *Bilingual Education*. New York: Avery, pp. 84–89.

Mehan, Hugh, Alma Hertweck, and J. Lee Meihls (1986). *Handicapping the Handicapped: Decision Making in Students' Educational Careers*. Stanford, Calif. : Stanford University Press.

Meltzer, Bernard N., John W. Petras, and Larry T. Reynolds (1975). *Symbolic*

References

Interactionism: Genesis, Varieties and Criticism. Boston: Routledge & Kegan Paul.

Messner, Michael (1988). "Sports and Male Domination: The Female Athlete as Contested Terrain." *Sociology of Sport Journal* 5:197–211.

Metz, Mary H. (1978). *Classrooms and Corridors: A Study of Authority in American Secondary Schools.* Berkeley: University of California Press.

Mills, C. Wright (1959). *The Sociological Imagination.* New York: Oxford University Press.

Mota, Clarice (1987). "As Jurema Told Us: Kariri-Shoko and Shoko Modes of Utilization of Medicinal Plants in the Context of Modern Northeastern Brazil." Unpublished dissertation. Austin: University of Texas.

Myerhoff, Barbara (1978). *Number Our Days.* New York: Touchstone.

Nelson-Cisneros, Victor (1975). "La Clase Trabajadora en Tejas, 1920–1940." *Aztlan* 6:21–55.

Oakes, Jeannie (1985). *Keeping Track: How Schools Structure Inequality.* New Haven, Conn.: Yale University Press.

O'Brennan, Junius and Nopal Smith (1981). *The Crystal Icon.* Austin, Tex: Galahad Press.

Ogbu, John (1974). *The Next Generation: An Ethnography of Education in an Urban Neighborhood.* New York: Academic Press.

——— (1987). "Variability in Minority School Performance: A Problem in Search of an Explanation." *Anthropology and Education Quarterly* 18 (4): 312–34.

Ogbu, John and Maria Matute-Bianchi (1986). "Understanding Sociocultural Factors: Knowledge, Identity, and School Adjustment." In *Beyond Language: Social and Cultural Factors in Schooling Language Minority Students.* Los Angeles: California State University Evaluation, Dissemination and Assessment Center, pp. 73–142.

Peña, Manuel H. (1985). *The Texas-Mexican Conjunto: History of a Working Class Music.* Austin.: University of Texas Press.

Persell, Carroll H. (1977). *Education and Inequality: A Theoretical and Empirical Synthesis.* New York: Free Press.

Poster, Mark (1981). *Critical Theory of the Family.* New York: Seabury.

Ramírez, Manuel and Alfredo Casteñeda (1974). *Cultural Democracy, Bicognitive Development and Education.* New York: Academic Press.

Rist, Ray (1973). *The Urban School: A Factory for Failure.* Cambridge, Mass.: MIT Press.

——— (ed.) (1979). *Desegregated Schools: An Appraisal of an American Experiment.* New York: Academic Press.

Rosaldo, Renato (1989). *Culture and Truth: The Remaking of Social Analysis.* Boston: Beacon Press.

Rose, Dan (1987). *Black American Street Life: South Philadelphia, 1969–1971.* Philadelphia: University of Pennsylvania Press.

References

Rosenfeld, Gerry (1971). *"Shut Those Thick Lips."* A Study of Slum School Failure. New York: Holt, Rinehart and Winston.

Royce, Anya Peterson (1982). *Ethnic Identity: Strategies of Diversity.* Bloomington: Indiana University Press.

Rubin, Lillian (1976). *Worlds of Pain: Life in the Working Class Family.* New York: Basic Books.

Samuel, Raphael (ed.) (1981). *People's History and Socialist Theory.* London: Routledge & Kegan Paul.

Sartre, Jean-Paul (1963). *Search for a Method.* Trans. Hazel E. Barnes. New York: Vintage.

Schofield, Janet Ward (1983). *Black and White in School: Trust, Tension or Tolerance?* New York: Praeger Press.

Schwartz, Gary (1987). *Beyond Conformity or Rebellion: Youth and Authority in America.* Chicago: University of Chicago Press.

Schwartz, Gary and Don Merton (1967). "The Language of Adolescents." An Anthropological Approach to Youth Culture." *American Journal of Sociology* 72:453–68.

Scott, James C. (1985). *Weapons of the Weak: Everyday Forms of Peasant Resistance.* New Haven, Conn.: Yale University Press.

Sennett, Richard and Jonathan Cobb (1972). *The Hidden Injuries of Class.* New York: Vintage.

Sieber, Timothy and Andrew J. Gordon (eds.) (1981). *Children and Their Organizations: Investigations in American Culture.* Boston: Hall.

Smith, Walter. E. (1978). "Mexicano Resistance to Schooled Ethnicity: Ethnic Student Power in South Texas, 1930–1970." Unpublished dissertation. Austin: University of Texas.

Smith, Walter E. and Douglas Foley (1978). "Mexicano Resistance to Schooling in a South Texas Colony." *Education and Urban Society* 2:47–61.

Spring, Joel H. (1972). *Education and the Rise of the Corporate State.* Boston: Beacon Press.

Stack, Carol (1974). *All Our Kin: Strategies for Survival in a Black Community.* New York: Harper Torchbook.

Steedman, Ian (ed.) (1981). *The Value Controversy.* London: Verso.

Taussig, Michael T. (1980). *The Devil and Commodity Fetishism in South America.* Chapel Hill: University of North Carolina Press.

Tedlock, Dennis (1983). *The Spoken Word and the Work of Interpretation.* Philadelphia: University of Pennsylvania Press.

Thompson, E. P. (1966). *The Making of the English Working Class.* New York: Vintage.

Tronti, Mario. (1973). "Social Capital." *Telos,* 17:98–121.

Trueba, H. T. (1988). "Culturally Based Explanations of Minority Students' Academic Achievement." *Anthropology of Education Quarterly* 19 (4): 270–85.

References

Tuchman, Gaye (1978). *Making News: A Study in the Construction of Reality.* New York: The Free Press.

Varenne, Hervé (1982). "Jocks and Freaks: The Symbolic Structure of the Expression of Social Interaction Among American Senior High School Students." In George Spindler (ed.) *Doing The Ethnography of Schooling: Educational Anthropology in Action.* New York: Holt, Rinehart and Winston, pp. 210–35.

Waller, Willard (1960). *The Sociology of Teaching.* New York: Wiley.

Weber, Max (1947). *The Theory of Social and Economic Organization.* New York: The Free Press.

Weis, Lois (1986). *Between Two Worlds: Black Students in an Urban Community College.* Boston: Routledge, Chapman and Hall.

Wilcox, Kathleen (1982). "Differential Socialization in the Classroom: Implications for Equal Opportunity." In George Spindler (ed.) *Doing the Ethnography of Schooling: Educational Anthropology in Action.* New York: Holt, Rinehart and Winston, pp. 268–309.

Williams, Melvin D. (1981). *On The Street Where I Lived.* New York: Holt, Rinehart and Winston.

Williams, Raymond (1977). *Marxism and Literature.* New York: Oxford University Press.

(1981). *The Sociology of Culture.* New York: Schocken

Willis, Paul E. (1976). *Profane Culture.* London: Saxon.

(1981). *Learning to Labor: How Working Class Kids Get Working Class Jobs.* New York: Teachers College Press.

(1982). "Cultural Production is Different from Social Reproduction is Different from Reproduction." *Interchange* 12 (2):48–67

(1990). *Common Culture.* London: Open University Press.

Willis, Paul and Phil Corrigan (1980). "Cultural Forms and Class Mediations." *Media, Culture and Society* 2:297–312.

(1983). "Orders of Experience: The Differences in Working Class Cultural Forms" *Social Text* 3 (7):85–103.

Wolfe, Thomas. (1973). *The New Journalism.* New York: Harper and Row.

Woods, Peter (1983). *Sociology and the School: An Interactionist Viewpoint.* Boston: Routledge & Kegan Paul.

Zamora, Emilio (1975). "Chicano Socialist Labor Activity in Texas, 1900–1920." *Aztlan* 6(2): 221–36.

Ziegler, Ralph (1966). *The Political World of the High School Teacher.* Eugene: Center for the Advanced Study of Educational Administration. University of Oregon.

INDEX

Index

Expressive culture concept, 77; in Willis, 167; in Marx, 174; in Goffman, 180; in folklore studies, 182; in Habermas, 185–86

Fiske, John, 189, 193, 198
Foley, Douglas, citations of *From Peones to Politicos,* 16, 66, 152, 196, 208, 214, 223
Fukumoto, Mary, 183

Gadamer, Hans-Georg: on hermeneutic interpretion 225, 227–28; on rationality and science, 231
García-Márquez, Gabriel, on solitude, 151, 153
Garza-Lubeck, María, 112
Gibson, Margaret, 203
Giroux, Henry, 162
Goffman, Erving: general dramaturgical view, 161, 176–79; social identity as misrecognition, 179; situational speech performances, 179–81
Gouldner, Alvin, 169, 171, 188
Gorz, Andre, 169
Gramsci, Antonio, 164, 189, 190
Grossberg, Lawrence and Carey Nelson, 173
Gruneau, Richard, 200
Guttman, Herbert, 183

Habermas, Jurgen: general perspective, 170–76; capitalist culture concept, 193; view of science, 229–31
Hall, Anne, 200
Hall, Stuart, 190
Hargreaves, John, 200
Heath, Shirley, 183, 190, 204
Henry, Jules, 65, 67, 204
Hobsbawm, Eric and Terrance Ranger, 16
Hollingshead, A. B., 72, 162, 169
Horkheimer, Max and Theodore Adorno, 189
Horowitz, Ruth, 70

Impression management: definition, 176–81; illustrations of, 62, 98, 100, 134, 155, 184–85, 231
Inkeles, Alex and Michael Smith, 183
Instrumental communication, 134, 155, 184, 230

Johnson, N. Brock, 104
Johnson, Richard, 16

Keil, Charles, 182
Kirst, Michael, 110
Kolakowski, Leszek, 188

Labor system, 14–15; migration north, 15–16
Labov, William, 82
Lawrence, Robert, 183
Larkin, Ralph, 162
Leacock, Eleanor, 104
Levine, Lawrence, 182
Lightfoot, Sarah and Jean Carew, 104
Límon, José, 182
Lynd, Robert and Helen, 162

MacLeod, Jay, 162
Making out games: definition, 112–14, 133–34; mutually constructed, 114–18; aggressive games, 122–26
Marcus, George and Richard Cushman, xvi, 223, 226
Marks, Elaine and Isabelle de Courtivron, 231
Marx, Karl, 174; on ideology, 168; on social classes, 169; as a hermeneutic thinker, 229
McDermott, Ray, 202–03
McLaren, Peter, 162
McNiel, Linda, 112
Mead, George, 171, 179
Meadowcroft, Jean and Douglas Foley, 108, 223
Mehan, Hugh, 191, 204
Meltzer, Bernard, John W. Petras, and Larry T. Reynolds, 178

245

Index

Memories of the author: picking on "band fags," 32; class bias in sports, 44; looking for a fight, 57–58; on being "in training," 60; classroom play and Mr. Dimmit, 127; social class experiences at Stanford, 161; social class experiences with Mr. Niel, 162; on the autobiographical mode, 227–28; a rationale for retrospective data, 230–31

Messner, Mike, 200

Metz, Mary, 104

Mills, C. Wright, xix

Mr. Niel (the banker), 162, 227

Mota, Clarice, 182

Myerhoff, Barbara, xvii

Narrative style, 223–226

Nelson-Cisneros, Victor, 15

New journalism, 224–226

Oakes, Jeannie, 102, 162

O'Brennan, Junius and Nopal Smith, 227

Observational methods: of student status groups, 216–19; of making out games, 219–22; of sex roles and gender, 222–23

Ogbu, John: on teachers' views of minority students, 103; on ethnic school failure, 202–03

Patriarchal order: sexist humor, 36–37; cheerleaders and male sexual fantasy, 32–34; powder puff football and gender socialization, 49–52; the politics of dating, 68–69; the male view of women, 56–57, 71–72; going steady and bonded sexuality, 70–71, 98; the general sports and dating scene, 99–100; the "dumb blond" routine, 115–16; working class women and their jobs, 137

Pedagogical formalism, 109, 113

Peña, Manuel, 182

Performance: a dramaturgical frame, 118–20; lines of teachers, 114, 133; straight, 112–18; hip, 128–32; nerdy, 126–28

Persell, Carroll, 162

Political leaders: Alonzo Alberto (county commissioner), 11, 12, 146–47, 150–52, 154; Esposito, Paulo (school board leader), 150–52; Gutíerrez, José Angel (Raza Unida founder), 6; Luna, Juan (mayor), 7, 12, 17, 35; Ramirez, Manuel (militant, 6–8, 17; Rapido, Francisco (justice of the peace), 147; Serrano, Beatrice (school board president), 147; Warren, Sam (county judge), 12, 154

Political machines: historical, 15; contemporary, 153

Political organizations: Better Government League, 3–5, 17–19, 42; Ciudadanos Unidos, 3–5, 10, 13, 19; League for United Latin Americans, 9–10; Raza Unida Party, 6, 19, 40

Popular memory, 16

Poster, Mark, 62, 183

Racial order: the northern migration effect, 14; working class challenges to, 15; cultural resistance to, 16, 196–97; changing social territories, 17; changing attitudes of youth, 144–46; changing altitudes of adults, 146–50

Racial relations: dating, 93–97; in classrooms, 102–08

Racial views: Anglo youth, 81–84; Anglo teachers, 102–08; Mexicano youth activists, 84–85; vatos, 86–88; Mexicana youth mainstreamers, 89–93

Ramírez, Manuel and Alfredo Casteñeda, 183

Rationalizing school authority, 19–24; as a system of discipline, 20; through multiculturalism, 21–22; placement and evaluation, 21; the limits of rationalization, 22–23;

Reciprocity and teaching style, 133–34

Rist, Ray, 104, 162

Ritual insults, 82

Rituals of reversal, 49–50

Role distancing, 131

Rose, Dan, xviii, 182

Rosaldo, Renato, xvi, 226

Royce, Anya, 180

Index

247

University of Pennsylvania Press
Contemporary Ethnography Series
Dan Rose and Paul Stoller, General Editors

John D. Dorst. *The Written Suburb: An American Site, An Ethnographic Dilemma.* 1989.

Douglas E. Foley. *Learning Capitalist Culture: Deep in the Heart of Tejas.* 1990.

Kirin Narayan. *Storytellers, Saints, and Scoundrels: Folk Narrative in Hindu Religious Teaching.* 1989.

Dan Rose. *Patterns of American Culture: Ethnography and Estrangement.* 1989.

Paul Stoller. *The Taste of Ethnographic Things: The Senses in Anthropology.* 1989.